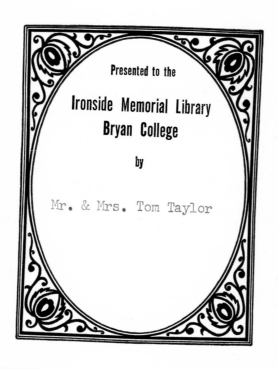

Russia in Flux

Russia in Flux

BEFORE OCTOBER

Sir John Maynard

COLLIER BOOKS · New York

First Collier Books Edition 1962

2nd Printing 1968

The Macmillan Company, New York

Printed in the United States of America

"Il se fera un énorme gaspillage de richesses,
de travail, et même de vies humaines; mais la
force de la Russie et le secret de sa destinée
ont toujours consisté en grande partie dans la
volonté et dans le pouvoir de ne pas regarder
à la dépense en vue d'un resultat à obtenir."

WALISZEWSKI
Pierre le Grand

"Enormous wastes of wealth, of work, and even
of human life may be necessary; but the
strength of Russia and the secret of her destiny
have always been largely made up of her
willingness and ability to disregard the cost
in view of obtaining the final result."

WALISZEWSKI
Peter the Great

Preface

THE TSAR HAD been the patriarchal house-father to a Great-Russian peasant family, which tilled its fields under his benevolent eye, fought at his command, and yielded obedience to those of the family to whom he vouchsafed authority, temporal or spiritual. The family was replaced by an empire of many races, in which the Great-Russian element was only the largest. The levelling rule of the house-father shifted, by successive steps, into a half-German Court, on a Finnish marsh, outside of Russia: with an official gentry, isolated by a widening gulf, a group of intellectuals troubled by cursed questions, a new capitalism which it was convenient to favour, and a peasantry no longer convinced of the duty of submission to its lords: a State which was not organically one with its people, and a people not organically one with itself. Great reforms, half carried through, were frustrated by reactionary misgiving. The denatured head of the new Russian State, obsessed by an illusion of proprietorship in human souls, made his people puppets in a game of empire: discarded his best, and set the unable in places of power. Two wars, the first disastrous but reparable, the second carrying ruin into the foundations of the State, exposed the sham behind the pageant of Orthodox Autocracy. As when Rehoboam's malcontents broke up the congregation with the cry: "To your tents, O Israel!" the people of Russia, by a common but unconcerned impulse, *stood out* from this State, of which they no longer had need: and, almost in a moment, it was not.

What followed was the beginning of a reconstruction on foundations new to the world's experience. The present study ends with the fall: but it was made by way of introduction to a longer one, of which circumstances did not allow the publication. Some day, the fall and the reconstruction must be exhibited as continuous. Otherwise we are in peril of apply-

ing the wrong standard to the new achievement: and of missing the true significance of such changes as the removal of
the capital to Moscow; and of the federal association of the
nationalities.

This study aims at presenting a clue of social and political
history, along with a glimpse of the currents of thought in the
Russia of the Tsars. At the end will be found a list of some
books useful to the student of peasant life.

I gratefully acknowledge my numerous debts to Sir Bernard
Pares, till recently Director of the London School of Slavonic
and East European Studies. Part of Chapter VII appeared as
an article in the *Modern Quarterly* for April, 1938. The Editors have kindly permitted its republication here.

Contents

Russia in Flux

Chapter 1

Introductory

"These poor villages, this niggard nature,
Land of long sufferings, thou art the land of the Russian
*   people.*
The proud eye of the stranger does not see nor value
That which shines secretly and modestly in thy meek naked-
*   ness.*
Thee, thee, my native land, the King of Heaven trod
In the guise of a serf, bowed down with the load of his cross,
And blessed thee in passing."

TYUTCHEV.

"Great God! Am I a patriot? Do I despise or love my country? I fear to say. It seems to me that I love her as a mother
loves, and despise as one despises a drunken thing, a characterless fool."

KONSTANTIN LEONTIEV.

WHAT HAVE THE Russian people been doing since they
emerged into view as something distinguishable from the
general mass of the Slav race? Let us begin by conceding the
claim that the history of Novgorod and Kiev and of early
trading adventure under Viking leaders and early contact with
Byzantine civilisation is part of their history. There is a story
that they begged a Scandinavian chief to rule over them, and
this was the origin of the House of Rurik. A similar tradition
exists in certain tribes of the Indus valley. Whether true or
not, there is a characteristic humility in it. What we first see
is a kingdom founded upon trade, and upon the warlike
prowess which primitive trade demands, and the deliberate
choice of one of the world religions—a choice which looks a
wise one when it is made, but is destined to erect a secular

barrier against brother Slavs, who made another choice. Then comes the rush of enemies, the road to wealth and civilisation is cut and the Russian people are back in the twilight from which they had hardly emerged. We have glimpses of them stealing off north-eastward, along the rivers and into the forests where they meet another race destined to add a new and strange element to their blood.

Brave and much-enduring soldiers though they have always been, neither then nor at any other time were they of the fighting sort. They had fought when they must. Otherwise they moved through the wildernesses, where weaker peoples made way or let themselves be absorbed, winning battles, not with man, but with unpropitious nature. Organised kingdoms have always called a long halt to their advance. But there was no natural limit to expansion except the frozen North, the Pacific Ocean, and the mountains and deserts to the South, and the forests were not of the impenetrable sort.

While this withdrawal is still in progress, the Mongol conquest bursts upon them: this time no invasion of barbaric tribes, but of a civilisation better organised than their own. At its best, it gives a Pax Mongolica, which makes the peerless river system of Russia a means of secure access to the trade of Asia and to Genoese settlements on the Black Sea, and supplies to the conquered a Chinese technique of administration and finance, with no touch of Chinese art. Some of the differences between Great Russia and Ukrain take their rise from this epoch, and the Orthodox Church gains strength from the Mongol policy of making it independent of the secular Princes.

Points of light begin to be perceptible in the twilight which covers the Russian people, and these points gradually concentrate upon Moscow. We see her growing rich upon trade, encouraged by the immense authority conferred upon her Grand Prince as the collector of the Mongol tribute from his brother princes, and strengthened by the adhesion of a national Orthodox Church—not yet the minion of an autocracy. The wise policy of able rulers helps this growth, till Ivan the Great, contemporary with the English Wars of the Roses, absorbs Novgorod and what is now North Russia, marries the niece of the last of the Eastern Emperors and sets Moscow on the throne of something which idealists will call the third and last Rome. And, while Moscow has been growing in greatness and unity, the unity which gave the Mongols their strength has been cracking. Quite undramatically, almost imperceptibly, we see the Mongol Empire crumble, leaving behind a barbarous off-shoot in the Krim Tartars, destined, as an outpost of the Ottoman Empire, to remain for centuries a terrifying menace to the frontier, and as effective an obstacle between Russia and the Black Sea as the Swedes and Poles between her and the Baltic. To the East, Ivan the Terrible confirms the end of Asiatic domination by his conquest of the Volga valley down to the Caspian Sea.

Now that the Mongol Empire is gone, we see more clearly that Russia's isolation was due to other and more lasting causes than her subjection to conquerors from the East. Teutonic Knights, Lithuanians, Poles, all of the Roman Confession, and easily aroused to a crusading hostility against the adherents of an Eastern Church, stand in the way of access to the west, and the civilisation of which it is now the centre, and the same sovereign who put an end to the last vestiges of Mongol rule finds himself balked when he tries to make a way through the cordon of opponents in that direction.

Russia had a golden age of painting, before an ecclesiastical decorum standardised the icon. It owed much to Greek, and something to Italian influence. Strangely enough, it was left to the Bolsheviks to discover and reveal the noblest examples of it. There was an indigenous and very attractive architecture, still to be seen in the wooden churches of the north-west and in the brick ones built under the influence of these prototypes. This was a genuine popular creation: for it seems that the villages built their own churches, and dictated full specifications to the builder guilds. The Church stopped the creative spirit in architecture, as it had stopped it in painting, by prescribing a standard form. Later on, Russia acquired unequalled architectural landscapes in her great cities. The craft was the craft of Italians, but there is nothing Italian in the results.

The semi-iconoclasm of the Church, which allowed representation of saints in the flat, but not in the round, explains why sculpture has never flourished.

Western civilisation owed enormously to Greek thought, whether it travelled in an Arab dress from Spain, or more directly in native form. Byzantium might have sent to Kiev or to Moscow the scholars and the manuscripts which she sent to Italy, and thereby made possible the revival of learning. Perhaps there was no Lorenzo de' Medici to welcome them, or the cold north smiled no invitation. Instead, Russia received what the Byzantine court and the monks of Athos and Sinai and the Oriental Churches could give: a conception of sovereignty in part late Roman and in part Biblical, but in all respects absolute, and confounding the Tsar's property with his authority: the Canon Law: a religious not a secular art, an ecclesiastical education: and the habit of secluding women, which the Mongols did not practise. Russian clerics did not even learn Greek, because Slavonic was the liturgic and literary language. Russia missed the Renaissance.

She had already missed the contact with that earlier and conquering Rome which gave so much to southern and western Europe: and she missed the other Rome, the ecclesiastical continuation of the first, which was the Roman Church. Thereby she went without the Latin language, the common tongue of European thought and learning, without the rationalistic training of the Roman mentality, which gave its colour even to religion in the west: and without the scholastic philosophers who applied reason to doctrine. That is perhaps why, at a later date, a Russian Churchman could boast, "The Russian Church knows no development." There was no Reformation, because the unity of civil ruler and Church was too complete, and the abortive attack which was made upon the wealth of the Church and its enslavement of peasants at the beginning of the sixteenth century was easily crushed; and there was no Counter-Reformation, so that Russia missed an educative influence such as the later and reformed Roman clergy exercised in the west, while her own clergy neither studied nor taught.

Russia had her magnificent rivers—the most perfect of inland waterways, if ice did not obstruct and if man did not stand hostile at the exits: but the seas were closed to her. Her physical isolation has been paralleled by spiritual. Having chosen her religious orientation to Byzantium and thereby incurred the hostility of western neighbours, she lost her civilising sun, when the Ottoman conquest eclipsed it. Even before that happened, the Greeks themselves had become suspect to her, by their abortive apostasy from the Eastern Church to win western support against the Turks: and this suspicion added venom to the schism in the Russian Church when Greek influences took part in the revision of the liturgy. From the early sixteenth century the country was practically closed to Roman Catholics, though its architecture was for long in Italian hands. Only English—precariously, by the difficult approach of the White Sea, where they established themselves as merchants—and Germans, Scottish and Swiss, as mercenaries, obtained access. Russia was cut off, almost as completely as the mythical realm of Prester John, from the influences which might have enriched her life. When the free flow of thought from without begins, we shall see that there comes a belated season of blossom and of fruit: but in the meanwhile a division has come between two sections of her people, which prevents the mass of them from sharing in the harvest.

From Peter the Great's time Russia—or Russia's upper stratum—has always had some European country as its fashion and its idea. In Peter's time the admiration was for technique and the economic life: and Holland, Sweden and Germany were imitated. France attracted admiration under the Empresses Elizabeth and Catherine the Great. After 1815, England, the House of Commons, Bentham, Byron, the dandies and Adam Smith, had their turn. Under Nicolas I, Germany became the ideal: her absolutism and bureaucracy attracted the official mind, her philosophy opened a new world to the intellectuals. But under the admirations and the imi-

tations has always run a current of adverse sentiment resent-
ing innovation, and claiming a primitive and non-European
source. The isolation, and the struggle to overcome it, and
the resistance to that struggle, make up the web of Russia's
history in earlier as in later years. They still make it to-day
when the loom clangs with the exchanges between rival political
and economic thinkers on the theme whether Socialism can
be built in Russia alone. Upon the shuttles of that loom, the
fingers of Russia's people are not often visible. The people
are the raw material from which other hands weave the fabric,
not the weaver but the wool. But there have been moments
when they have taken their place beside the loom, have sent
the shuttles flying with a mighty clangour, and have changed
the pattern and the fabric. There is one such moment when
Ivan the Terrible, after great thoughts and great deeds, smitten
by that madness which seems to be the nemesis of unchecked
power, destroys his own dynasty by the destruction of his heir.
He leaves to his people the legacy of the "Time of Troubles":
something like that "Ram Raula" of civil war, marching and
counter-marching, raid and foray, which came upon North
India in the decay of the Mogul Empire. It was a stranger
nation which ended the Indian "Time of Troubles": but the
Russian people ended their own. In the Red square at Moscow, near to the black and red marble of Lenin's tomb, stands,
and has stood for more than a century, the monument to
Minin and Pojarsky, a butcher and a noble, who called together the popular forces and drove the Poles from Moscow.
In the group, it is the butcher who is pointing the noble to
his duty: and always (and not only since the revolution) it is
the butcher who is named first, though the two are remembered together.

It was not to be imagined that Russia should be without a
Tsar, and greatly to be desired that he should be of the old
stock. Young Michael Romanov, of the family of Ivan the
Terrible's first and dearly loved wife and son of the Metropolitan, was set on the throne by popular acclamation. Tsar and
Church were the institutions which typified national existence
for the Russian, and gave him his ever-deferred hope of redress

and deliverance: till each in turn shrivelled into a lifeless husk.

1675. It is now that we begin to distinguish clearly that feature in Russian life which has done most to make Russian destiny. The land is wide: eastwards, almost boundless: and empty. Hands, whether for weapons or the plough, are precious. There is a struggle to keep the labourer in his place: and, on the other side, to find more freedom or a larger life by flight. The Cossacks have their origin in settlements of runaway peasants: and the economics of under-population and of labour flux, as a modern economist might express it, are apparent from an early date. The "Time of Troubles" gave special opportunities and motives for flight, and the new dynasty's needs made it inevitable to bring the elusive peasant under control. Elsewhere, where similar restrictions on human liberty have established themselves, the historian is dependent upon uncertain inferences and hypotheses. In Russia we can see and hear the successive blows which rivet the chains: until the sale of the peasant, without the land on which he works, is recognised by law, and finally the gentry are set free from the obligations which were the original justification of the restrictions put upon the people. In the meanwhile, and long before the establishment of serfdom is completed, Russian colonisation, started by a Cossack brigand, has reached the Pacific, with Government limping heavily behind it: a people's conquest.

1762. We see a succession of fierce struggles to throw off the yoke. The manifesto of Stenka Razin—the ballad of whose deeds is still sung—calling upon all broken men and debt-slaves to join him, has the true Spartacus ring. Emilian Pugachev—the Revolutionary Government has named a town in southeastern Russia after him—kept the Russian armies occupied for two years, and Moscow itself was in terror. It is significant that he hanged priests as well as gentry, for by this time the Church was no friend. It had played a noble part in earlier Russian history, confirmed, if it did not create, the greatness of Moscow among the lesser principalities, pointed the way into the fruitful wilderness for the advancing pioneer, offered in its walled monasteries centres of refuge and resistance. A Metropolitan dared to rebuke Ivan the Terrible and died for it. It was another Metropolitan who uttered the trumpet call to which Minin and Pojarsky responded. By a singular irony, a correction of the Liturgy, which seemed to involve nothing more fundamental than a return to a more accurate scholarship, effected by a tactless and stiff-necked Patriarch, became the occasion of a rift between the Church and its sources of popular support. But there were deeper causes for this alienation. Then, as later there must have been among the clergy, white and black, humble and pious followers of Jesus the carpenter and zealous successors to Paul the tent-maker. But the monasteries were great landowners, and had at least their full share of debt-slaves and serfs. It has been stated that the monks in the sixteenth century were the most intelligent merchants in the country. The power and the glory of the Church—as later of the State—rested upon the necks rather than upon the hearts of the people.

In the reign of Tsar Alexis, father of Peter the Great, a new thing happened. The Tsars did not allow foreign travel. It was treason, or something like it, to wish to go abroad. But the young son of the Minister Ordyn Nashchokin, sent by the Tsar with a message to his father, a youth of brilliant prospects, as this commission proves, fled across the frontier, first to the King of Poland, then to the Holy Roman Emperor, finally to Paris. His father was one of the early admirers of Western civilisation, the boy had been an associate of Polish prisoners, he had been inspired by a passion for something which Russia did not give. His flight was the first overt sign of a rebellious yearning which was afterwards to become characteristic of a large part of thinking Russia. The youthful fugitive is the spiritual ancestor of the Intelligentsia, with its aspiration toward the west, which only a small portion of his successors was ever able to gratify.

When the first Peter begins that tremendous career in which he wore out the heart and muscles of a superman, we seem to see what was the choice which lay before Russia. She might have been the amorphous mass of village communities, laborious, peaceful, sundered from contact with European civilisation, open to the raid of every man-hunting horde, and to the ambitions of every vigorous ruler on her borders. Something like this is what Leo Tolstoi would have had her be, meeting oppression with the Christian virtues. Peter was not the first to decide against this alternative, but, the decision being made, he was completely ruthless in his acceptance of the consequences. The primary need for him is the military need; and from this flow all his reforms. His people must bear the burdens of a race without natural frontiers, isolated among enemies: must stretch out hands to Europe, reach and use the sea, build up a great military power, and (since industrialisation was an essential to war then as now) must acquire and apply the technical arts. Hence a more rigorous serfdom, and a people divided into occupational castes. All must work: the gentry as educated leaders in civil and military tasks, the people, even the beggars, monks and nuns, in their humbler functions, and he himself hardest and most unsparingly of all. It was an early vision of the Totalitarian State, in which every part must be sacrificed to the greatness of the whole. When Peter became Tsar, his dominion, landlocked except to the frozen north, included the old Russian realm, the conquered Tartars of the Volga, and some nomad tribes of the north, east and south-east, all of them inferior in culture to the Russians themselves, and his capital lay at the heart of the Great Russian people. He was the ruler of Muscovy, and of the half-waste places on the skirts of Muscovy, not of subject peoples equal or superior in civilisation to his own. The Orthodox Church was still actually, as in theory, the Church of his people, and the Great-Russian language its speech. With his foundation of St. Petersburg, the window upon Europe, his acquisition of Baltic lands and his adoption of the title of Emperor, he began the fateful change which converted the Tsardom into an empire over many peoples and many cults, in which the original kernel of Great-Russians was less than half, and not the most cultured half of the whole, and the unforced followers of the Orthodox Church perhaps not more numerous. Russian subject, and Orthodox, and speaker of the Great-Russian language, henceforth cease to be synonymous: but some of his successors will embark

upon a policy of making them artificially one, and will add to
the number of their enemies in doing so.

What was it that made Peter an unforgettable figure in the
memory of a people not susceptible to the influences of tradition, so that his Bolshevik successors in the work of unmaking
and remaking a world spoke of him with admiration as "the
real one"? For one thing, he put an end to the Church as something claiming to be a State within the State. Not an originator,
he yet carried adaptive energy to the point of originality, and
did what less audacious predecessors had only thought of
doing. He tried everything, and failed in much: yet much
remained accomplished. A whirlwind of will-power, he yet
could wait and be cautious: as the twenty years of sapping
and mining which preceded the destruction of the ecclesiastical
Patriarchate would show us, if the organisation of an army
out of a mob of musketeers and pikemen, and the conversion of
defeat into victory over the greatest soldier king of Europe, had
left any doubt. A part of the impression which he made on
the Russian imagination may be due to the violence with
which he forced on his people his caprices along with his
reforms, dividing them into worshippers and haters; to his titanic debaucheries, and the organised horseplay of his public
buffooneries over the false Patriarchate. Yet duty was a passion
with him. The supreme leveller, he levelled himself like the
rest. The hardest and most devoted of his own workers, he
accepted for himself subordinate rank, lived on his salary,
applied to his own officers for promotion, and acquiesced in
their refusal of it. He took a congeries of patriarchal families,
in which the Tsar was the mystical house-father, and began to
make of it a European State. He put new European limbs to
the old Asiatic trunk, and though it was a strange hybrid
which resulted, something passed out of the new graft into the
old stock. He made an administrative machine, and fought the
tradition that office was a benefice, but did not hit upon the
modern device of taking away temptation by sufficient pay. He
brought the women of the capital out of the Asiatic Terem, and
tried, but failed, to build a middle class with self-governing
institutions. He tried to organise finance, and succeeded so far

as to introduce the principle of strict accountability and to reform the monetary system. He failed to create an educational system, but communicated, perhaps as a permanent gift, to his subjects something of his own universal and insatiable curiosity. He left the still living, but for him barren, glories of Moscow, to found a new world on a Finnish marsh, and it was no mad folly, but the inspiration of a statesman's genius, which took him there. He made a new script, almost a new and more flexible language, founded the first newspaper, dug, or began to dig, the first of the great navigation canals, developed the mineral resources of the Urals, taught the peasant to plant potatoes, acclimatised the vine, bred sheep, started the protection of forests, tried to establish industries—tried to drive capital into the linen industry with a club, says Pokrovsky—but failed because compulsion in that field is ineffectual: but where is the list to end? The superman proceeded by trial and error: unmade and remade everything: left a partially depopulated and ruined Russia, and forgot to provide for a successor to continue his work. To uncertain heirs, more German than Russian, he leaves a great idea, partially realised, of a Russia in Europe, the inheritrix of the arts and wisdom of civilisation, of an Empire which is more than and different in quality from the old Muscovy, of an imperial machine immensely strengthened and organised, of a Church without a voice against the errors and excesses of the autocracy: foreigners in the high places of the realm, and a people groaning under burdens not understood, and already divided into two nations, beardless and bearded, gentry and serf.

The prominence of Germans in the Russian State was increased by Peter's personal predilection for skill and capacity, and by his Baltic acquisitions, with their large upper stratum of German landowners and townsmen, until it reached proportions which gave point to the regrets of the Slavophils and to the desire of a return to ante-Petrine conditions. Repressed, yet vital, the protest of the older Russia found an outlet in the next century in the race-worship of the Slavophils. Germanism passed into the ruling dynasty, when Peter's daughter Anne married the Duke of Holstein-Gottorp, and their son, afterwards Peter III, married Princess Sophia Augusta of Anhalt-Zerbst, famous under a different name.

It was in this German princess, selected with unconscious perspicacity by a Prussian King, that Peter the Great found the true continuator of his own westernising policy, and the most resplendent of his successors, "great Catherine, whom glory still adores". A genius of many facets, she writes incomparable letters and shows the qualities of a brilliant diplomat: forestalls the centuries by keeping Russia and herself in the world's news: has dazzling dreams and realises some of them: conquers and colonises: shares the plunder of a Slav Poland which should have stood, one and inviolate, by Russia's side: tolerates all confessions, and, in a magnificent vanity, introduces the germ of liberal thought, while rebel Pugachev is hanging priests and gentry, and the generals sent against him find a "universal indignation" which hampers their task; and then—abandons her project of freedom of the press in the terror caused by the French Revolution, and falls sick with the news of Louis XVI's execution. A dazzling orgy of pyrotechnics, leaving the ground strewn with the sticks. What are the people doing while it proceeds? Some, of course, are gaping and whooping at the fireworks. But the mass is painfully wresting from nature the wherewithal to pay for them, in the black distance outside the circle of light.

If glory still adores the genius of Catherine, there is a reason for the idolatry. She opened her palaces to a west wind, a wind which was the trumpet of a prophecy, though only courtiers and parasites first heard it. The correspondence with Grimm, Diderot, Voltaire, and the rest, the encouragement of European studies for the gentry and their daughters, the choice of a woman to preside over the Academy of Arts and Sciences, formed habits and scattered seeds of thought which were to contribute not only to the movement for political reform, but to the outburst of literary genius among the *noblesse*, which began in the reign of her grandson.

1812. Something—accident, and yet more than accident—confirms after Catherine's death the accession of prestige, which her dazzling personality has given to Russia, and creates a legend of invincible latent strength. It was a legend which has been responsible for some later political mistakes, and for one great political obsession affecting the British Empire. Her grandson, Alexander I, with a reflection of her brilliance, but with genius far inferior to hers, after vacillations of policy which seem to justify the criticism that he was unable to pursue steadily one line of thought, finds his country invaded by the greatest army of the centuries before our own. A battle in which the Russian soldier shows heroic capacity for self-sacrifice is followed by Napoleon's occupation of Moscow, with the confident expectation of a treaty of peace such as his entry into other capitals had obtained for him. The Russian people at first show little national feeling: they use the confusion of war to rebel against authority and to plunder the estates of the gentry: they accept money from the French and confirm Napoleon's hope of an easy triumph. But, when Alexander rises to his great decision to hold no parley while an enemy remains on Russian soil, Tsar and people speak one language, and work together with Generals November and December to inflict on the invader such ruin as Xerxes suffered. It was an uprising of a people. Herzen tells us that, six months after the evacuation of Moscow, bands of men from the depths of Siberia were still appearing on the European frontier of Asia to defend the ancient capital, which they regarded as the true one.

1825. Let us not stop to ask what Napoleon might have done in Russia, and whether the serf would have been the happier without a Russian victory. Raised to splendid heights as the arbiter of an admiring Europe, Alexander's generous impulses spent themselves in sentiment. He did more for the Poles than he did for his own people, and yet failed to secure for them the unity which was what they wanted. A recent Russian writer says that, as a Liberal, he remained always an amateur, attracted by the theory and unable to master the practice. His policies at home passed into those measures of compulsion in spiritual and intellectual activities, for which the name of his friend Arakchéev has become a Russian byword. His Holy Alliance became a league of sovereigns against the aspirations of peoples, and his dream of emancipating the serfs ended with freedom—without land—to the peasants of the Baltic Provinces, that is to say with nothing for the peasants of Russia. His reactionary brother Nicolas, sworn foe to the philosophers, did far more for the serfs, though he smothered in blood the revolutionary movement which flared up, like the crackling of thorns under a pot, at his accession.

The most judicious of the foreign observers of nineteenth-century Russia, Donald Mackenzie Wallace, writing in the seventies of the last century, tells us that Russia has accomplished, and can accomplish again, political and social evolutions of a dangerous kind, *provided the autocratic power is preserved* and the people remain politically passive. He goes on to probe the weaknesses of English Liberalism. Russians, he says, believe that they are champions of social equality and enemies of feudalism, and that they will come as deliverers to the lower classes in a country organised on English principles: and he asks whether "the present Liberal principles of liberty and reform may one day come to be regarded as somewhat superficial". To this question he gives a topical application by observing that the Russian peasantry have reason to congratulate themselves that they are emancipated by a Russian autocrat and not by a British House of Commons.

1861. The Emancipation Law was superior to what a British Parliament would have done, because it recognised, in principle, that freedom is not freedom without the means of subsistence. A British Parliament, at all events one of the nineteenth century, would have rejoiced in an opportunity of emancipating the serfs. But unless they had been under the influence of some such exotic genius as Disraeli, in a mood of exceptional illumination, can we doubt that they would have given them the status of agricultural labourers, free in the British sense, with legal but not economic liberty, at most with a modest provision of quarter-acre allotments? The Russian autocrat did better than that. Perhaps he should have done either less or more: and have made either proletarian workers without rights in land or a nation of peasant proprietors. It was a fateful decision: for it was the peasants and their grievances that made all the Russian revolutions.

There were palace revolutions enough in Russian history to remind the autocrat that his strength was not his own. A Marxian might say that he was the trustee of a class, and that the class removed him when he disappointed it. The Tsar Liberator, though he headed a revolution of his own subjects, freed the serf, gave him land, and carried out some of the complementary reforms—a herculean task—had in him something of his predecessor and namesake Alexander I. He was no Peter, to force the fulfilment of his will against all the opposition of advisers, through the misgivings and dangers caused by the impatience of political zealots, through the weariness which comes half-way towards the completion of heroic tasks. The work remained half done.

The newly emancipated were burdened with redemption dues, often in excess of the value of their land, and in reality the price of their own thews and sinews. These dues fell upon an illiterate people, most of whom were unaccustomed to cash obligations of any sort, and delivered them into the hands of those to whom arithmetic was not a mystery. The land would have fed them if the systems of tenure and of agriculture had progressed with the growth of the population. But it was less by a fifth than what had been enjoyed by them before, and the portions taken from them consisted largely of grassland, without which the cattle—the heart of agriculture—cannot fulfil their function. The lack of the balanced holding was an even worse disability than the scantiness of the arable. The emancipated serf retained much, though not all, of the old legal inferiority, the old liability to special and degrading punishments, the old insecurity against the arbitrary treatment of official oppressors, the old status with its deprivation of opportunities, with a new multiplicity of masters to replace the old serf-owner. He had become the dependent of the Commune —the Mir—of which he was himself a member; unable to move without its consent, he still worked for his old proprietor, because he needed the wages of labour to supplement the earnings of a scanty holding cultivated in the primitive way;

and hired from him the grasslands which he had looked upon as his own, though the law assigned them to the landlord. The need of advances often caused him to bind himself for a period of service, which was a temporary renewal of the obligations of serfdom. These were not conditions in which a large and rapid improvement of peasant agriculture was to be expected. Yet, the economic pressure did result in a measure of improvement, though not on a scale commensurate with the rapid growth of population.

The defects of the great emancipation, after the first flush of disappointment over the redemption dues was over, were not immediately apparent to the mass of the peasantry. It was otherwise with the eager radical publicists who had watched the progress of the scheme. They could not forgive the disappointment of hopes which had been pitched so high: and a passion of sympathy with the peasant drove them out into the country-side and fostered the growth of a bitter revolutionary conviction. To the peasant it seemed—vaguely and inarticulately—that the Tsar had meant something better and the gentry had thwarted him: even that the gentry were seeking to injure the Tsar because of the good that he had done. It was not long before the countryside was full of rumours of a new "black partition", which would give all the land to those who worked it: the one solution which seemed equitable to the peasant.

1881. In the meanwhile, amid the misgivings and tergiversations of timidity and reaction, with the most influential classes clamouring that the emancipated peasant had fallen into drunkenness and laziness and must be disciplined before he would work, the Tsar Liberator carried through reforms which produced the equivalent of County Councils in Russia, years before they were set up in Britain, made the judges independent of the executive authority, and established a corporation of the bar, set up new law courts with a public procedure and a jury system, and put the army on a democratic basis, at least on paper, with the equal liability of conscription for all and a shortened term of military service. But the appetite grew faster than that upon which it fed: or the emancipation had removed a keystone and made the work of reconstruction too heavy for a weakening resolution. Reactionaries took back with one hand some at least of what was given with the other. The realities of oppression and inequality clashed irreconcilably with the ideals which concessions had encouraged. The most dangerous moment for a bad Government, writes de Tocqueville, is when it begins to reform itself. A Turkish war, made by Panslavist sentiment, ended with a military victory and a humiliating diplomatic defeat. A terrorist party pursued with self-sacrificing fanaticism the Tsar who had done much, but not enough, for liberty, and something, but not enough, for discipline: and, after a series of audacious attempts which speak eloquently for the weakness of the Police State, at length achieved his destruction: victim of a revolution which he began and did not finish.

We must probe deeply indeed to find the reasons of the unconcern with which the public watched the struggle between the autocracy and the terrorists in the period preceding the murder. A sense of religious duty may sometimes supply the lack of sense of responsibility in public affairs. Russian society had never had the latter, and they had very largely lost the former. It was replaced in a number of individuals by an uneasy conscience, which caused them to see their duty in revolution rather than in the support of the Government. There was no sense of solidarity between Government and society. Even the officials, or some of them, were not always certain that they were on the right side. The preachers of non-resistance, or the greatest of them, were revolutionists in their hearts, ready to change all things, by negative if not by positive action. We are told that the conscience-stricken gentleman, the man of gentle breeding who felt that his privilege was sin, was active among the prophets of change, but the negative attitude of those who lacked confidence in their titles was more wide-spread. As for the mass, what was their concern with this quarrel between an unintelligible Government and its unintelligible enemies?

We are left with the sense that this much-enduring people is suffering, and not making, its own history, and that there is no contact or sympathy between them and the protagonists, whether these are to be found in the machine of the autocracy, among the Liberals, or in the ranks of the terrorists. On a superficial examination, the Russian public seems to be like the audience in a theatre, perhaps laughing or weeping with the actors, but not dreaming that it is for themselves too to play a part on the stage.

But is it nothing to have occupied a sixth of the earth's dry surface? A peasant people have filled these great spaces, kept at bay their nomad enemies, and brought under tillage so much as is culturable by primitive methods. Nature had made a testament in their favour, and attached a condition to it: that they must earn their inheritance by occupying it, be fruitful and multiply, and replenish the earth. The fulfilment of the condition was the restless labour of centuries. With immensely added quality of performance, with motor and aeroplane and ice-breaker and steam and electricity, it continues to be the labour of to-day. Over all of us hundreds of thousands of years passed without emergence into history; but great preparatory tasks were performed in that seemingly dead interval. Russia has been a few centuries later in passing out of the stage of unconscious instinctive preparation. In the meanwhile, there have been rare moments when tragic crises have compelled attention and life itself appeared to be at stake. All else, except the call of the land, has passed over the heads of this peasant people, as if it has been a dream.

It is a people which the rigours of still unconquered nature and the cruelties of man have schooled into an infinite capacity for suffering: not into a love for it, as some fanciful interpreters have asked us to believe. Tolerant, pitiful, Christian in the spirit of the Sermon on the Mount, it has yet been capable of outbreaks of savage and horrifying violence, when the cup of unconsciously accumulated rage was full. Certain rudimentary social institutions it has made its own: the family: the village commune: the working partnership with chosen comrades. Beyond these it has been non-political: and towards the institutions of the State, with one exception, it has been anarchical, submitting only to the sense of helplessness and to fear.

Round and over this people, but not of it, is sketched the

political fabric, State and Church in one, with the most imposing of façades, and foundations, partly Byzantine, partly Tartar, partly German, whose strength is still taken for granted. The Emperor Pope, as—not correctly—he has been called, is still the benevolent Father and Protector, who would set all things right if the cry could reach him. He has first made, and then unmade, a nation-wide bond of service discipline. The ground is still strewn with the ruins of this outgrown system, and the eye detects the beginnings of another in which the landlord and the factory employer are taking the place of the serf-owner, and economic pressure is replacing patriarchal or feudal compulsion. The task of government is grown vastly more complex. The ruler is to be judged by a more exacting standard. The abolition of serfdom has left a void into which will rush spirits of evil worse than the first, unless it be filled with a new kind of wisdom and a new kind of justice. In the transition, altogether incomplete, from old to new, Alexander II, the Tsar Emancipator, has fallen a victim to newly awakened and half-satisfied aspirations.

Chapter 2

The Peasant in the Nineteenth Century

"Eternal is the cruel way of life,
In which generations of mankind
Live and perish without trace,
And leave no lesson for their sons."

N. A. NEKRASOV.

"The peasantry is the true autocrat of Russia."

VICTOR CHERNOV.

IF WE EXCLUDE the northernmost third as generally unfitted for agriculture, most of the remainder of Russia in Europe falls into two regions: a region of food deficit, where the crops do not—perhaps we shall soon be able to write, *did not*—suffice for the food of the inhabitants: and a region of food surplus to the south and south-east of it. The region of deficit is, as regards soil and the length of the open season (in the north, as little as five months), the less favoured by nature. But it has the more equable climate and the greater supply of moisture. It contains the capitals and the manufacturing centres, a larger proportion of the people have learned to supplement agricultural earnings, first by home industries and later by factory labour, and the agriculture is not so nearly universally concerned with cereals, because the nearness of industry has encouraged dairying and the growth of special crops, including

33

flax. The region of surplus includes the famous Black Earth zone. With a far better soil and a longer agricultural season, extending in the south to nine months, it has wider variations of cold and heat, and suffers from recurring deficiency of rainfall, tending to be more acute towards the east. Historical reasons have made a portion of it, especially north-eastern Ukrain, a land of small holdings and overpopulation, and much of the soil has been exhausted by excessive cereal cultivation. Almost one might say that man has done better where nature was less kind: but this is not the whole truth, for the hot winds and the drought, which periodically bring famine to the so-called granary of Europe, have hitherto been beyond the control of man, whatever the future may have in store in the way of dry farming, drought-resisting plants, afforestation, and irrigation canals.

The region of surplus has been the scene of the worst famines. It was also the scene of the most violent agrarian outbreaks of the early part of the twentieth century. We arrive at a rough demarcation between the two regions if we draw a line, much curved and much indented, from south-west to north-east, starting from a point just south of Kiev, to the junction of the Volga and Kama rivers south of Kazan, and prolong it across the Urals into Siberia.

As in all countries before the scientific engineer gets to work on them with his artificial drainage and artificial irrigation, his communications and supply of power, land and water in Russia are unevenly mixed and badly distributed. Ample moisture, extending to swampiness, prevails in one part, while drought parches another. Rivers carry unused floods to the sea, while deserts adjoin their banks. Here is room for large-scale remedies such as only the highly developed State has the knowledge or the means to apply. The causes of agricultural poverty are partly explained by this inevitable postponement, partly by institutions and practices which affect the processes of agriculture. The Commune, known to many English, but to fewer Russians, as the *Mir*, plays a large part among the latter.

This institution was latent, or at least happily concealed from the eyes of administrators, till the forties of the last century, when a German traveller, Baron Haxthausen under the inspiration of Slavophil friends who yearned for something characteristically Slavonic, dragged it to light. Whatever its true history and origin, it was an inevitable accompaniment of the open-field system of agriculture, which demands an authority for the determination of the leading agricultural processes and their dates. It had an Executive in the Elder, and it expressed itself through the Village Meeting, an assemblage of heads of families, not numerous in the days of the patriarchal household, but multiplying, and becoming more widely representative, as the large joint-families broke up after emancipation. It proceeded by a rough method of acclamation, not by formal voting, and, in its palmy days, enjoyed confidence and commanded acquiescence. It must often have been overruled by the squire or his manager when the members were serfs: but, more often, it must have been found a convenient and representative instrument. One of its prime functions was the redistribution of land, to adjust burdens and rights to changes in numbers and working power. General redistributions had entirely ceased over a third of Russia and had become rare elsewhere: but partial redistributions were constantly occurring.

When we first get our view of the Mir—for this is the name by which I shall call it—rights in land are held in common: but possession and cultivation are separate. There are no private grazing grounds, but some private hayfields, and no practice of stall-feeding of peasants' cattle except in winter. Since all the cattle must graze together over the stubbles of all, and over the fallow land, and since the hay of the common hayfield was generally cut by the joint labour of all, the village meeting decided when to plough, when to mow, when to reap, and was the means of perpetuating the almost universal three-field rotation, which obstructed novelties such as the growing of clover.

Whatever further functions the pre-emancipation Mir may have discharged in addition to the redistribution of the land, and the regulation of agricultural processes and dates, we see it, in its nineteenth-century form, acting as an organ of village self-government: distributing among its members the customary peasant-duties of repair of roads and bridges, escorting of holy icons and the like, forming by collection from all a reserve of corn for insurance against need, allotting his subsistence farm to the priest, managing the communal field when there was one, organising fire-fighting and protection against thieves, enforcing the patriarchal authority upon contumacious sons, and settling minor disputes among its members. It even made separation orders for quarrelsome spouses, regardless of the law which gave the monopoly of divorce to the ecclesiastical courts—but the peasants were always half outside the law. It was the maid-of-all-work for the miscellaneous demands of a busy administration, and we are not surprised that more tasks were soon laid upon it by the State.

Before Emancipation (and indeed after it too) the peasant—of course without any clear conception of the juridical meaning of ownership—believed that he, or his Mir, was the owner of the land which he cultivated. This belief was expressed in the famous plea of the serfs to their squire: *We are yours, but the land is ours*. Nicolas Berdyaev puts it that the peasant regarded the land as God's, and the right of using it as belonging to the man who gave his toil to it. In this conception there was no room for the rent-receiving landlord. Whatever the historical justification for this, the law held that the land, or rather the land which was not the property of the Crown or the Church or the appanage of a member of the Imperial House, belonged to the squires. Under the Emancipation law a large part of it became the prospective property of the peasants: and the Mir became the *ad interim* proprietor of the peasants' share till all dues were paid off. It was convenient also to put upon the Mir the responsibility, which had formerly rested upon the serf-owner, of meeting all payments due from its members to the State. This included, along with the poll-tax and other imposts, the new item of the redemption-dues on account of emancipation. The transfer of responsibility necessarily involved a transfer of power, and the Mir was empowered to prevent its members from travelling more than twenty miles away without passport. Since the possession of land, in the deficit area, was often rather a burden than a right, this power gave opportunities of blackmailing the adventurous peasant. There were even cases in which a Mir sentenced a recalcitrant member to exile in Siberia, and the authorities upheld and enforced the order. At the same time administrative convenience made a subtle change in the position of the Elder, who had been the officer, rather than the head, of the Mir. The Government gave him a clerk, known as the Writer, ordinarily brought from outside the village. The Elder was empowered to put an end to a village meeting by withdrawing from it: so that he obtained a virtual veto on decisions. He became an official personage: and cases of whipping for insolence to the Elder were not unknown. He was evidently in process of transition to the position of official master.

The Mir was the darling of the Slavophils for its specifically Slavonic character. The Populist-Socialist loved it because he saw in it the germ of a peculiarly Russian Socialism, which would give the go-by to the proletarianism of towns and the capitalism which oppressed Western Europe. The conservative politician saw in it the hope of keeping the peasant (presumably loyal and religious) apart from corrupting influences. But, all the time, life—or death—was too strong for all three, and the object of their affections was decaying before their eyes. The vitality of the Mir depended upon a virtual economic equality among its members, which made a reality of village democracy. The cash-nexus which established itself with the introduction of cash obligations, put an end to the equality, by giving scope to the talents of the more astute for self-aggrandisement: and the end of the equality meant the domination of the village meeting by the more prosperous, and the beginning of a class-struggle in the village. After it had lost its equalising function, the Mir retained that power of obstructing agricultural innovations which made it odious to the agricultural reformer, and its tendency to hold back the more active and enterprising of its members. But we shall err if we suppose that it was unpopular with the mass of its members. Most peasants did not expect to benefit by the withdrawal of restrictions and had neither energy nor cattle nor implements to do so. To the poor there seemed always the possibility of benefiting by a redistribution; and, even when landless, they retained their rights of common pasture, and feeding, though it were only for goats or poultry. The Mir remained in idea what it had long ceased to be in fact, an agent of equalisation; and equality made a stronger appeal than freedom: a fact which explains some things which would otherwise be unintelligible in the more recent history of Russia.

Two pieces of legislation of the year 1893 show the meeting of the two currents: on the one hand the recognition that the Mir had had its day: on the other hand, the attempt artificially to give life to it. In June the lawgiver diminished the Mir's authority of redistribution. In December he limited the right of the individual to secure separate proprietary rights in his own share of the land by prepayment of his redemption dues, and insisted upon the Mir's authority to prevent it. We shall see that the principle of separate individual property in land won an apparently conclusive victory in 1906, but the struggle was renewed, with varying fortunes, in and after 1917, the more prosperous peasants standing for the one solution and the less prosperous for the other.

The love of equality is illustrated by the tenacity with which the peasant has clung to a practice which has greatly embarrassed his agriculture. It is not exclusively Russian, nor even exclusively Slavonic, except in its exaggeration. When the crops were standing, the traveller of yesterday, in areas where collectivisation was not complete, noticed a streaky appearance about the cultivation. These were the "strips", often not more than three or four paces wide, and maybe a quarter of a mile long. They were particularly narrow and numerous in the north, where soil is of uneven quality, and in the agricultural centre with its dense population and small holdings. They were wider and less numerous in the more uniform steppes of the south and south-east: but the scarcity of water there and the necessity of locating the village near the source of supply made the distances to be travelled by the cultivator long and exhausting. A monograph on a village in the Valdai hill area, compiled in the early period of the revolution, says that each peasant in each of the three "fields", winter, spring and fallow, has seventy strips of arable and seventy-six of hay, and each strip is only one-seventh of an acre for a whole "soul", and half of that for half a "soul". In such conditions, one-fifth of the whole land went in boundaries, and it was hard to get the plough round at the end of each strip. The peasants said you could take the hay of one strip under your arm, and carry it across to the next one. Mistakes, and cultivation of the strips of others, were very common. It was calculated by a revolutionary commission that a man had to walk twelve hundred miles, on an average, in the agricultural season, to get round his own holding. But the tradition, and the passion for equality, were so strong, that when the peasants got their additional allotments at the expense of the landlords and other individual owners in 1917 and 1918, most of them divided the new areas into strips—and re-established the inconvenience.

The love of equality naturally shows itself most in those who are not confident of possessing the means to excel. It is negative rather than positive, and is perhaps at bottom a hatred of being surpassed, combined with a doubt of the fairness of the competition, in which particular qualities are marked too high. It existed in the peasant, if we are to trust our authorities on peasant life, along with an admiration for the man who had emerged from the mass, whatever the means which he had employed. There is something of the *kulak* in every peasant, we are told. He is a stubborn individualist who will not share his resources with anyone, will not take part in common tasks, and as soon as he becomes more successful than his fellows, finds the Mir a fetter upon his energies and wants to leave it. But these facts have to be reconciled with others which apparently contradict them. The workers' fellowship of chosen comrades— the *artel* as Russians call it—was a well-established institution, extending to agriculture as well as to industrial and other tasks: and co-operation in production, consumption and credit attained widespread success in the twentieth century. It seems plain that the peasant, in spite of his individualism, was capable of being convinced by the prospect of tangible advantage: but that he preferred the voluntary association, from which the less eligible were barred, to that in which custom gave equal rights to all members of the community.

The history of Russia in the past has been for the most part that of an underpopulated country: and land, at all events arable land, was less important than labour, in the region of deficit: but a part of the Black Earth zone has suffered from the contrary evil. The serfs here had very small holdings, because their masters wanted all their labour on their own rich estates, and many of them were shortsighted enough to accept the "pauper lots", of one-fourth of normal area, without obligation for redemption-dues, which the Emancipation Settlement offered to them. This is why we see the peasants of Poltava and Kharkov burning the houses of squires, and dividing up their cattle, implements and grain stores in 1902: and why the seizures of land in 1917 and 1918 came near to doubling the peasant holdings of Ukrain, while they added but a small additional fraction to those of some other regions.

We do not find the peasants of the Black Earth refusing their Emancipation allotments, or paying to be rid of them. But this not infrequently happened in the region of deficit, before the value of land increased in the closing decades of the nineteenth century. The flight of a whole village from its allotment of marsh land, with the Police Officer pursuing, as Pharaoh and his host pursued the Children of Israel, is the subject of a story by one of the many writers who have left us pictures of peasant life. The novelist Korolenko tells us of a village in the Nizhni Novgorod area, which had been in rebellion for thirty years against the Emancipation Settlement. There was a legend of mysterious strangers who had left a "golden letter", bidding the people to resist. For twenty years they held out, and would neither take possession of their land nor pay their redemption-dues. Once the judge of the Rural Court visited them with a posse of police: tied them to their ploughs, and dragged them over the land, by way of symbolical investiture with possession. But, even when they had thus "accepted" their land, they continued to refuse payment; and, despite all methods of pressure, beating, withholding of passports, and proposed withholding of relief in the catastrophic famine of 1891–2, they had still not paid in 1892, though by this time they were cultivating the land.

The police were the collectors of taxes, and the responsibility of the village up to 1903 was joint. The Mir paid, and recovered the shares from its members as best it could. The State did not ask how. A story-writer, who was a genuine student of village life, has depicted for us the working of the system. The Village Meeting gets the money from a contractor, one of the local "rich", and makes the defaulters over to him to work off their debts. They pass into a sort of temporary slavery, where they have to work up to their knees in water. Two of them are a young married couple. The contractor forces his attentions on the wife, the pair run away, the police bring them back. The contractor is found in a ditch with a cracked skull, and the young husband is convicted of his murder. At the end we see him being led off to the "column of disgrace", a sort of stocks, to be exhibited to the people before being taken to the galleys. If the evil did not often go as far as this, the working off of arrears by personal labour was common. Whipping was even commoner: but, in spite of the vigour of the police, enormous arrears accumulated, which it was ultimately necessary to remit.

Beside the taxes, there were other liabilities such as attach to the ownership of land in all mainly agricultural countries, where there is no reserve of general wage-labour; the mending of roads and bridges, the clearing of snow from railway lines, the breaking up of blocks in the timber floating down the rivers, the cutting of drains for the escape of floods, the running of official messages; at which no one dreamed of grumbling so long as the customary limits were not seriously overstepped. There was virtually no law for peasants. They did what the Elder, or the Meeting, or the Police told them to do, or suffered the usual physical admonitions for recalcitrance. The vagueness of the law for peasants extended to more serious matters than these. In the great majority of cases questions of succession were settled on the spot. But if they reached the Courts, the law of succession showed itself to be completely chaotic: and the decisions of the Supreme Court were so confused and con-

tradictory that the fundamental question, who is the owner
of a peasant holding on which the redemption-dues have been
paid in full, was practically insoluble before the Stolypin legislation of 1906.

Some of the serf-owners had been sadistically cruel. Still
more had lost their mental balance from the exercise of a virtually unrestricted power. In a few, the very best, power had
developed a grandeur and generosity of soul. Dostoievsky's picture of old Karamazov and his sons shows how isolation and
irresponsibility worked upon human nature. It seems that the
human will needs to have fixed limits set to it, if it is to be
saved from overbalancing; for power, like solitude, makes a
man either a god or a beast. In its more grotesque forms the
master's mania took the form of brutal practical jokes: such
as fastening the parish priest's beard to the table, when the
ecclesiastic had indulged too freely: and throwing the policeman into the pond. The old spirit in some measure survived
serfdom, for it takes generations to give sanity to a tyrant class,
as it takes generations to change a slave morality. Gleb
Uspensky, our most convincing source for rural Russia in the
seventies, tells us that the peasant is sure that the gentleman
understands nothing, and this is because of the lack of any
ordinary human relations between the two. There were exceptions, of course, but one of the best of them, Englehardt, who
has left a rural diary, got tired at last of the attempt to be a
good landlord without spoiling his peasants, and took refuge in
pure research. We see Count Leo Tolstoi, in the character of
Levin in *Anna Karenina,* struggling with a similar difficulty.
That remarkable movement of "going to the people", which
absorbed the attention of so many intellectuals in the seventies,
was in large part an effort of the conscience-stricken to restore
the broken links of a human relationship: but there was another element in it too, for by that time the revolutionary conviction was widely established.

Some of the squires, particularly in the region of deficit,
where labour was all, were hard hit by the Emancipation.
These withdrew to the towns to take up Government service,
which had begun to be better paid during the period of Alex-

ander II's reforms. A considerable number sold their land, sometimes to peasants, but sometimes to new owners who were often no improvement on the old. In the region of surplus the terms of emancipation were more favourable to the squires, who continued to cultivate their estates, and "drank beer and kept accounts", as the saying was, that is to say reduced the old lavish scale of their establishments. But everywhere difficulties of labour embarrassed the farming squire, particularly in good seasons when the peasants were occupied with their own land and not hard put to it to find a living. Towards the end of the nineteenth century there was a great extension of the practice of short leasing to peasants in the surplus zone, particularly in the Central Agricultural and Middle Volga regions. This practice exhausted the soil because the lessee had no motive for sparing it. It also encouraged the notion, already firmly established among the peasants, that the landlord, a mere parasite, had no rights in the land; and must bear its share of the responsibility for the peasant disturbances of 1902 and 1905.

Those squires who continued to farm were put to all sorts of shifts to find labour. In seasons of scarcity they had no trouble, and the practice arose of hiring in advance. In return for a payment down, the peasant bound himself to future service. When the time came for fulfilling the undertaking, he sometimes found himself too busy with his own crop. In the local society of doctor and schoolmaster and police superintendent, the squire was a personage. It was not difficult for him to set the administration—it would be a mockery to call it the law—in motion; but the peasant had a gift for passive resistance, and the local influences were not always successful. The complaint was therefore carried higher, and, in 1886, when reaction from the reforms of Alexander II was at its height, the Government legislated against what we may call criminal breach of contract of service. The police were empowered to bring back fugitives who had broken the conditions of their labour contracts. The landlords, on their part, were empowered to dismiss labourers for "rudeness"—an authority difficult to distinguish from a discretionary power to annul a contract. Rural Russia had evidently travelled part of the way back towards serfdom. A Provincial Conference on agricultural labour said in 1897 that relations between employer and worker were nowhere so strained as in the agricultural industry: "the one is forced to hire, the other is compelled to serve: and each suffers the other as an unavoidable evil."

The peasant, on his part, was conscious of no moral obligations either to the Government or the squire. Nicolas Lyeskov tells a story which shows where his sense of duty lay. One of his characters, an "intelligent", makes a journey by rail, passing three principal stations where tickets are inspected. At each of these he sees a long-bearded peasant dragged from the train and beaten by the railway staff. At the Moscow terminus he sees the same passenger beaten again, and sympathises with him on the treatment he has received. "God be praised!" says the peasant, "they only beat me four times at the large stations. They pulled me out and I got into another carriage each time. And here I am (showing a full purse) without having paid anything. All that I have earned is here. I take it to my little ones: and perhaps I shall give some to the Church." The "intelligent" says: "But it's stupid to give to the Church." "Don't you dare say that," says the peasant, putting his fist under the nose of the unbeliever.

The legal status—one might almost say the outlaw status—of the peasant affected his social position. The inn parlours had "black" half, where the "black people" sat, isolated from their superiors, the merchants and officials. The kind of work which peasants did was called "black work", unfit for those of higher status: and when an "intelligent" started a farm of his own near Ufa, under the inspiration of the teaching that "intelligents" should work with their hands, the local Colonel of Gendarmes, hearing that an "intelligent" was doing "black" work, called him up and suggested that he should join the Service—with a capital S. He was a member of one caste, doing work which properly belonged to another. Good people do not break the rules of caste: unless, indeed, they are nihilists.

The "black" people were a caste too, not quite untouchable, but near it. The peasant who had just returned from acting as a juror at a trial for arson or robbery, might find himself whipped for arrears of tax or for impertinence to the village Elder. The contradictions between the functions and the status, and between one part of the status and another, and their effects upon peasant psychology, have been subjected to analysis by Karonin, one of our painters of peasant life. His Michael Lunin is a sort of peasant Hamlet, conscious that the times are out of joint. He has arguments with his father about his father's right to beat him, grows moody with thinking about the freedom given in 1861 and the beatings which the rural Court administers. It is characteristic of the important part played by bread, that one of the things which he contrasts with his theoretical freedom is the adulterated bread which he and his kind have to eat. He wants to live like a man, and finds it impossible. After a humiliating collision with the Elder and the usurer (the village already calls the latter by name of *kulak*), he persuades his father to get him a passport (there was no getting one otherwise, for patriarchal authority was still a reality), and leaves the village. In a second story, we see him making friends with a studious locksmith, with whose help he educates himself. He marries a village girl, who cannot understand him, and remains an unhappy man, all the more unhappy for his glimpse of the book of enlightenment: and the beatings administered to his likes continue to torment him. It is the story of the broken road. "Yegor, the free man" is another of Karonin's peasant figures. Yegor was born something of a precisian. He wanted to "live by the rules". In particular he likes to pay his dues punctually, and this love of punctual payment becomes an obsession. A shipshod landlord, for whom he has worked, withholds his wages, and he fears that he will be late with a payment. He goes to the landlord's house to demand his money, when the landlord has guests, and makes a disturbance at the door. The guests comes out to back their host, Yegor is hustled, and the police officer, who is one of the party, locks him up in a cell. The shock of this injustice makes him ill: and, when he recovers, he is completely changed in appearance and character. He gives up all notion of being a "free-man", and endures casual beatings with the dull resignation of his fellow-peasants.

In a third story a book-loving peasant, much occupied with "cursed questions", falls into arrears from too much attention to his books. He gets the usual beating: and the shock causes him to take to drink. In Russia, as elsewhere, drink is the refuge of those whom life defeats and puzzles. The indignant squires and officials said there was more drinking than ever in the famine year 1891–2: and our inclination to disregard them, as mere praisers of the past, is contradicted by Leo Tolstoi's statement to the same effect.

The bitter cry of the possessing classes against the indiscipline, indolence, and drunkenness of the emancipated peasant caused Alexander III, in 1889, to establish a new network of rural officials known as the Land-Captains. They have been described as "official squires", and had indeed a general and vague mandate for doing many of the things which the serf-owners did before emancipation. They had a summary authority for the decision of partitions and of certain land disputes, and a general control over all rural institutions. The State regarded with a very jealous eye its own recent creation of the elective rural Councils, and from their very inception, hampered them and restricted their functions and authority. The Land-Captains served as an instrument for these purposes. Thus, the vital function of victualling in famine was transferred from the rural Councils to the Land-Captains, or divided uncertainly between the two, so as to cause a maximum of friction. The Land-Captains were generally military officers. Korolenko came across many of them in his experiences of famine relief, and has left us some thumb-nail sketches. There was the nice-soldier-boy, with a good military education, who set up a secret society to make relief lists, because someone had broken the windows of the parish priest for missing out his name. Another could not speak to an ordinary peasant without spitting objurgations at him, but had so high an opinion of the village Elders that he left everything in their hands. A third, with Slavophil sympathies, insisted that all who appeared before him should wear the old Russian peasant dress, and bow down to their waists in the old Russian way. A fourth, evidently a senior officer, with some control over the other Land-Captains, had been jobbed into his place in order to satisfy a pique against the rural Council and withheld the money which had been collected for it. We frequently hear that such and such a village was too remote for the Land-Captain to visit: and the touring habit, which is the saving virtue of bureaucracies in primitive countries, because it takes the official away from his papers into contact with life, was evidently perfunctory. Transfers were frequent, and officers did not know their territorial charges: two complaints which have been heard in another great agricultural Empire, having some remarkable resemblances to the Russia of the opening twentieth century.

The same writer has drawn for us a picture of the "old hand" in the police. He makes no bones of exceeding his authority, for who shall say where it ends, when no official superior is at hand? He looks upon the peasant, in the mass, as a rogue who is only awaiting his chance, and he is convinced that the district is being spoiled by indulgence. In famine times he is quite ready to collect, not only the current taxes, but also the arrears of past years. His report on conditions is always: "All is well": while the rural Council's doctor reports a raging epidemic of typhus. It is no novelty to the old hand. Typhus? Every year. Weeds in the bread? Always.

And there was truth in what the old hand reported. Famine is not a sudden apparition out of the void, but rather an intensification and extension of normal conditions. There always is typhus. There always are weeds mixed with the bread to adulterate it. Some degree of scarcity, affecting a smaller or larger number of individuals, is endemic. You no more get rid of famine, inchoate, incipient, demonstrating itself among the more helpless and incapable, from a purely agricultural country, than you get rid of the relieving officer and his unlucky applicants from modern industrial England. Good times show a shorter list. The name of famine, the name of slump, is kept for the worst times. But the spectre is always at the door, *for some*.

Poverty, bitter and grinding poverty, was always present in peasant Russia. The books are full of it: the landless peasant, perhaps not the most ill-starred, for he at least was not tied to a farm and its obligations: the peasant with a non-economic holding, which does not yield a living, without a change of methods beyond the wits and the means of the occupant: the horseless peasant, who must lay on the backs and arms of himself and his wife burdens too heavy for any but animal strength: the peasant in arrears, and the peasant in debt: the peasant at the drink shop: and, at the back of it all, the miserably inadequate yield, rarely as much as six or sevenfold of the seed, and smaller than in any other long-settled and populous country, including India. Even the occupant of an average holding of twenty to thirty acres of good agricultural land in the Black Earth zone had to look for outside earnings: and numbers in the rural areas could not find employment. The break-up of the joint-family, to which Emancipation gave an impetus, increased the economic strain by adding to the cost of living.

In judging the Russian standard of living, both at the time with which this chapter deals, and at a later stage, we must begin by banishing from our thoughts all comparisons with the United States of America, with Britain, and with Western Europe. Northern India, indeed, is more germane to the case, despite the contrast of temperature which makes the needs in housing and clothing widely different. There were gleams of something better: as when flax cultivation introduced a comparative prosperity into central Russia. Incipient industrialisation, which formed nuclei of special types of consumption, was the principal cause of improvement. Accessible markets for something other than cereals were a condition of a better life for the peasantry.

A monograph of a village eighty miles from Moscow, and sixty from the nearest railway station, shows us the people in the 1860's living in wooden huts with a floor space of about 240 square feet, thatched with straw. Prosperous villagers had two such huts, separated by doors with wickets. The poor had one. The stoves were great erections of clay, upon which some of the family slept. Many had no chimney. There was a little opening over the door near the roof, which let out the smoke after it had warmed, and blackened, both walls and people. The hut was lighted by burning splinters of fir. The kerosene lamp (without a globe) came in during the eighties. Clay was the material for cooking vessels, and clay or wood for plates and dishes. China was a rarity for holidays. Splinters of wood supplied the function of forks. The general sleeping place was the floor, on straw, which was brought in each night and taken out in the morning. All clothes were home spun. The men wore blue linen or hempen trousers and shirts with gussets under the arms: red ones for holidays: and the women wore *sarafans* (sleeveless dresses of printed linen, without buttons, but fastened by strips of stuff and girdles of coloured yarn; and bodices of home-made stuff, either wool or linen and wool mixed. For winter they wore trousers of the same material. Both men and women wore jackets of untanned sheepskin. The usual footgear was birch-bark sandals: leather boots only on holidays, and to church, and a pair lasted more than ten years. In the seventies when the village had taken to flax-growing, felt boots also made their appearance. For a long time there was only one cloth coat in the village: it was borrowed by friends for festive occasions.

The bridegroom had to pay a bride-price (a practice which was still common in 1934). The bride brought with her a linen bed-cover and bedding of coarse materials. After the marriage feast, *a whip was given to the bridegroom, as an emblem of power.* At meals the women stood while the men sat down to eat, and kept their heads bowed and their hands folded, not speaking till they were spoken to (survivals of this practice also are to be found).

The first samovars appeared in the seventies, but tea was only drunk on holidays. An infusion of dried apple-strips and St.-John's-wort was often used as a substitute. About 1890 when a dairying economy was being introduced, and the standard of prosperity was rising, the practice of daily tea-drinking began in this village. Meat was a rarity. The rye-bread was supplemented by cabbage-soup and barley-porridge. In autumn they added mutton fat or hemp oil to the porridge; in the spring, milk. Crushed hemp-seed was eaten with radishes; steamed turnips, and a *purée* of oats and peas, were eaten; herrings, biscuits, and sweets, were *only dreamed of,* says our informant.

The profits of the dairying brought about changes. In 1898 all the huts had a stove-pipe and some of them had two rooms. The only furniture, except the benches fastened along the walls under the icons, was a table. About 1900, wooden beds for the children made their appearance. After the Japanese war manufactured goods spread more widely, and returning soldiers introduced certain luxuries.

An official report of the early twentieth century on the needs of agriculture in a province of the Black Earth zone gives another picture, which will serve as a general one: though the absence of bath-houses was not universal.

The dwelling is usually a cottage of eighteen by twenty-one feet and about seven feet high. . . . Cottages having no chimneys are still very common. . . . Almost all have thatched roofs which often leak, and in the winter the walls are generally covered with dung to keep the place warm. A peasant family, sometimes a large one, lives in a space of some 2,400–3,000 cubic feet. They sleep in two tiers—on benches and on bunks—behind the stove. . . . In the localities which have no forests, the peasants use straw for fuel, and in years of poor harvests even dung, thus depriving their fields of much-needed manure. . . . Bath-houses are practically non-existent. . . . They almost never use soap. . . . Skin diseases . . . syphilis . . . epidemics, under-nourishment. . . . Such foodstuffs as meat, meal, bacon, and vegetable oils, appear on the family table only on rare occasions, perhaps two or three times a year. The normal fare consists of bread, kvas (a kind of weak beer brewed from rye) and often cabbage and onions, to which fresh vegetables may be added in autumn.

One might wish that the reporters had said something about windows. After the Civil War, at all events, window holes were often boarded up or stuffed with clouts. In Siberia we hear of the use of mica instead of glass. As to the prevalence of syphilis, Korolenko, writing of 1891–2, describes whole villages stricken with it, so that it was impossible to establish famine kitchens in them. The use of dung as fuel was, and is, more common than the description suggests. The cockroach behind the icon, and the bed bugs on the wall, were commonplaces of village life.

A long series of authorities, spread over a century, convinces us that bread, mere bread, has been, as it still is, the Russian staff of life. Subject to some modification among the working people of the towns, and to some very recent importation of town habits into the country, meat and fish have been rarities for holidays and festivals. Cabbage, potatoes, garlic, cucumbers and onions have been, and are, the only vegetables in common use. Milk and butter have been, and are, little consumed. The cooking has been, and is, done with hemp oil or sunflower oil, and not with animal fat. It is a myth that tea was ever widely drunk. There were all sorts of substitutes in the form of infusions of dried apples or dried radishes and the like. A writer who was a peasant agriculturist himself, and was taken up by Count Tolstoi because of his literary promise, tells us that, before the flax cultivation began, there were only three samovars in his village, and one of these was kept for show, as being the smart thing. A budget for a middling peasant in a year of good harvest on the Black Earth zone shows, as items of food expenditure, only bread, salt, meat for three holidays, fish for Shrove-tide, vodka for two holidays. The peasant probably obtained, in addition, onions, potatoes, and part of his bread supply, off his own land. Kvas was the common drink. One authority, indeed, tells us that vodka was drunk once or twice a day during the heavy work of harvest: but her example must have been something of a *viveur*. Meat, as a regular diet, comes in only when the peasant leaves farm work for some other occupation. Thus Count Tolstoi, whose special familiarity was with the provinces of the Black Earth, tells us in the *Kreutzer Sonata* that the usual food of a strong peasant, when engaged in light field labour, consists of bread, kvas, and onions. When he enters into the service of a railway company, his food is porridge and a pound of meat daily.

We have said that bread is the Russian staff of life: but it is not the bread, "water taught to stand up", which passes for such in Britain or the United States of America. At its best it is of excellent rye flour, not deprived of its nutritive constituents, stiff, solid, with an acid tang in it: stuff for unspoiled digestions. Two pounds of it are a fair daily ration, but larger amounts are eaten during heavy field work, and the soldier's ration is more. Baron Haxthausen, after a journey made in 1843, says that five pounds was the harvest ration, and that, in White-Russia, a man would eat seven pounds. As we learn that harvest work often lasted eighteen hours out of the twenty-four, this occasional heroic consumption is not impossible.

Bread kept a man in working, or in fighting, trim—if there was enough of it. There is abundant testimony in our writers on Russian peasant life to show that there seldom was enough, even if statistics of the balance remaining after exportation did not raise a suspicion of deficiency. The first question which is put to the peasant jurors, in a story already cited, by their fellow villagers who have taken up work in town, is about this primal need. "Is there bread?" Precisely this question was put to the present writer in 1933 by an old woman in a Moscow church, who wanted to know conditions in England. She moistened her lips as she put it. In the story the answer is: "By God's blessing, it will last till the Great Feast (Christmas) if we are careful with it." There was no question of it lasting all the year round till the next harvest, at least in the deficit provinces. Some exhausted their supply within a few weeks after harvest: some had enough till Christmas: some till Lent. Bread was a thing to be treated with respect. The loaf must be stood upright on the table. It must be broken, not cut. Cutting was disrespectful. A generation earlier, the opinion still survived among a few that it was a sin to sell corn.

The most provident began from the outset to mix adulterants (sometimes bran, sometimes a bitter weed which our dictionaries translate as pig-weed) with their flour. In a bad season all had to do this.

When the bread supply failed, the household, or some of its members, began to "go out for morsels", to wander and ask their more fortunate fellows to supply their need. This was not regarded as ordinary beggary. All the poorer peasants did it in their turn. It almost approached to a system of mutual insurance. A asks from B, this year, knowing that B will ask from A next. There was no disgrace in asking, but it was bad to refuse, so long as there was anything in the bin. A few, of course, abused the practice by asking while they still had a remnant: and we may guess that it did not survive the general practice of marketing the surplus.

In the villages of central and north-central Russia cottage handicrafts were well established and had been exploited by merchants from the eighteenth century onwards. Baron Haxthausen, nearly twenty years before the Emancipation, found whole villages of smiths, curriers and linen makers, who received advances on condition of supplying the dealers. Even at this early date there were complaints that the Government was favouring the factory at the expense of cottage industry: and it is not long before we hear of the handicraftsmen falling hopelessly into debt to the merchants. The Populists, who believed that Russia would circumvent the economic developments which had created the capitalist system in the West, disliked the factory and hoped much from the small handicraft. But it seems likely that in Russia, as elsewhere, cottage industries could survive only in so far as they possessed special artistic value, or supplemented factory production with cheaper goods for local consumption. The numbers finding employment in this way continued, however, to be large at the end of the period with which this chapter deals: and, as late as 1911, Mr. Monkhouse puts them at three and a half millions in summer and eight millions in winter.

We are not surprised to find that the peasant was brutalised by the conditions of his life. One of our writers, whose Siberian

stories had great vogue in the seventies, describes the roast-
ing, by their captors, of horse-thieves over a slow fire. This
was the revenge for losses caused to peasant transport-drivers.
Fire-raisers were often beaten to death, and this was in the
comparative civilisation of the Moscow region. The treatment
of women was coarse and cruel. The woman was "unclean",
and many of the old men would not enter the bath-house
after her. Wife-beating was entirely approved, by public opinion, and a particular kind of possession or hysteria, supposed
to be due to grief and ill-treatment, was common among
women. Life, and the land, made such pitiless demands that
there was no chance of the growth of any finer feelings.
"Peasants marry their girls in autumn, rather than in the
spring, for the same reason that they sell a cow in autumn
rather than in spring—to save winter keep." This is how
Englehardt follows up his story of a handsome girl, the darling
of her parents—till she fell seriously ill. Then she was sent
back, before she had fully recovered, to the tremendous tasks
of the village woman, caught a chill and grew rapidly worse.
The mother was philosophical and calculating. "She'll die:
that's all about it. In autumn we should have had to marry
her, so she would have been out of the house then. She'll die:
and there'll be less cost." In other words, a burial costs less
than a marriage. It is the deer, smelling her dead fawn, and,
assured of its death, springing away into the forest: but the
deer that has learned to speak and count.

It is a relief to turn to a picture, by Tolstoi's peasant protégé, of the high jinks of the young people in the Moscow
region, in the dead season between spring sowing and hay-
cutting. They did not worry themselves with the hoe, or indeed with weeding in any form. They meet at Church after
mass and on holidays. It's all picnicking and dancing in the
open, to the music of the concertina, with the lads from the
factories coming home for the Easter holiday, and, with their
fine city ways and smart city clothes, disturbing the hearts of
the village lasses, and arousing the emulation of the village
boys. Then comes the hay-cutting, and with it the beginning of
the summer's heavy tasks, when manual work often lasts

longer than the sun. Admirers of the peasant life, who have never felt the ache in their shoulders, nor the calluses on their hands, have talked of the joy of work. If there ever was such joy, it was not for the Russian peasant, when once his time of "suffering", as he calls it, that is of harvest work, was upon him. It was a time of dust and heat, when the children, neglected for many hours, fell ill and languished. All but the strongest were at the very end of their strength, and those pretty dancing girls aged cruelly fast. It often happened that grain was left uncut or uncarried, when the short open season came to its end.

The rough and inconsiderate treatment of women did not mean that they had no influence in the peasant home. Under the patriarchal system of the joint-family, the house-mother was as much the queen, as the house-father was king, of the household. She had her way over the marriages of the young people, and ruled the daughters-in-law with a rod of iron. A Smolensk landlord, whose experiences we have already had occasion to quote, tells us that in introducing any agricultural novelty, such as flax cultivation, it was essential to look closely to the interests of the women. Woman had her separate pecuniary interest, because the "woman's box", as it was called, was by custom her inviolable property, and even the husband was punishable, by the practice of the rural Court, if he took anything from it without permission. The wages earned by a woman in summer, when she worked in the field alongside of her husband, belonged to the household: but winter earnings went into the "woman's box". Englehardt got the women on his side over the flax cultivation, because the kneading or stripping of the product to extract the fibre was done after St. Philip's Day, in the winter. One of the factors of the Bolshevik success over collectivisation is similar. It secures a separate dividend to the woman for the work which she does.

Another of our authorities who is describing the ways of the middling peasants in the Black Earth belt, about the turn of the century, tells us that hens belonged entirely to the woman. The cow was not precisely her property, but she had special rights in the milk. The spring wool of the sheep belonged to the woman, and the autumn wool to the man. The man sowed the flax. The woman gathered it and stripped or kneaded it. There were mutual thefts between the spouses, and not at all uncommon either. So much for the picture of the completely patriarchal household, with the man as ruler of it. Pigs were so much a special department of the women that the Bolshevik agricultural authorities have in some areas experienced difficulty in persuading the men to attend to them: for these habits are stronger even than revolutions. The title of pig-breeding expert has, however, assisted the process of conversion.

Disappointment with the results of popular education has given currency to opinions which emphasise the mental vigour and originality of the untaught. It is necessary therefore to remind ourselves that literacy is (or was, until broadcasting became common) the sole passport to the thought of those with whom we cannot converse: in other words, the means of widening and varying one's experience of other men. The rural Councils of Alexander II achieved an increase of literacy in the village, but it remained low among men and all but non-existent among women. It is not surprising therefore that superstitions were firmly established. As superstitions mean that true causes are unknown and unsought, the effects on health and economic conditions were destructive. The troubles of a farmer who wished to work on Saints' Days, and not to lose agricultural opportunities by escorting the holy icons from village to village, are vividly described by Count Tolstoi's peasant protégé. His fellow villagers said he was responsible for the lack of rain, and he was prosecuted for offending the religious feelings of other persons. The diseases of human beings and of animals were often attributed to the evil eye, and treated with charms.

The "darkness" of village life was proverbial: a darkness which was more than ignorance, for it included a mass of false knowledge. It was worse, of course, in the women: for the woman's path was "from stove to threshold": she came into contact with no outside experiences except the gossip of her kind. We see her at her darkest in that horrifying tragedy of peasant life, Count Tolstoi's *Power of Darkness*. The murderer man in that drama can have the consciousness of sin, and can repent. The women show an animal-like unawareness of wrong: but a skill in planning and executing it which no animal could possess. This was one of the unintended revenges which woman took, upon man and his offspring, for domestic slavery and brutal treatment. She became a citadel of darkness in his household, and made a prison for her captor.

What did the Church do for the peasant? The Black Clergy, who filled all the important posts in the hierarchy, hardly touched the village. But every village, that is to say every Church-village, for villages within a radius of a dozen miles or more were grouped round a settlement having a Church, had its married parish priest. At some time in the past he had been an elected functionary, and there was a traditional memory of his status as a servant of the Mir. Once by law a member of a hereditary class, he continued for long to be in practice the successor of his father or his father-in-law in the "living". There was normally no salary, the State's subvention for priests' pay being mainly expended *in partibus infidelium*, or among those whom the law recognised as unorthodox. He lived on the land allotted by the Mir, and Englehardt tells us he was often a very good farmer and a "knowledgeable" man. For the rest, he received fees for his spiritual ministrations, and there was notoriously much bargaining over these. He was weak in the article of preaching, and did not make a great success of the pedagogic function which began to be thrust upon him by the State in the latter part of the period which we are considering. He was not quite a representative of civilisation in the village, and yet his ways were a little superior to those of the peasants about him. His reputation, if we are to believe the proverbial philosophy of the people, included greed (be it remembered that he was very poor) and drunkenness (life was hard and dull). One of our diarists tells us a story of a holy icon, left under a tree in the forest by the young people who were escorting it on its round of visits, and forgotten by the clergy, who were rather tipsy from the entertainment they had received. Gleb Uspensky perpetrates the somewhat cruel epigram that the priest is wanted, as the post-master is wanted, drunk or sober, to send off the letters. In the period of repression which began after the murder of Alexander II, he was used for police purposes, to report political secrets discovered under the seal of confession, and to watch the schoolmaster of the rural Council school. But the ecclesiastical seminaries were themselves hotbeds of revolution, and the poverty of theological students and of priests fomented discontent in the class. Stalin was a student in the Tiflis seminary in the middle of the nineties. The village priests were open to bribes, and often attested, for a consideration, the participation in the sacred rites of persons who neglected them or belonged to other confessions. As to their cost to the people, one of the few budgets which we possess shows us the middling peasant of the Black Earth zone, about the turn of the century, paying six per cent of his income in Church charges.

The same authority who gives this budget says that the children are rapidly infected with freedom of thought and do not take the priest's denunciation of the wrath to come very seriously.

The contribution made by the village priest to peasant civilisation was not, on the whole, a great one: and he did not hold very high the banner of the Church. But he was very human, and very like his flock, perhaps a little better, and he dealt humanly and not oppressively, very rarely refusing the consolations of the Church to the really poor. Sometimes he rose above this standard. In his famine work in the Nizhni Novgorod neighbourhood Korolenko met three parish priests of the higher type, and one of them he calls a true pastor. A little sin makes for the virtue of humility, and perhaps for that of charity too: and a little sin was quite common among the parish clergy.

A great reform is often followed by a tendency to rest upon the reputation of what has been achieved. After the Emancipation, and the accompanying reforms, the conscience of statesmen was not entirely asleep over the backwardness and poverty of nine-tenths of the population: but neither was it entirely awake, or at least not awake till mischief had already been done. In 1880 the repeal of the Salt Tax, and two years later that of the Poll Tax, were important measures of fiscal relief. Soon after, the Peasant Bank was established to facilitate purchase of additional land: and the more enterprising and thrifty of the peasants benefited greatly by the opportunity: though, for the mass, this only meant the growth of inequality in the village. The remarkable growth of internal colonisation in Russia attracted the notice of foreign observers. Nicolas II himself intervened to support emigration to Siberia. But the great developments there fall outside of the period of the present chapter. In 1893 a special Ministry of Agriculture was set up. It had a miserably inadequate budget; but Russia was not the only country which was slow to recognise the needs and opportunities of agriculture. Up to 1897 Agricultural Cooperation, which at a later date extended itself very widely, was suspected by the Russian State of a dangerous political tendency: but a start had been made with it before the Revolution of 1905. If industrial development was the remedy of agricultural poverty, as the historian of Agriculture before the Revolution says it was, Count Witte's work during the eleven years of his administration of finance, laid a solid foundation for agricultural prosperity. Not only the material, but also the moral and civil disabilities of the peasant began at this time to receive the attention of the more farseeing: and, in 1898, Witte, then at the zenith of his career, addressed to Nicolas II a letter in which he recounted the grievances of the class. His list included corporal punishment, arbitrary taxation by the Mir, arbitrary restrictions on leaving the home-village, the entire absence of legal definition of rights and liabilities, and even of the laws of peasant inheritance, and oppression by the Land-Captains and other officials. It was only for those included in the legal category of peasant that these grievances had their full significance: though arbitrary, and extraordinary, laws existed for the whole population.

The rural Councils, established by Alexander II, or, more correctly, some of them, were zealous in their attempts— sometimes thwarted by the State—to ameliorate the lot of the peasant. Those of the Moscow province busied themselves with the encouragement of the cultivation of grasses: a fundamental need of an agriculture dependent on cattle. An expert who had distinguished himself by his success with clover, found himself in prison. We are not told why: but, recalling some of the things which have happened to the experts and the "intelligents" of a later and less orthodox epoch, we may be pardoned for thinking that we can guess. The State, then as now, is a jealous State: and it changes less than some suppose.

The rural Council of Tver, as well as that of Moscow, established agricultural advisers: but the Governor of the province vetoed the expenditure. When the members protested, the executive was replaced by obedient nominees.

The chief items of expenditure of the rural Councils were schools and hospitals, and their primary schools obtained a good reputation. They aroused the suspicion of Government, which aimed at transferring educational work to a subservient Church: laying a great stress upon religious and "sound" political teaching; but a very large proportion of the whole expenditure on primary education continued to be that of the Councils.

1780–1847. A feature of the period which we have under consideration is the growth in the educated class of a sense of duty towards the peasantry, and the direction of that sense of duty towards the study of facts. In the pictorial art we leave altogether behind us the imaginary shepherds and shepherdesses, copied from the French, of an earlier epoch: and, by way of Venezianov with his much idealised *Girl on the threshing floor* and somewhat more natural *Shepherd boy asleep*, we arrive at Miasoyedov, depicting, in 1872, the peasant members of the rural Council taking their meal of bread and onions on the flagstones outside the Council building, and at Savitsky's picture of the peasants kneeling down by the roadside to receive the visiting icon. In literature we pass from the exquisite artistry of Turgeniev, describing—from the distance of the cultivated man and the artist—the peasant in the latter days of serfdom, to the balder, more realistic tales of Gleb Uspensky, who might perhaps have been an artist if he would, but chose to be an analyst and a recorder of fact, and a formulator of social theories. Other writers, of less literary merit, but almost equal sociological interest, take up the tale of peasant life: and diarists and recorders of the facts of village work and of agriculture begin to swell the volume of information. Even statistics, always a weak point in Russia, receive the attention of some of the rural Councils, and Gleb Uspensky makes a gallant effort to put flesh and colour upon the disjointed and misjointed skeleton with the sketches entitled: *Figures come to life.* Finally, the Government, frightened by the hoarse murmur of rising discontent, begins to study the awakening Demogorgon, and the reports of Commissions of Inquiry begin to pour from the official presses. Of that strange idolisation of the peasant, which was of the essence of the Populist faith, of its share in the revolutionary movements, and of the formation of the Social Revolutionary party, we shall have occasion to speak elsewhere.

From 1871 to 1896 was a period of fall in the price of cereals: and Russian wheat in the latter year was selling for little more than half of its earlier price. This change was not accompanied by a corresponding cheapening of manufactured commodities. The protective policy, compelled by the fall in the value of the principal medium of payment for imports, kept up the prices of the latter. The deficit food-grower, that is to say the bulk of the poor peasantry, should have gained by the low price of grain. But his taxes and dues compelled him to raise money in autumn, when harvest prices were at their lowest: and he had to buy seed again later when the approach of the sowing season made it dear. After 1896, when the general trend of cereal prices was upwards, the position of all buyers of food or seed grain was even worse: and, along with the rise of rents which accompanied the rise of prices, this was a factor in the peasant disturbances which preceded and accompanied the revolution of 1905.

In 1902 there were disturbances in the Black Earth zone, particularly among peasant communities adjoining large estates and linked with them by the practice of leasing land, which was cultivated by means of peasant stock and equipment. In northeastern Ukrain, Poltava and Kharkov, and in parts of Saratov, a Volga province, they took a systematic form. On eighty-two estates of the Poltava and Kharkov provinces, the people—all classes of them, it appears—assembled to the sound of the bell, which was the ordinary method of summoning a village meeting, divided up the animals, implements, grain and fodder stores of the squires, burned their houses and outbuildings, and dispersed quietly before the defenders of law and order arrived. The Danish official who made the agrarian settlement, known by the name of the Minister Stolypin, says that these disturbances were worse than anything since the rebellion of Pugachev: but the rebels of 1902 never kept the field, and they committed no murders. The object was to frighten the squires into abandoning their estates: and this was in many instances achieved. The systematic procedure is indicative of organisation: and the participation of the Elders and of the middling peasants is a portent of the troubles that follow. Evidently the Mir—the hope of conservative idealists—is beginning to play them false. Repression was rigorous, and village constables were now introduced in forty-six provinces of the empire: but the Government judged it wise to abolish the system of joint responsibility for taxes, which was a particular grievance.

1905. We are now in a position to suggest some of the reasons of the peasant discontent, which expressed itself in ever-present rumours of an impending redistribution of land by the Tsar, before it took the violent form. There was an actual shortage of land in part of the Black Earth zone: in all parts there were many peasants with non-economic holdings and with no land. Over large areas the landlords seemed to have abdicated all responsibilities for the land except the collection of its rents. The unbalanced holding, deficient in pasture or in hayfields for cattle, was, to the deficit zone, what the smallness of arable holdings was to the surplus zone, a means of reducing the amount of fruitful labour which the peasant could expend on his land. The yield of the land, owing to general economic conditions, among which was the still backward though advancing state of industry, was so low that an average holding was insufficient to keep a family in well-being. Rural unemployment and under-employment, except in the neighbourhood of the manufacturing centres, were rife: though excessive work, at busy seasons, was usual owing to the scanty supply of animals and improved implements. Indebtedness was widespread. There was no capital for improved methods, except at the command of the squires and a minority of prosperous peasants. There were few centres of demand for any variety of local products, outside of the market for cereals. Up to the time of the remission of the Redemption dues, the imposts on the peasant were heavy, and the method of collecting them was harsh and inelastic, varied by spasms of wholesale remission at coronations and the birth of heirs. Not least important, though not most frequently mentioned, was the outrage upon human dignity which the legal and illegal status of the peasantry continued to tolerate. The law for the peasant was the will of the official and of the landlord.

Such were the grievances which, taking the compendious form of a demand for more land (very much as the early English peasants asked for "the laws of King Alfred"), set in motion the elemental force which was to shake and finally overthrow the fabric of Tsarism. That force might have exhausted itself, as formerly in the rebellions of Stenka Razin and Emilian Pugachev, in a temporary orgy of ill-directed destruction, if it had not been supplemented and guided by another, far weaker, but also far better organised, than itself. The town-workman, himself part-peasant, or at most a townsman of not more than a couple of generations' standing, is now on the point of emerging as the leader of the malcontent peasantry; and the intellectuals have for some time been doing for the peasant a better thing than idolising him: they have been attempting to understand.

Chapter 3

The Revolution of 1905

> "An incompetent Government is being opposed by an ineffectual Revolution."
>
> A Japanese Observer, quoted by
>
> MR. MAURICE BARING.
>
> "Russia was and still is being played with like a toy. In the eyes of our rulers was not the Japanese campaign itself a war with toy soldiers?"
>
> COUNT WITTE'S MEMOIRS.

THE PASTORAL LIFE makes men companions of the stars and wild associates of their own cattle. Agriculture brings them nearer to one another: and, as soon as the earliest stage of the woodland-clearing is past, combines them into communities. But the communities are small and scattered because, until much has been learned of the means of controlling nature, a square mile can barely hold half a dozen families. Industrial tasks draw them closer. But the final concentration comes with the rise of the factory, and is most complete when machinery begins to be operated by power. In this new phase of human existence, man lives in a crowd of other men doing like work and having common interests. If the farmer learns by looking over the hedge, the factory hand sees more and at closer quarters across his bench.

It has been calculated that there were ten millions of male

non-agricultural workers in the Russia of 1905. They were for the most part scattered over the rural areas, and employed in small handicrafts. But a substantial fraction was employed in factories of exceptionally large size, and these workers were more closely massed together than those of any of the great industrial countries. The proportion employed in large works having more than a thousand hands apiece was in Russia three times as great as in Germany. The less industrialised country had the larger proportion of the largest-scale industry.

Karl Marx, who got his industrial facts from England, noted that the factory was a potential centre of social life, of play and study and thought and action, as well as of industrial production. In the early days of the industrial revolution in every country, when hours were too long for play or study or thought, it was, at least, a centre for the exchange of grievances as well as for work, and that formidable weapon, the strike, was forged on its stithies.

In Russia the factory originated with serf-labour, but Emancipation gave to its growth a greater impetus. Moscow became a centre of the textile industry: and iron and steel established themselves in St. Petersburg. In 1884 George Plekhanov was demonstrating to the Populist Revolutionaries that the Capitalism, which they believed that Russia could evade, was already upon them both in town and in village. Between 1887 and 1898 the output of iron and steel almost trebled, and that of textiles almost doubled itself. A prosperous class of owners and middlemen came into existence, having no concern with their workers except as instruments of profit. The factory worker, at first a seasonal hand more interested in his land than in the factory, and returning periodically to his village, became, in an increasing degree, particularly in the metal trades, a permanent, even a hereditary, townsman. The abuses which characterise the early stages of industrialisation were not less gross in Russia than elsewhere: exploitation of female and child labour: hours of enormous length: wages on a tropical scale in a rigorous climate: no guards on the machinery, and accidents common, with no compensation: heavy and capricious fines: an oppressive truck system: housing which was not housing at all, but meant, at best, a share in a common barrack, at worst, sleep beside the machine: all the familiar accompaniments of the worst wage-slavery, relieved only by the possibility of return to an even more precarious existence in the village. There were higher and lower grades of labour, and some of this is not fully applicable to the iron and steel workers of St. Petersburg or to the railway men: but such was the lot of the mass, and the luckiest fared little better. Much of the capital was foreign and its owners absentees.

The story-writer Zlatovratsky, gives us a glimpse of the bachelors' quarters in a tannery in a provincial town of the Moscow region. It is a holiday. The men are lounging on benches round the walls. Light and ventilation are bad and "they get used to the smell". In one corner are five workmen with a fat, dishevelled, red-faced woman. "Shall I let your underlinen down for you?" says one of the men: and there is a scuffle and a laugh. Further on, the visitors tread on a drunken workman, and help him on to a bench. The others say that this man was homesick for his wife and children, but could not earn enough to keep them in town, when they came to him: so sent them home again and began to drink. The visitors say he should be sent back to the land. "The land, it's God's job." "Aye, boys, but you go away from the land when it doesn't feed you." They go further, and come upon a consumptive youth spelling out a novel: and so on and so on, a Hogarthian picture, with someone picking out the notes of a sentimental song on a cracked harmonium.

Mr. Monkhouse, whose experience was later, tells us of bad sanitary conditions and excessive drinking and says that living and working conditions varied greatly. Another foreign engineer, Mr. Rukeyser, describes pre-revolutionary workers' houses in St. Petersburg as having less than three hundred square feet of floor space for more than twenty workers *of both sexes* and all ages, which gives barely room to lie down: but it is likely that the shifts prevented them from being present all together at the same time. The windows were incapable of being opened. The shifts were of ten, eleven, twelve, even fourteen hours. In Moscow a woman's body was used to clean a chimney flue, as children's bodies were used in the England of the first half of the nineteenth century. In his own asbestos factory, before improvements were made in 1929, the living space was six feet by twelve for a worker's family. As in the dismal cellar described by Maxim Gorky in his *Down and Out,* the beds were boards covered with rags. There were no latrines (better than bad ones, if there was accessible space in sanitary conditions outside). In the Moscow of 1896 the present writer saw young women queuing up with men for access to latrines. An English writer describes a gold-field in Siberia, with no police or sanitary arrangements and an enormous death-rate: like one of the worst American mining camps, before the administration caught up with the boom.

The workmen were not allowed, before the Revolution of 1905, to form their own organisations. But they actually adapted a practice brought from the village, and elected their own elders (Starosta), who became the germ of the later Soviets. From the seventies strikes became frequent, generally for the payment of withheld wages or by way of protest against excessive or capricious fines. In the latter half of the nineties they were declared on a large scale, and the demands included the limitation of hours.

There is nothing surprising about bad conditions in factory labour. Most of them can be paralleled in present or very recent Bombay, and they tend to come into existence everywhere till the operations of large-scale industry are brought under control. One competitor cannot afford to be more considerate than another. Only the public authority can force them all to be considerate. The indictment against the Tsarist Government is that it did not, except spasmodically, attempt to deal with the evils of industrialisation. Nicolas Bunge has left behind him a noble memory of his tenure of the portfolio of Finance in the eighties. Beside the abolition of the poll-tax and the foundation of the Peasant Bank, he set limits to the practice of fining factory hands, provided for fortnightly payments of wages and for a fortnight's notice of dismissal, and secured liberal factory legislation. The legislation was made nugatory by inadequate inspecting staff. It is said that there were only two inspectors for the two thousand factories of the Moscow region. To propose additions was regarded as sympathy with subversive tendencies, as Count Witte found when he broached the subject with Nicolas II. Bunge was dismissed "for socialist leanings".

A German historian of the revolution has said that Tsarism under Alexander III and his unfortunate successor, became the policeman of Capitalism. An incident recorded by Madame Krupskaya, Lenin's widow, helps to illustrate the epigram. A young worker, who had been in her Sunday-school, argued with the manager of a factory in St. Petersburg against an order to change over from two mules per worker to three. He was deported under police escort to his native village. On small provocation the Cossacks were called in and used their whips. It was as though the Government had wished to establish the Marxian thesis that every State is a class-State. Whether as cause or as consequence of the policy, or both, there was a close connection between factory discontent and revolutionary aims: and the Figner sisters and others of like subversive convictions were employed in the factories from the middle of the seventies. Of the singular device of "police socialism", which attempted to convince the workers that the Government was their friend, I have something to say elsewhere.

Count Witte was Finance Minister from 1892 to 1903, a period of extraordinary developments, in the railway system and in industry, with the establishment of a gold standard, the encouragement of foreign and domestic capital, and the intensification of protective tariffs. Wages rose and strikes multiplied. Two large strikes in 1897 led to legislation for the limitation of hours. Adults were to work not more than eleven and a half hours, or not more than ten if nightwork was included. But secret instructions nullified the law. The temptation to pursue "prosperity" (for the rich were growing richer and the resources of the State were being doubled) was too great to allow of interference with the freedom of employers. By this time the young Lenin was busy in the St. Petersburg factories, illustrating the teachings of Marx with the every-day occurrences of working life: and we can imagine the reactions of him and his hearers to the secret instructions.

The boom of 1897 was succeeded by the slump of 1899, and the *Novoye Vremya* most conservative of newspapers, said that unemployment was reducing the workers to despair, and called for reforms *"from above* as in 1861" (the year of the emancipation of the serfs); and was punished by suspension for a week. The first political strikes came after 1900. In 1901 the demand for an eight-hour day put the onus of decision not upon individual employers but upon the Government itself. The first general strike, which took place in South Russia in 1903, and included the great oil centre of Baku, shows how far general organisation had progressed. The movements of rural and urban discontent were converging upon one another. At this moment a sketch of two reactionary figures will help us to understand the conservative side of the case. One is that of Konstantin Pobiedonostsev, who had been the tutor in succession of the two princes who became Alexander III and Nicolas II, and also helped to instruct the twenty-two-year-old Empress Alexandra Feodorovna, when she arrived in Russia as the bride of Nicolas, eager to understand the inner significance of the Orthodox Church and the Autocratic State. A man of strong religious convictions and of lofty personal character, he had assisted to draft the judicial reforms of Alexander II, and had been the translator of Thomas à Kempis. He became the lay chairman of the Synod of Ecclesiastics which governed, under the supreme control of the Emperor, the Orthodox Church. He has left on record reflections which read like a Commination Service. He condemns democracy, elections, eloquence and representative institutions: the jury system, the press, free education, obligatory school attendance, all education (except "real education in the sphere of domestic, professional and social life"): institutions devoted to charity and beneficence (on the ground that love cannot be organised): justice (when it takes the form of a judicial machine): reform (except in periods when reform

is the "ripe fruit of social evolution"): devotion to knowledge:
and the doctrine of evolution. He complains that we see authority abusing its mission: the unjust distribution of honours:
wealth acquired by rapine over-mastering power itself (very
like the Marxian theory that the State is always a class-State):
thousands and millions sacrificed to the god of war: the innumerable multitude vegetating in insensibility, racked by pri-
vation, living and dying in wretchedness. As for the Church,
its clergy is rude, inactive, ignorant, without influence on its
flocks, teaching little and seldom: to the illiterate the Scriptures are unknown: in remote districts the congregation understands nothing of the words of the service, or even of the
Lord's Prayer.

Finally he condemns the sins of the Intelligentsia: *welt-
schmerz*, pessimism and nihilism: but the reader cannot but
feel that the writer of the reflections himself suffers from some
or all of these. Through it all there runs a note of despair.
All this tangle of evils he does not expect to unravel. The mischief is done. The dissolvent acids are at work. He can only
look on, lament, and denounce.

True, he still believes in Autocracy, provided that it is unlimited by law: although "the violence, abuse, folly and selfish-
ness of power raise rebellion, and humanity has suffered dis-
enchantment, betrayal, affliction from it". And, in spite of the
weaknesses which he has revealed, he believes in the Church,
whose duty it is "to inspire the people with respect for the
law and for power, and to inspire in power respect for human
freedom": brave words.

He draws a harrowing picture of the evils which need
amelioration: so that for a moment we think that he is condemning the Tsarist administration. There are faults in schools,
hospitals, libraries, sanitation, justice, church-worship: and
these faults need—something, but we must not call it reform:
probably a universal change of heart: perhaps more and better officials to put them right.

Konstantin Pobiedonostsev cannot always have been like
this: but his arteries were hardening when he began to influence Nicolas II, and still more when he came in contact with

the Empress. What he taught to his pupils was the mystical faith in the Autocracy, as having a religious efficacy undiminished by the impotence of its wielder: as though tne holy oil which the priests prepared with myrrh and frankincense, text and psalm, for the coronation ceremony, conveyed with it a quality of godhead. To forgo any portion of the divine gift and its obligations, could be no less than sin. And yet he was capable of seeing that the Emancipation of 1861 had left the peasant "only a half-personality" and of saying that he ought to be made more like a complete one.

We have another example of the Cassandra type in M. Pavlov, a landlord of the Volga valley, who was gathering his experiences from the middle of the eighties, and wrote them down about the time of the first Revolution. The profligacy and hooliganism of the village; the difficulty of obtaining labour; the indebtedness both of gentry and of peasants; the usury practised by lawyers, doctors, bank employees, shopkeepers, priests, Jews, even peasants, as well as by merchants; the exodus of the gentry to the towns; the maintenance of the three-field system of cultivation; the multiplication of useless cattle; high prices and extravagance; general incapacity for business; tango-dancing and social visits; are some of the items on his condemnatory list. We are not surprised that the strike movement, the growth of socialism, liberal legislation, Justices of the Peace, Rural Councils, and the absence from the ranks of the legislature and administration of steady defenders of "our class", are disapproved. But it is a little startling, in this period of reaction, to find so round a condemnation of the weakness and bad judgment of the Government and of the apathetic administration of the laws. "God grant," says he, "that our generation may not see the retribution of this anarchy."

There is one good thing amid this welter of evil. That is the landlords, their land and their cattle. And the practical lesson of the book is the need, for Government, of ending the talk about the expropriation of the most valuable class in Russia, and of building a better State upon the firm foundation of property rights. Pavlov claims that he and his landlords' asso-

ciation (which was dissolved by the Government in 1907 because some of its members could not keep off politics) were
the originators of Peter Stolypin's agrarian reform, of which
we have more to say in the next chapter.

What was the grain of truth in all this sackful of denuncia-
tions? Probably it was a sense of growing indiscipline, which
arbitrariness and violence did not correct: of gross inefficiency
and absence of stable principle in the Tsarist State: in the
State itself, rather than in the character of any particular ruler.
Imbecility, in the original sense of the word, is characteristic
of the Government of the Tsars in their latter days. It seemed
as though the structure were crumbling.

Alexander III was a man of steady convictions, though not
of steady nerves, who followed with tenacity the policies with
which Pobiedonostsev must have inspired him. In an age when
the Empire of all the Russias had grown far beyond its primitive kernel of Great Russian Orthodoxy, and included nationalities of older and superior cultures, and other faiths and confessions having claims not less venerable than those of Orthodoxy, he sought to bring all alike within the framework of a
sort of glorified Orthodox Muscovite Tsardom. Autocracy,
Orthodoxy, Nationalism, were the bases of his policy, and
Russification was his instrument with the non-Russian peoples, who were more than half of the whole. The Russian
language is everywhere imposed. Cathedrals of the Russian
type are built in all non-Orthodox centres of culture, none but
Orthodox can acquire land in the western provinces, Catholicism is the worst treated of all the tolerated confessions. Russian administration and justice are introduced into Poland
and the Baltic Provinces. Even the Armenians, the most pro-
Russian of the subject nations, are driven into opposition.
Cultivators of the non-Russian races are ousted from their
lands to make room for Russian colonists. When, at a later
date, we find that the non-Russian nationalist is often the most
active in the revolutionary field, we see the fruits of a policy
which attempted to thrust Russian Orthodoxy and nationhood
upon unwilling peoples.

In Alexander III these policies were accompanied by a foreign policy firmly resolved upon peace. The dynasty would have survived—who can say for how long?—all the weaknesses of Nicolas II, if he could have kept out of war. But, from the first he played with fire. He had hardly come to the Imperial throne when he accepted a plan to bring about in Constantinople a situation which would have given a pretext for the landing of Russian troops. Fortunately he wavered, or Europe would have been at war in 1896. The miserable story of the Japanese war cannot be retold here. But those who fancy that autocracy is a guarantee of continuity of policy may well glance at the events which led to it. For years, military preparations had been directed against the dangers of war on the western front, and railway policy had been largely, though not exclusively, inspired by that prospect. But Nicolas, as Heir Apparent, had visited the Far East and become interested in its possibilities. It was the policy of the German Kaiser to divert Russia from too close an attention to European affairs. A camarilla, having corrupt interests in Korea, established itself at the Russian court. The Ministers stood for one policy, and that a cautious one. An adventurer—we need not enquire how his influence began—stood for a different and a rasher policy. The Foreign Minister lost all influence upon diplomacy in the Far East, and the Emperor corresponded direct with a man of little judgment or experience who had been made Viceroy of the Eastern territories. After an attempt to reach a settlement at St. Petersburg, the Japanese began the fighting *(1904)* used their sea-power to cut the Russians off from Korea, inflicted a series of military defeats, obtained the surrender of Port Arthur, and destroyed the Baltic Fleet at Tsushima. By the Peace of Portsmouth the Empire of Peter and Catherine abandoned Korea and Southern Manchuria, and ceded half of the great island of Sakhalin, to a power which Nicolas had been convinced would not dare to proceed to the extremity of war against him. The issue of paper money in Russia had been doubled, the credit of the Empire abroad was impaired, and when Count Witte passed through France he saw signs of the disgust and contempt with which the collapse of the great ally was regarded. An unnecessary and filibustering war had exposed to the nations the weakness of Russia, had imperilled the dynasty, and, but for the hasty conclusion of peace, might have come near to overthrowing it in 1905.

The lack of co-ordination in the body politic is not less apparent in internal than in external affairs. The idea of a Social Revolution from above had for some time been in the air of Russia. It was a police officer named Zubatov who put in practice the plan of harnessing the workers' movement to the police-machine. Co-operative Societies, like Trade Unions, had hitherto been discouraged by authority. They smacked of self-government. Now they were established under the patronage of the Police, who also assisted the workmen in their preparations for the general strike of 1903 in Southern Russia. This was no momentary escapade of an individual, but a policy aimed at convincing the proletariat that the Government was their friend. The employers were so much alarmed by this disconcerting reinforcement to their workers, that they begged for the legalisation of strikes, and of the election of shop-stewards by the men, as the lesser evil. Only the second of the two requests was granted, and the practice of keeping one foot in each of the two camps of capital and labour was continued for some time.

Another bizarre device of the administration was the patronized *pogrom*. In its origin the *pogrom* was the smashing of the window of a pawn-broker's shop by any angry borrower, promptly punished and having no political importance. The Minister Von Plehve, who first rose into distinction as the efficient prosecutor of Alexander II's murderers, and had, in 1903, prescribed a "small successful war" as the remedy for internal troubles, used the *pogrom* as a lightning conductor for diverting popular discontent upon Jews. The *pogrom* of Kishinev led to the murder of Von Plehve himself in the following year. The murder was organised as an act of vengeance by a Jew named Azev, whose history is a compendium of the ramifications of the police administration. He was a police-agent: and, when the peasant disturbances of 1902 encouraged the formation of the Social Revolutionary party, which succeeded the Populists in the championship of peasant rights, the police secured his nomination as the head of the new Socialist organisation. For years he hovered between the revolutionaries and their natural enemies, effecting selected betrayals, and alternately, or simultaneously, deceiving both.

1904. Immediately on the outbreak of the Japanese war, internal troubles began, with Polish resistance to mobilisation. Peasant disturbances followed in March, and continued at intervals, inspiring terror among the landlords.

July 1904. Von Plehve's murder was followed by a swing of Government to the left when his successor, Prince Svyatopolk Mirsky, "opened a ventilating hole for public opinion" by the relaxation of the censorship. The Holy Synod proposed the convening of a Church Assembly to discuss the restoration of the Patriarchate, always a symbol of the freedom of the Church from the domination of the State. A decree of December 12th gives us a glimpse of some of the burning questions of the day. The Committee of Ministers was required by it to make proposals for the *establishment of legality* (that is to say, for the removal or limitation of arbitrary and extra-legal powers), for the extension of freedom of speech, for religious toleration and self-government, for diminution of the disabilities of non-Russian nationalities, and for the abrogation of extraordinary laws. The only legal measures which resulted from this inquiry were an alleviation of the position of the dissenters and the removal of some Roman Catholic grievances in respect to schools in the western provinces. At the same time a conference of rural Councils was permitted to meet, and to make proposals which included an elective national assembly with legislative powers, but without responsible government in the British sense of the phrase.

This swing to the left was soon followed by a swing to the right. One of the "Police Socialist" agents was a priest known as Father Gapon, who exercised a great influence with the workers of St. Petersburg. They had recently suffered a fall of a quarter to a fifth in their real wages, and Father Gapon, though evidently vain and accessible to flattery, was moved by a genuine sympathy for their cause. When Bolsheviks and

Mensheviks were at logger-heads over a plan for a grand demonstration of workers, the priest assumed the leadership, and took a procession to the Winter Palace, with a petition for a general amnesty for political offenders, a Constituent Assembly to be elected by universal suffrage, and an eight-hour day. There is evidence that he contemplated a disturbance in the event of the rejection of this petition, but there were no preparations for anything more than unorganised violence. Some arms were taken by the crowd from policemen. The Emperor was absent at Tsarskoye Selo, and the Grand Duke Vladimir had been entrusted with the preservation of order. There was some firing on the crowd at the city gates but there were no preventive arrests: the procession was not prohibited: when a considerable part of the workers reached the Palace Square there was no summons to disperse. The troops were posted to receive the demonstrators, a bugle sounded, and firing began. Dr. Dillon, who was present, estimates the dead at seventy odd, and the wounded at two hundred and fifty. Afterwards, there were attacks upon individual police officers, and barricades were erected on Vasilievsky Island, but were easily captured by troops and police.

The facts show that the authorities were right in anticipating disorder, and would have acted appropriately in preventing the procession and arresting its leaders. But the Grand Duke Vladimir elected to wait, and "to give the people a lesson". This "Bloody Sunday" may be taken as the beginning of the Revolution of 1905.

1905. Popular indignation was already high owing to the surrender of Port Arthur in circumstances pointing to treachery. It rose to fever heat. A general strike was proclaimed in Poland, always in the van of the workers' movement. Such respectable bodies as the Moscow Agricultural Society and the Unions of professional men joined in the angry chorus and in the demand for a Constituent Assembly. In February the Grand Duke Sergius, uncle and brother-in-law to the Emperor, and Governor-General of Moscow, was assassinated by a Social Revolutionary. In March western Georgia expelled the Russian officials and formed a local government of its own which lasted till December. Peasant disturbances of a violent type were chronic throughout the year, in the seasons for such disturbances, which are always limited by agricultural conditions. In the industrial areas, strikes demanding a Constituent Assembly and an eight-hour day culminated in the formation of a Union of Unions, which acted as a Central Strike Committee. On arrival of the news of the destruction of the Baltic fleet, this Union of Unions demanded an end to the war, and the crew of the battleship *Potëmkin,* mainly Volga peasants, mutinied in the Black Sea, and carried the ship to a Roumanian port. A gesture of conciliation, ill-judged in the opinion of Count Witte, granted self-government to the Universities: and the students' meetings in these asylums of free speech attracted revolutionaries from outside and became centres of agitation.

1905. In August, the Government disappointed the demand for a Constituent Assembly by proclaiming the intention to convoke a consultative assembly so composed as to establish the preponderant influence of landed proprietors—the so-called Bulygin constitution.

The war was now over; but its authors and conductors were not forgiven. From September, the newspapers, even the conservative *Novoye Vremya,* were in open revolt against what remained of the censorship, and by tacit agreement ignored its orders. A Peasant Union, with a programme of expropriation without compensation, began to meet at Moscow under the eyes of the authorities. Lenin was not then a name of power: but the fact that he was able to return from exile, to address large audiences at St. Petersburg, and to publish articles in a daily newspaper founded by Maxim Gorky in the interests of revolution, is an illustration of the hesitant temper of the authorities.

Count Witte says that they were frightened, and that terrorism played a part in frightening them. He adds that the administration was in a state of chaos. For instance, during the demobilisation and the return of the troops from the Far East, the military authorities themselves did not know where their men were: and in some places, at the very height of the troubles, there were no police at all. What contribution the new rich, who had drawn their wealth from his economic policy, were making to the solution of the difficulties of Government, is suggested by his story of the chairman of the Stock Exchange who asked him to use his influence with the Imperial Bank to reduce the rate of discount. Witte said he could not interfere with the Bank's rules: whereupon the worthy financier affected an attitude of despair, and said: "Give us the Duma!" Some millionaires contributed to revolutionary funds, and the general attitude of employers, at this stage of the revolution, was hostile to the Government, or hopeful of extracting concessions from its difficulties. Later, when the interests of employers appeared to be threatened, they too became frightened, and withdrew their support from strikers and agitators.

The remaining, and the most important, events of the first Revolution fall under the headings of the formation of the St. Petersburg Soviet of Workers' Delegates, of which Trotsky was first the Vice-Chairman and afterwards the Chairman, with corresponding Soviets in almost a score of other towns: the General Strike: the issue of the October Manifesto, and the withdrawal of middle-class support from the strikers: the insurrections of the peasants in the Black Earth zone in October to December, of the Baltic peasants in November, and of the Moscow workmen in December: the announcement of the Witte franchise: and the assemblage of the First Imperial Duma in an atmosphere of counter-revolutionary triumph.

Of the Soviet I shall have something to say elsewhere. The General Strike was effective in securing what may be called an ostensible surrender on the part of the Government, mainly because the organisation of the Railway workers prevented traffic, even between St. Petersburg and Peterhof, except by water: but it was effective only because it was backed by a renewal of peasant disturbances. Officials of the most reactionary complexion were at this time discussing plans of expropriation of the large estates in order to restore order among the peasantry: which was plainly the most urgent consideration. Witte had not, of course, the advantage which we have, of knowing the subsequent course of the urban workers' movement. But he had all the sources of contemporary information at his disposal: and he is quite clear in the opinion that the peasant movement, which wrecked two thousand estates in 1905 and spread terror in the most influential part of society, and not the Soviet of Workers' Delegates, now established at St. Petersburg and directing the General Strike, was the cause of the Emperor's Manifesto of October 30th. The one was a nation-wide danger, the other only a serious inconvenience. Trouble with urban workers seemed a normal occurrence, and was in some degree discounted in advance. But the peasantry was still regarded as the backbone of the Empire, and its defection as a peril to the Orthodox Autocracy. There is no doubt that this was a just estimate of the two forces.

1905. The Manifesto of October 30th was not a Constitution. As ultimately interpreted it was not even the promise of one. It promised civic freedom on the basis of inviolability of the person, freedom of conscience, of speech, of assemblage, of association, and it promised an elective Duma with legislative power (without mention of legislative initiative), and with a real participation in the control over the legality of the behaviour of the officers of State. As to the franchise, it promised, *without stopping the elections appointed under the previous Bulygin constitution,* "to admit to participation in the Duma those classes of the population which have hitherto been deprived of the franchise, so far as this is feasible in the brief period remaining before the convening of the Duma, leaving the further development of the principle of general suffrage to the new legislative order". Whatever may have been the precise meaning of these words, they seemed to concede a Duma, with at least a veto on legislation, and with a right to public discussion of the conduct of officials, to be elected on a very wide franchise, and to be authorised, subject to the concurrent authority of the Council of State, to widen the franchise yet further. There was no mention of any reservation of autocratic authority. On the other hand there was clearly no concession of legislative control over the executive power. It was far from being the Constituent Assembly for which the strikers and a large part of articulate Russia were asking, but it seemed, and perhaps was, much: and the St. Petersburg Soviet—under moderate or Menshevik influences—at once called off the General Strike. The manifesto made no reference to the land question: and, when it reached the peasants, their disappointment was the occasion of additional disturbances: and either this, or a general impression of the abrogation of authority, may account for the outbreak in the Baltic Provinces, where the worst outrages of the revolution were committed, between the Lettish population on the one hand and their German masters on the other. Political autonomy was restored to Finland: but the working class, which had formed a Red Guard there, remained under arms. Measures of Russification generally were withdrawn, all claims on account of the redemption-payments required by the Emancipation law were cancelled, and the reorganisation of the Peasant Bank, to allow of the more extensive purchase of land, was promised.

What did Nicolas II actually mean by the Manifesto of October? When a deputation from the *Union of the Russian People* (recently formed under the patronage of the Grand Duke Nicolas to support the principle of autocracy) visited the Emperor and asked for assurances, he told them that the religious principle of absolute autocracy remained intact. The new fundamental laws published before the opening of the first Duma were issued by the absolute Autocrat, and a chapter of them expressly reserved the validity of the ancient Statutes relating to the Coronation, the Anointment, and the Faith. Within a year an example of the significance of these reservations was given by the publication, when the Duma was not sitting, of the Ukaz establishing the basis of the highly controversial agrarian reform of Peter Stolypin. It has been suggested—and such must have been the early teaching of Pobiedonostsev to his imperial pupils—that the Tsar could not have abandoned his Autocracy without violating his religious oath, and that the manifesto could only have ended absolutism, for the imperial conscience, if it had been accompanied by a corresponding declaration of the Tsar as head of the Orthodox Church.

The *Union of the Russian People*, which interested itself so deeply in the preservation of the Autocracy, had other items in its programme. It claimed a superior status for Russians over non-Russians in the Empire, and represented the Jews to be the main source of its troubles. It turned back to a patriarchal ideal of the Russian State and deprecated the influence of the bureaucracy: points which seem to have Slavophil origin. It appealed to religious reformers by a demand for the convening of a Church Council to restore the Patriarchate, placed in commission by Peter the Great: to the peasantry by the claim to access to more land: and to the general public by asking for equalisation of taxation. It is easy to detect resemblances to what was elsewhere and later called National Socialism. The programme seems to have been very well-considered, as a reply to revolutionary tendencies, and on the surface at least, the Union was a sort of Primrose League, enjoying conservative and official countenance of an unimpeachable respectability. But it had a Mr. Hyde to its Dr. Jekyll, in the shape of the so-called Black Hundreds, which were the agents of *pogrom*. By no means all officials, not even all Ministers, were aware of the aristocratic and official backing to these more disreputable activities. Witte has described to us the shock with which he, the chief Minister of the Empire, received the information that a hidden hand was behind the hooligans. He is so malicious in his comments upon his sometime master, Nicolas II, that we must not overrate the value of his statement that, at heart, the Emperor's ideals were those of the Black Hundreds; but the highest quarters were not unsympathetic to the "loyalists" who beat up "the disloyal": and there was an embarrassing dichotomy in the administration.

I have spoken before of a kind of paralysis in the body politic, of a disco-ordination in its various limbs. Trotsky, who was imprisoned when the St. Petersburg Soviet was broken up, tells us of the discovery, in the prison, of a cache of tools intended to facilitate escapes. The prison authorities hushed up the incident, because they believed that the Police had put the tools there, in order to get them into trouble and facilitate a change in the prison administration.

A Ukrain landowner tells us how a Jew of his—landowners had their Jews who did business for them, and were regarded as a useful sort of dependants, receiving protection in return for dirty work—was beaten up in a *pogrom*. The landowner went to the local Governor to ask for protection for his Jew. The Governor reflected, and then said, with a cynical grin: "Go and complain of me at St. Petersburg. I shall get credit as an energetic officer in my dealings with Jews. And you will get the protection that you ask." We recognise the old official hand here.

The Black Hundreds started their operations on the very morrow of the constitutional manifesto: and over a hundred *pogroms* took place, the worst being at Odessa, where seven hundred persons were killed, and at Tomsk, where many perished in a conflagration. Maurice Baring tells us the story of a Moscow police officer who, being asked to stop an attack on the funeral cortège of a dead revolutionary, replied, with a shrug: "Liberty." One consequence of the non-interference of the Police was that it was impossible to enforce the restrictions upon the sale of arms and many persons obtained supplies which contributed to the disorders of the period which followed. It was said of Ivan the Terrible—said perhaps by a chronicler whose interests he had offended—that he had "become a rebel in his own land". Something like that was true of Nicolas II, or of his government as represented by Von Plehve.

The war was over, and resentment over a humiliating peace was not so effective a grievance as war. The Manifesto had taken the edge off popular feeling. Many thought a constitution had been granted. When the Soviet attempted to renew the general strike, the response was a cold one. The employers and the monied people were satisfied, or frightened, and withdrew their support. At a later stage, under the evident influence of the youthful Trotsky, the Soviet declared a repudiation of Romanov debts and called on the people to withdraw their deposits from the Savings Banks. But it was clear that neither this body, nor the workmen whom it represented, would have supported any attack upon the authority of the Tsar: and that the town-workers had shot their bolt, for the present at all events.

The peasants resumed rioting in 1906, and again in 1907,

producing renewed panic among landlords and a rush to sell estates. But there are well-recognised limits to peasant disturbances: since agriculture is literally the life of the people, and the seasons will not wait for man. Peasants can be active in the dead time, between spring sowing and hay cutting. They can act again with effect when the harvest is cut and carried. The winter limits their activities to their own near neighbourhood, and the thaw makes roads and rivers impassable, and reduces the country for a time to an archipelago of mud. They are irresistible rioters till the troops arrive, but there is no organisation and they are overpowered in detail—free, of course, to resume action when the military detachment has passed on—unless spirit has been completely crushed by the terror. Armed resistance to punitive columns in 1906, when the Government had recovered the initiative, was rare and feeble. With the months of October and November 1905 the moment of combination between town and country had gone by. Between peasant and Government the position was almost one of stalemate.

The soldier, in the mass, is a peasant in uniform, and his grievances were the peasant grievances, with the addition of some of his own, among which delayed demobilisation played a great part. Like his brother peasant, the soldier did not dream, in 1905, of the displacement of the Tsar, or even of his replacement by another member of the Imperial family. He wanted land, and he wanted an end to arbitrary officials, and to the special civil disabilities and inferior legal status of the peasant. There were eighty-nine outbreaks in the Army in November and December 1905, accompanied with much disorder along the line of the Siberian Railway: troops at Sevastopol fraternised with the revolting Black Sea Fleet: a military gathering at Irkutsk demanded a Constituent Assembly, as well as military concessions, and threatened a peaceful strike. But the Army, however undisciplined, was loyal, as it was soon to show in the crushing of the belated, ill-judged, and ill-managed rising at Moscow in December, when the authorities, for once, showed both judgment and energy.

Dec. 24, 1905. The interest of the Moscow insurrection,

which lasted only ten days, lies in its illustration of revolutionary tactics. While it was in progress, Counte Witte's franchise
law was published, giving effect to the promises of October
30th. It provided for indirect election, and the proportions in
the electoral assembly were such as to favour the peasants
rather than the urban workers. But it gave the vote to city
workers occupying separate lodgings, though not to those living
in factory barracks and approached sufficiently near to male
adult suffrage to be a contributing cause of the Empress's
enmity to Count Witte. The latter has explained (and, unless
the Duma was to be a Sovereign Parliament, the reason is convincing) why he urged the publication of fundamental laws—
in the language of to-day they would be called "safeguards" or
"reserved powers"—before the assemblage of the Duma. Without these, he justly argued, the new body would assume the
functions of a Constituent Assembly, and so encroach upon the
imperial prerogative as to compel, or excuse, the abrogation
of the new constitution by force. The Ministers were to be
solely responsible to the Emperor. Foreign policy, defence,
currency and privy purse and court departments, were made
"reserved" subjects, and the Emperor's powers in respect to
maintenance of order and general welfare were secured. The
Judges were made inviolable, and a clause was inserted guaran-
teeing liberty of conscience. The Emperor's powers of issuing
decrees was restricted to periods when the Duma was not in
session, and the endorsement of the Council of Ministers to
such emergency legislation was made necessary. The Council of
State, now to include an elective element equal in number to
the nominated, was to have parallel powers with the Duma in
respect to legislation and budget.

Expecting that the new legislature would meet in an ugly
mood, Count Witte borrowed largely both in Russia and abroad
before the elections were held: a piece of judicious hedging
which expresses the extent of his confidence in the new institutions. The part taken by the French people in providing this
money was remembered against them by the Russian Liberals;
and Maxim Gorky exploded against France for having thus
closed the road to liberty: "As for me, O my beloved of yore,

I spit my gall at thy face." But we need affect no surprise that a statesman trained in a school so entirely dissimilar from the parliamentary one was cautious. The Constitutional Democratic party—the Kadets—made no secret of their intention to propose the expropriation of landed property, and there was an understanding among the Ministers that the Duma would be dissolved if this question were touched. In an atmosphere of punitive expeditions, with the "loyal" Black Hundreds co-operating with military and police to restore order, the elections took place, and the first Duma began its sittings on May 10th, 1906, in the Tavrida Palace at St. Petersburg.

Mr. Maurice Baring, a candid and careful observer, tells us that, in 1914, Russia was being worse governed than under Alexander II. Count Witte, always bitter against his successors in power, writes about the same time that the concessions of the revolutionary years existed only on paper or had been retracted. There are those, on the other hand, who point out that it is not the worst, but the weakest, rulers upon whom the nemesis of bad government falls, and that the Tsarist Government had made, and was making, substantial improvements in itself when it fell. The truth, as it appears to the present writer, is something different from either of these opposite opinions. The appetite comes with eating: and the standard which people apply to their Governments is a progressive one, advancing with the amelioration of the administration. The achievements of the year which centred upon the Revolution of 1905, some temporary, some permanent, were real: and the administration of 1914, with some qualifications, was absolutely better than that of twenty years earlier, but not better relatively to the expectations of the Russian people. In particular they had ceased to regard the power of the Autocrats to involve them in war as a part of the necessary order of things.

First among the benefits conferred by the Revolution of 1905 was the existence of the Duma, even after the limitation of the franchise, which deprived it of its claim to speak for the whole people. It fell far short of the hopes of those whose eyes were fixed on the Parliaments and Congresses of the West. That was inevitable, since the so-called political parties were mere bodies of thinkers having no organic root in the electorate. But it was a training-ground for a limited class, and that an important one, capable of representing a portion at least of the aspirations of the people. It was a platform of free speech, giving opportunities for the ventilation of abuses and the exposure of highly-placed offenders. The support given by some of the authorities to the hooliganism of the Black Hundreds was revealed in the Duma in 1906, and the prosecution of a former Director of Police followed the disclosures. On this platform Alexander Guchkov could denounce the Court favourite, Rasputin, Paul Miliukov could ask whether the conduct of war by the Ministry was madness or treachery, Grand Dukes could be told that they were out of place in high Army-command. That the speeches in the Duma caused alarm in the highest quarters is made plain by the letters of the Tsaritsa begging the Tsar to prevent it from meeting. Finally, the elective body gave an opportunity for the free play of a moderate Liberalism, capable of carrying out valuable, if minor, reforms. Another change of the period was the establishment of the office of Prime Minister: which introduced an element of potential—not always of actual—coherence and stability into public business.

The peasants, proverbially "dark" and "deaf", suffered under wrongs for which they could not find the right name. Their demand was expressed as a claim for the land held by the landlords. That would not have solved the problem of their poverty, as subsequent history showed. One cause of their poverty was excessive demands from the State, another a primitive system of land holding and of agriculture, a third was the national character. Character is the product of history and institutions, and an element in the Russian peasant character was certainly the inferior legal and social status which had survived serfdom. These things were remediable, if only slowly: and the period of the first Revolution brought some palliatives. The landlords kept their land; but, frightened by the attacks upon their estates, increased their sales of land and reduced their rents. The reorganisation of the peasant bank was carried out. The way was opened to a wider policy of colonisation. If the mass remained as poor as ever, the "strong and sober" received a magnificent opening in the Stolypin legislation of which we speak in the next chapter, and in the encouragement of Agricultural Co-operation. If it be true that the best way to help the poorer is to make the less poor prosperous, then the first Revolution and its sequelae helped the peasantry as a whole. The abolition of the redemption-payments due under the Emancipation Law of 1861, was a very great boon. If we calculate the burdens on the peasantry at different epochs—the thing was done by a qualified Russian economist in 1924—we find that they were not, taking a general average, excessive in the years immediately preceding the Great War, and the old reproach against the Tsarist administration of over-taxation of the peasants had been by that time removed.

The moral burden upon the peasantry, the inferior legal and social status, the liability to arbitrary treatment and to exceptional punishment, was only in part removed by the Revolution of 1905. From 1906 they ceased to be debarred from the higher institutions of learning, and were able to rise in the services to posts from which they had previously been excluded. The Land-Captains remained, and continued to exercise illegal and arbitrary powers. The Rural Courts remained unchanged, and corporal punishment, though restricted by law, continued to be practised on the peasants. But that they themselves saw in this Revolution some improvement in their status, is shown by their name for it, *"ravneniye"*, the levelling.

It was not only the peasant who needed assurance of inviolability of person. The ordinary citizen was also subject to arbitrary interferences, and the promises of 1905 did not put an end to these. In 1913, Stephen Graham tells us that "anyone is liable to arrest at any hour of the day or night at the instance of a stupid or corrupt police". The exceptional-status-regulations of Alexander III which expired in 1906, were renewed by an Imperial Ukaz for an additional period of three years: and exceptional laws and exceptional jurisdictions continued to be a cause of complaint up to the outbreak of the War. In 1912 Count Witte tells us that the police still have unlimited authority, including the right of administrative exile: that correspondence is still unreasonably examined: that laws regulating association and meeting exist on paper only. It seems, indeed, to have been impossible to any Russian police, *then or afterwards*, to accept, *in practice*, any limitation upon their authority. We shall miss some of the lessons of Russian history unless we realise that the outlook on law, and on the liberty of the subject, is fundamentally different from that which, in theory at least, prevails in the Anglo-Saxon world.

The guardians of civil rights—without which, anywhere and everywhere, such rights exist upon paper only—are the Courts and the Press. The Bar, at least the Bar of the great cities, had always enjoyed a high reputation since its organisation by Alexander II. Judges were made inviolable by Imperial decision under the Fundamental laws of 1905: but it was the practice to make temporary, instead of substantive, appointments to the Judicial Bench, so that removal was a simple matter. On the other hand there was a real relaxation of the censorship. Maurice Baring tells us in February 1906 that "every case of oppression is now reported in the newspapers as it happens", and that "some of the comic and satirical papers might have Marat for their editor". Before 1906, Kluchevsky's history of Russia could be circulated only in manuscript notes, like Peter Chaadaev's Philosophical letters seventy years earlier. The relaxation was no merely transient feature. Books now begin to appear which were formerly unprintable, and the Bolshevik newspaper *Truth*, though often suspended, begins to have a continuous life as a legal journal from 1912.

Except as protégés of the police, during the bizarre episode of Zubatovist Socialism, both Trade Unions and Co-operative Societies had been frowned upon by authority, as likely centres of disaffection and conspiracy. Both now received authorisation, which in the case of the former was precarious and short-lived, though the law was on the Statute book. But the strikes of 1905 secured a ten-hour day to the metal workers and an eight-and-a-half day to the textile workers. Sick benefit funds, established under a law of 1912, were more fortunate than Trade Unions, and had two million members at the outbreak of the War. Co-operation obtained more than a nominal blessing. In the forms of Producers' and Credit Co-operation it rapidly demonstrated its adaptability to the conditions of the Russian peasantry and was more swiftly successful than in any other country. In 1914 there were 33,000 societies with twelve million members, and the butter of the Siberian Co-operatives had become famous on the western markets. The producers' Co-operatives did particularly valuable supply work during the Great War.

In the early phases of the Revolution of 1905, religious teaching was declared to be free, and certain remissions were conceded to the Jews. The position of the Old Believers was alleviated, and we see them hereafter holding regular annual religious conferences, attended by delegates from North Russia, the Urals and the Caucasus. Some of the grievances of the Roman Catholic schools were removed. The prison at the Suzdal monastery which was used by the ecclesiastical tribunals for clerical and dissenting offenders, was emptied of prisoners after the Manifesto of October 1905: but soon began to be again occupied by priests, who had denounced the death-sentences pronounced in the Field-Courts-Martial of the counter-revolution. Self-government was granted to the Universities.

The non-Great-Russian nationalities also benefited by the temporary liberalism of the Government. Autonomy was restored in Finland, and was, for a time, a reality, so that Finland became a refuge for the disgruntled politician and the revolutionary, beyond the reach of the Tsarist police. Poland was also to have enjoyed political concessions, but these were declared, as early as November 14th, 1905, to be postponed, because of the renewal of unrest after the issue of the October manifesto. Active measures of Russification were generally withdrawn. Up to 1906 the use of the Ukrainian language was prohibited in schools, courts and public offices: and, even after the withdrawal of this prohibition, books in the language were not allowed in public and school libraries.

The Revolution and the repression that followed it had a demoralising effect both upon officials and people. The habit of resort to exceptional laws, and of employing irregular auxiliaries in suppressing disturbances, affected the official balance. Violence is not discipline, any more than a man is a good rider because he jerks at his horse's mouth. The agrarian disturbances, continued into 1907 and 1908, the violence of the Black Hundreds, and the practice of revolutionary "expropriation" of funds, which melted imperceptibly into unashamed robbery, were equally demoralising to the population. In the words of a peasant, quoted by Sir Bernard Pares, respect for the State was gone and only fear of it remained. Even the fear must have been partly gone; for the people had seen that ministers and officials, as well as landlords, could be frightened. The experiences of the first General Strike of 1905 and of the operation of Soviets of workers in St. Petersburg and other important towns, were fraught with lessons which the revolutionaries did not forget. 1905 was a step towards 1917.

Chapter 4

Counter-Revolution and Revolution

"Be more autocratic, my very own Sweet-
heart, show your mind. . . . Ah, my Love, when
at last will you thump with your hand upon the
table? . . . Oh, Lovey, you can trust me. I may
not be clever enough—but I have a strong feeling, and that helps more than the brain often."

The Tsaritsa's letters to the Tsar.

"As poor peasants, how happy, how worthy,
had ye two been! But, by evil destiny, ye were
made a King and Queen of: and so both are
become an astonishment and a by-word to all
times."

THOMAS CARLYLE: writing of Louis XVI and
Marie Antoinette in *The Diamond Necklace*.

"When I think that our autocratic régime
ends in this impotence, I become republican."

A Russian Grand Duke, quoted
by M. MAURICE PALÉOLOGUE.

"Russia, alas, is the classic model of a state
where many people are not where they belong.
It is a country where there is a general complaint about the lack of good men, but where
no attention is paid to the good men who exist."

Speech in the Duma, Aug. 14th, 1915.

WHEN A PEOPLE enters upon a career of industrialisation, it has two primary needs, besides that of technical skill: the need of capital and the need of consumers to take the products. If it is fortunate enough to find a world of consumers open to it, before the competition of rivals has developed, the two needs are solved together, by the profits derived from the great open markets. Russia, when she commenced industrialisation in earnest in the eighties of the nineteenth century, had neither capital nor consumers. It was necessary to borrow the capital largely from abroad, and to find the effective demand for the product largely in the State's own needs of railway development —and in further industrialisation: which involved the encouragement of industry by subsidies and protective tariffs. Her own peasants, however greatly in need of the products, could offer no considerable effective demand for them. In such conditions, if the process of development received a check, the restriction of demand was likely to hold up industrial production altogether. A normal demand for the products of industry could only be established by an addition to the purchasing power of the peasant: which might mean a solution of the agrarian question in terms of political change, and a loss of support for the autocracy among the landlord class.

Who paid for Russian industrialisation, for the service of the foreign debts, for the gold reserve which was necessary to stabilise the currency and establish Russian credit, for the lag between outlay and realisation? There was only one source of payment, and that was the product of the soil: the grain, the flax, the timber, the oil. Of these things, the grain was the largest item, and the burden of Russia's great export trade, by which a "favourable" trade balance was maintained continuously from the eighties onward, in bad years and good, lay ultimately upon the peasant whose daily ration was the less because of it. There was a long tradition in Russian history of heavy exports of grain. In these latter days when, to the luxury needs of a small circle and the elementary equipment required by a primitive State, was added the vast growth of railways and industry, the strain upon the food supply even in favourable seasons was much increased. Economists may tell us that the export of grain increases production by developing a market for surplus, and therefore does not diminish the amount available for home consumption. But Russia, as an exporting country, was producing less grain per head of its population than other European countries which were importers. Either the latter were wasting their food, or the former was, for some reason, presumably some compulsion, going short.

The compulsion which reduced the ration was the heavy drain of payments to the State and to property owners. Before the abolition of the redemption-payments this drain was enormous. A trustworthy calculation made for the year 1912 shows that it was still eighteen per cent of the gross income of the peasant, of which less than twelve per cent was on account of taxation levied by the State. The latter figure corresponds with remarkable closeness to the general average of the land revenue and cesses raised in British India. In return for this the peasant received the potential benefit which extended industrialisation was likely to bring to agriculture by the enlargement and variation of its markets.

For the extension of industrialisation, and for the abolition of redemption-payments, he was indebted to Count Witte, an economic and financial genius, who showed, in the later days of his power, that he might have saved the Tsardom or postponed its fate. He was not ignorant of the danger of stripping his country of her food to pay for his policy of industrialisation. But he saw that a country which lacks industries is at the mercy of its neighbours, because there is neither wealth nor successful war without them, and he held that it was necessary to build up national industry before dealing with the agrarian problem. In effect, his policy for his country was one of compulsory saving, taking the form of investment in railways and in industrial plant, similar in kind, if not in degree, to that pursued under revolutionary planning. Later, if time *and peace* had been allowed to him, it is plain, from the efforts which he made to provide for the needs of agriculture and from his abortive efforts at a solution of the agrarian question, that he would have approached with equal determination and re-

source the more difficult and dangerous part of his problem.
Alexander III understood, and supported, Witte; and Nicolas
II, in the first years of his rule, at least did not effectively
thwart him over the great essential to his design. For a country
still fresh upon the path of industrialisation, with an agrarian
problem clamant for solution, and foreign payments dependent
upon a dangerously large export of food and raw materials,
peace was essential. Witte therefore set his face against all adventures. Alexander probably owed to him his title of Tsar
Pacificator, it was Witte who must have initiated the plan of the
Hague Conference, which led in 1898 to the establishment of
the permanent Court of Arbitration: and, though he secured
by doubtful methods the concession of the Eastern Chinese
Railway, he opposed the Far Eastern folly which led to the
Japanese war. He made the Peace of Portsmouth, and must
have known that the humiliating terms would be remembered
against him. He stood (along with Rasputin, a singular combination) against war in 1909, when Austria annexed Bosnia
and Herzegovina, and Ferdinand of Bulgaria assumed the title
of Tsar. It is plain that in July 1914 Russia would not have
championed Serbia against Austrian aggression, if Witte had
had his way: and therefore that the Great War would not have
taken place when it did. Rightly, or wrongly, he had no respect
for Russia's supposed mission to protect the Slavs of the
Balkan peninsula, or for the dream of a Russian Constantinople. What he knew, better than anyone else, was the precarious prospect for Russia in a war with a highly industrialised
country such as Germany, under conditions of virtual blockade
separating her from her own industrialised allies. His policy
would perhaps have established Germany, in her shining
armour, dangerously close to the outlets towards the Southern
Sea: but it would have saved that collapse of Russian economy
and administration which made the revolution of 1917, and
would have given to the autocracy another *locus paenitentiae*.

1905. Witte, seasoned administrator as he was, and evidently
not too skilful a manager of political parties, had no liking for
Constitutions. He is reported to have expressed his feelings
about them, in the coarse manner natural to the old station-

master, to a British interviewer. But he was a realist, and a statesman; and, when he returned from making the Peace of Portsmouth, and found all Russia in dangerous turmoil, he told his Imperial master that he must choose between a constitution and a military dictatorship. He was premier when Nicolas issued the Manifesto of October 30th: and must have advised him to yield whatever that manifesto did in effect yield. In December he issued the regulations which made the franchise all but universal and took the wind completely out of the sails of the revolutionary movement: and was never forgiven for it by his Imperial master and mistress. Then he set to work to minimise the danger of the impending Duma, by issuing the fundamental laws, by making the Council of State into a Second Chamber alongside of the democratic assembly, and by protecting the military budget against political interference by a very large foreign loan. Given the disbelief in democracy and parliamentarianism—and it would be absurd to affect surprise at this disbelief for such a country as Russia—this was statesmanship. Witte's way was to establish a fresh basis for the Imperial authority by economic development, and, in the meanwhile, to maintain peace, to avoid quarrels with the Jews and with the non-Great-Russian nationalities, and to frustrate the encroachments of politicians upon the executive power, while giving them the consultative assembly which could no longer be withheld. Think as we may about the ultimate wisdom of this policy, it would have given to Russia a very different history in the twentieth century.

We hear nothing of a broken heart. Rather, Witte withdrew into a corner to snarl: to dip his pen in gall and to dissuade the Japanese ambassador from the proposal to send a Japanese army to Europe to help the Allies: and to die when the economic machine which he had equipped and set going was already being driven to destruction.

None of the Socialist parties took part in the elections to the first Duma. Otherwise there was general participation, and no more interference than the sporadic operations of punitive forces made inevitable. According to all the rules of the game —as practised in the west—the legislative assembly should have had widespread support in the country. The largest party in it consisted of the Constitutional Democrats, the "Kadets"— the Liberals, we may call them—versed in the best models of western Constitutionalism. The Duma discussed the Black Hundreds and their *pogroms,* the abolition of capital punishment, an amnesty for revolutionary offences: and the programme of the Kadet party showed that they had other proposals unpalatable to Government, including the abolition of administrative punishment, of extraordinary Courts, and of the passport system, and the incorporation of guarantees in the fundamental laws. The Emperor had not pretended to concede responsible government, but the parliamentarians endeavoured to make the Government responsible to the Duma by passing a vote of censure on the Tsar's Ministers, as a majority in the British House of Commons might have done in the days when majorities were not subservient to ministries. The Ministers ignored the claim, and walked out. The critical struggle was over the land. The Kadets proposed expropriation, and rival proposals of a less drastic kind were put forward on behalf of the Government. The Duma was dissolved: and the Kadet and Labour members retired to Finland, and appealed to the country to withhold co-operation and to repudiate foreign loans concluded without the Duma's consent.

There was no response. Liberalism had called spirits from the vasty deep. They did not come when called. All the power was on the other side, and the constitutional forms were no more than forms. Externally, the protesting members had reproduced the constitutional procedure of the western democracies. The vital difference was that they had no roots in the electorate, which did not regard them as its own, but looked on, as at a spectacle.

The Minister who was selected to carry out the dissolution of the first Duma was Peter Stolypin. A lesser brain than Witte, he was nevertheless the monarchy's second chance of escape, and the second chance that the monarchy threw away. He came to note as the strong man in the time of trouble, who controlled disorder in 1905 in the provincial government of Saratov. As a Minister of the Crown, he resisted a proposal for the appointment of a Liberal ministry from the ranks of the recalcitrant Duma—which would have conceded the claim for responsible government—and was made Premier to carry out his own alternative policy. He took up with vigour the task of restoring order in a desperately disordered country, and established, under the authority of the fundamental laws, the Field-Courts-Martial, known as Stolypin's *neckties*, which summarily tried and hanged robbers within twenty-four hours of capture. This was the period of the expropriations, the "Exes" as they were familiarly called, acts of brigandage for the collection of revolutionary funds, which were not in practice, nor always even in motive, distinguishable from ordinary crime. The number of executions on account of these expropriations, and of armed resistance, is variously put at figures ranging from six hundred to three thousand five hundred. Liberal opinion was indignant and the Emperor Nicolas himself was perturbed. It is said that there were ten thousand victims during the repression of the disturbances in Latvia in November 1905. But, as usual in Russia, executions in legal form, even when the procedure was that of a Field-Courts-Martial, were more shocking than mere slaughter in hot blood with no form at all. People talked of a Stolypinshchina, as they had talked of a Pugachevshchina in the days of the great rebellion. But, if we admit that Governments must either maintain order or abdicate, it does not appear that Stolypin's Courts-Martial were unnecessarily severe. Over eleven thousand persons were condemned to various penalties in 1907, the largest number of cases being in the Baltic provinces and in the regions of St. Petersburg and Moscow, and we hear of villages in which every tenth man was whipped. But disorder was in some areas so widespread that whole villages were concerned in it.

This drastic visitation was only a fraction of Stolypin's policy: which, viewed from the standpoint of the revolutionary, was a doubly dangerous one. Not only did he seek to repress disorder by severities (which, in a greater or less degree, is the way of every Government) but he aimed at finding a new basis of strength for the monarchy in a class of new rich, reinforced by the addition of a well-to-do peasantry. It was to this that his agrarian legislation was directed.

At the height of the disturbances in 1905, the Emperor's own *entourage* was discussing the compulsory expropriation of the large estates to meet the peasant demand for more land, and a similar proposal, in various forms all more or less drastic, was widely canvassed. Such a measure would have been quite in keeping with the methods of the Tsarist Government, which had sequestrated the landed property of the Church under Catherine the Great, bought out the squires on a large scale at the Emancipation Settlement, and, at a later date, reduced the holdings of the old-established settlers in Siberia to forty and a half acres per male soul in order to make room for new colonists. The conception of the sacredness of property, subject to certain strictly limited overruling rights of the State, was replaced in Russia by that of expediency, and in this respect the revolutionaries were in the legitimate order of succession to the Tsars. The advocates of expropriation were naturally met with the argument that more land was not the remedy for the troubles of the peasant. If we are content with bare averages, we find that in 1900 the peasants had just under seven acres per head for men, women and children. So far from this average being inadequate, it is, on the peasant scale of subsistence, almost handsome. We may agree with those who tell us that, for one reason or another, it was impossible to utilise more than a third or a half of this area in any given year. But this is an argument, not so much for adding to the land, as for adding to the means of cultivation and improving its conditions.

If we leave general averages, we find a different story. The word *peasant* was an elastic one. A man might be legally a peasant when he had become a large proprietor. The historian of Russian Agriculture before the Revolution tells us, in connection with the large purchases made by "peasants" after the establishment of the Peasant Bank, that a whole third of the area was bought by men who held from a hundred and thirty-five to two thousand seven hundred acres apiece. Again, the regional averages go down below five acres per head and up to twelve or thirteen: and the provincial averages vary much more widely. M. Köfod, who made the Stolypin Settlement, tells us of 560,000 whole households which had no more than five and a half acres apiece, that is, perhaps, a little more than an acre per head: and of two and a quarter millions of households, in which the average per head would range from this figure up to two and a half acres. Prima facie, there was need here for more land: but the question was complicated by the fact that many of the non-economic holders lacked cattle and equipment, and many more had no intention of living by agriculture, so that the best solution for them might be to be bought out.

The nature and value of the large estates proposed for expropriation were also to be considered. In 1905 the panic among the landlords was already causing many of them, especially in the Black Earth zone, where holdings were smallest, to sell their land to peasants. It has been calculated that, even if the expropriation of the landlords were complete, the addition of new cultivation to be made to the average peasant holding would be less than thirty per cent.

The quality and nature of the farming on landlord's estates differed widely. Much of their land was already leased to peasants, who cultivated it in peasant fashion, with peasant knowledge and peasant means, and, because of their transient interest, produced yields smaller than they obtained on their own allotments. But some of the larger estates were valuable to agriculture. The general average of the yield upon them, taken in the mass, was substantially higher than that on peasant holdings: and the best of them observed superior methods. Wholesale expropriation would therefore injure the interests of agriculture, and reduce the food surplus, with which Russia paid for her imports and met the service of her foreign debt. These considerations led M. Chuprov, a contemporary advocate of expropriation, to limit his proposals to estates upon which no measures of improvement had been taken. It was the same distinction which the Bolsheviks proposed in 1917–18 to observe between ordinary estates at the disposal of the local land authorities, and improved estates and superior stock which were to form the nucleus of model State farms. But, in proportion to the amount of such reservations, the area available for increasing peasant holdings would be reduced, and the addition to be made would therefore be nearer to fifteen than to thirty per cent of the existing average.

In his provincial government of Saratov, Peter Stolypin had been in contact with peasant disturbances only less threatening than those of Ukrain, and with a body of landlords ready to defend their rights. He conceived the idea of calling in a new world of individualist peasant proprietors, freed from the control of the Mir, consisting of "the strong and the sober", to strengthen by their self-interest the principle of landed property, and of thus putting an end for ever to the talk of expropriation. What he expected to happen to that unfortunately large section which was neither strong nor sober, we can only guess. Presumably he expected it to sink into the ranks of the rural proletariat, which already existed in considerable numbers. It is plain that he attached no value to the Mir, which had played its part as soon as common responsibility for taxes was gone, and that in his condemnation of it to extinction, he made no difference between its agrarian functions and its work as an organ of village self-government, in which it was difficult to replace. His aim was not less political than economic: to create a new and stable conservatism in the village.

Those who are accustomed to the gingerly approach to great problems of Governments of a different type, can only gasp at the speed with which Stolypin flung himself into the task of revolutionising the agrarian system of an Empire, while conservatives and socialists alike protested. It was only a few degrees less drastic than the Bolshevik plan of the general collectivisation of holdings: and its revolutionary swiftness helps us to understand some subsequent history. Within five months of his appointment for the purpose of dissolving the first Duma, an ordinance was issued, under a clause of the Fundamental Laws, without reference to either House of the Legislature, which envisaged the end of the Mir and the establishment of individual peasant property in land, and entrusted a Land Settlement Commission with the task of consolidating the new farms out of the old strips. The Revolutionaries of November 1917 were less bold, for, in their first agrarian legislation, they at least acted upon the ascertained wishes of the great mass of the peasantry.

The instructions to the Settlement Commission, when the Stolypin legislation was completed, contemplated three stages in the operations. The first was the affirmation by certificate of proprietary right in the strips as they stood at the time of the new settlement, together with emancipation from the authority of the Mir. The second was the consolidation of the scattered strips into integral holdings, a process to which we might give the name of enclosure, if enclosure did not appear to imply fencing or hedging. This second stage might obviously involve compulsory measures against persons other than the applicant for consolidation, but it did not include the redistribution of the farmhouse-lots (what Russians call *usàdba*) in the village-site. The third stage involved complete separation from the village and from the village-site. The man who entered upon this third stage included his farmhouse-lots in the consolidation, left his home on the common village-site, and established himself in a new farmhouse on his own consolidated and independent farm, away from all the common organisation of village life, including water-supply.

The Stolypin legislation would be wrongly described as establishing free trade in land, for it maintained the existing restriction upon the sale of peasant land to non-peasants and, by a clause inserted by the third Duma, when a bill on the subject was before it, forbade the acquisition of more than a limited maximum of peasant land by any one purchaser in any one district. The social danger of the buying out of poor peasants by richer peasants, or by non-peasants, was thus provided against, in so far as legislation on such a matter can be effective.

Like most Russian legislation of the Tsarist, no less than of the revolutionary, epoch, the law showed less regard for individual rights of property than is normally shown in Britain. The rights of the peasant in land had been—so far as Russian law was definitely ascertainable—rights of the whole house-

hold. The new law transferred them to the head of the household. The old rights in land were subject to redistribution,
general or particular, carried out by the Mir. At the moment
of the operations under the new Settlement, a peasant might
have more or less than his normal share. But the measure of
his new rights was his actual possession, subject to payment
for any excess on a scale fixed in 1861, when the value of
land was very different.

There was another respect in which the Stolypin legislation,
as completed in 1910 and 1911, treated existing rights in a
more summary way than a British legislature would be likely
to treat them. In a considerable part of European Russia, peasant land covering nearly a quarter of the whole area of peasant
allotments had already become separate heritable property,
not subject to redistribution by the Mir. This would normally
have stood in the way of the consolidation of holdings which
it was desired to effect. The law of 1910, which was passed
by the third Duma, provided that the owners of such separate
heritable property in a village might decide by a bare majority in favour of the consolidation of their separate strips
into integral holdings. It will be noticed that the dissentient
minority might thus be compelled to exchange land which
they had hitherto, on solid grounds, considered to be their
separate heritable property, not liable to redistribution. The
law of 1911 went still further in the direction of authorising
the compulsion of minorities.

The head of the Settlement, M. Köfod, was an enthusiast for
the individualisation of the landed property of the peasants,
and all the influence of the Government was at this time
thrown into the same scale. In case of opposition, recourse was
had to the clause of the Criminal Code under which forcible
resistance to a person exercising his lawful rights was declared
punishable at law: and the Land-Captains exercised pressure
of an effective kind upon recalcitrants. On the other side, conservative influences were strong, legal devices were employed
to hamper the Settlement proceedings, and we gather, from
the journals of Semyonov, Count Tolstoi's peasant protégé,
that the Banks sometimes exercised an influence opposed to

that of the Government officials. Outside of the Black Earth belt, and particularly where the factories competed with agriculture for labour, the squires sided with the opposition, because they feared the detachment of the peasants from the land as a consequence of the break up of the Mir.

The proceedings of the Stolypin Settlement were brought to an end during the Great War, because of the large number of mobilised soldiers who were nervous of changes affecting their rights. In the upshot, out of the twelve million peasant households included in the scope of the operations, over two and a half millions obtained separate proprietary rights in their strips and emancipation from the authority of the Mir. One-half of these carried the matter no further, and did not proceed to the second stage of consolidating their holdings. It may be that some of them were prepared to go further, but that survey operations were too slow and were still incomplete when the war ended the proceedings. One million and a quarter households obtained consolidation of their arable holdings into integral blocks, eliminating altogether the stripping which handicapped agriculture. But woods and ponds were never divided up, and in many cases pastures were still left common. Mr. Lancelot Owen, who has recently made a valuable study of the Stolypin Settlement, tells us that at most three per cent of the original peasant allotment holdings proceeded to the third stage, of the establishment of the farmhouse on the consolidated estate outside of the village: in spite of pecuniary encouragement given by the Government to the building of new dwellings and the sinking of wells. I suspect that the actual proportion was even smaller than this. Difficulties of an individual water supply, and fears of an isolated life, were generally conclusive against removal from the village-site.

The new system met with the greatest success where the maritime trade routes were nearest, and the habit of production for export most firmly established. By far the greatest amount of consolidation of holdings—what we have called the second stage of the Settlement proceedings—was done on the south-west and on the southern and south-eastern steppes, where wheat cultivation had long been practised on a commercial scale on level lands of uniform soil. In "New Russia" (southern Ukrain), in White-Russia, and in the central provinces of the Black Earth zone, the proportion of peasants leaving the Mir was about one-third, and reached almost a half in the south-west. In the Volga region the proportion was about a fifth. Outside of the Black Earth the proportion leaving the Mir never exceeded a sixth, and in the north it fell to six per cent.

A substantial proportion of those who availed themselves of the new Settlement sold their land at once, either because their holdings were too small to be economic, or because they wanted to emigrate, or because their main interest was in the wages of labour rather than in agricultural earnings, and they had secured proprietary right only with the object of selling it to advantage. The alienation was not on a scale to constitute a widespread dispossession of cultivating peasants. Of the million and a quarter households which proceeded to the stage of consolidation, there is reason for believing that about four-fifths did so in order to be free to improve their agricultural methods. To this million of improving households we must look for the principal agricultural advantage of the Settlement proceedings.

The pressure brought by Government to encourage the consolidation of holdings was great, and it had more than one unfortunate result. In the distribution of land, there was a tendency to give the better land to those who fell in with the wishes of the authorities. The opposition got the worse land, and great bitterness of feeling resulted. Those who separated from the Mir or broke it up, tended to be favourites with the landlords, as well as with the local authorities, and to be employed in charge of forests and in other ways which brought them into conflict with the rest of the peasantry: the land seizures and the Revolution of 1917 undid all but a little of the work of the Settlement: and a temporary revival of the movement for the individualisation of land-holding started with the New Economic Policy of 1921, but was brought to an end in 1926. This later history is an unanswerable demonstration of the failure of the political aim of creating a strong conservative nucleus in the peasantry: for it was the peasantry which made the Revolution, and the land was the motive of it.

During the brief currency of the Stolypin Settlement and probably, at least in part, in consequence of it, agricultural statistics show improved conditions. There was an increase in the importation of agricultural machinery and artificial fertilisers, a general increase in the acreage under crop, apparently indicating that land formerly regarded as unproductive was being tilled, and a slight increase in the yield per unit of area of rye, oats and barley, but not of wheat. Emigration to Siberia and Central Asia which had previously been very active, amounting to seven hundred thousand a year both in 1908 and 1909, fell off between 1909 and 1914, presumably in consequence of improved conditions at home. In spite of an industrial slump which lasted till 1910, industry produced, between 1905 and the War, double its earlier production. Such significant figures as those for goods carried by railways and for the production of pig-iron went up; and people were using substantially more sugar and more roof-iron just before the War than they were using in 1905. On the other hand, an increase in agricultural indebtedness attracted attention in 1910 and there was a severe harvest failure, amounting to famine, in 1911. Between this calamity and the outbreak of the Great War, was a period of prosperity, in which a part at least of the peasantry, and certainly the "strong and sober" among them, had their share: and there were great developments in agricultural co-operation, especially in Siberia. The State finances prospered, and the revenues of the last year before the Great War amounted to £370 million, of which £95 million were derived from the liquor monopoly.

March 5, 1907. The second Duma, a more extreme body than the first, because of the exclusion of the constitutionalists who had appealed for non-co-operation with the Government, was soon dissolved in an atmosphere of police prosecutions. A large proportion of its Socialist members were exiled, to return in triumph at the fall of the monarchy ten years later. Then followed the new Electoral law *(Nov. 1907)*, which made the conservative "Octobrists" the leading party in the third

Duma, and gave predominance to the propertied and Great-Russian elements of the population. This was characteristic of Stolypin's policy of political and economic nationalism, with a constitutional or quasi-constitutional monarchy, but without responsible government. He leaned, or wished to lean, upon the Duma, whose support he ultimately used for his agrarian legislation, and upon the middling landowner and the middling capitalist, and upon the patriotism, not to say the chauvinism, of Great-Russians against the federating tendencies of the other peoples of the Empire. The reactionaries might have recognised the constructive statecraft which framed these plans, but they were not grateful to their second potential saviour. The Court, always blind to its friends, and having perhaps an instinctive sense of the tendency of his measures to convert the Orthodox Autocracy into a sort of Louis Philippe monarchy, could not abide Peter Stolypin: and when he was murdered in 1911, the Tsaritsa said: "He is gone: let us hear no more of him." As for the inchoate class of capitalists and bourgeois, whose interests would seem to have dictated a warm support, they did not at any time show willingness to put up an energetic struggle either for themselves or for their friends. Throughout this period of revolutions, attempted or achieved, the middle class in Russia seems to have expected to have its battles fought for it by the official machine. Its activities did not go beyond those of the *Union of the Russian People* and the less reputable performances of the Black Hundreds.

The period of the third and fourth Dumas, starting in 1907 and carrying Russia into the beginning of the Great War, is one which leaves the inquirer with a sense of unexplained contradictions. It begins with a spiritual depression and disillusionment, along with which violent disorder continues to prevail, so that something like stalemate appears to be reached, between a Government which cannot enforce peace and a people which will not submit to repression. The counter-revolution is so far successful, that many socialists are in despair and withdraw from their activities. The literature either does not serve as a mirror for the life out of which it springs, or truly represents a chaos of conflicting tendencies. There is a revival of religious thought and interest springing from Dostoievsky and Vladimir Soloviev. A band of liberals, former Marxians, bring religion, without reaction, for the first time into politics. Artsybashev publishes *Sanin* and preaches in it a kind of anarchy of sexual behaviour—which at a later date proved too strong a dose for Bolshevik ethics, so that *Sanin* was excluded from circulation and Artsybashev expelled from Russia: Vyacheslav Ivanov, mystical anarchist and adept of the cult of the Divine Wisdom, demands like Dostoievsky's Ivan Karamazov, the non-acceptance of the world. The poet Andrei Bely immerses himself in a mystical eschatology with all, and more than all, of the imagery of the Book of Revelation. It is, in part at least, a literature of escape, from which the realism of an earlier generation has entirely departed: perhaps an interval of sultry hush and tension before the breaking of a storm.

In the meanwhile the Duma has ceased to be representative of the population as a whole,—if indeed it ever was so—and yet is doing work of an effective kind: co-operating in the land-settlement: improving the schools and the pay of teachers: making itself felt in the administration of finance, and improving Russian credit by the publicity of accounts and statistics. Incidentally it is showing a very lively interest in military expenditure, and improving the military administration with an evident expectation of occasions for putting it to practical use. It is even developing a constitutional technique of its own, by dealing with business in separate commissions, each of which makes a special study of its own subject, and becomes qualified to speak with the ministries in their own official language.

In 1912, with the disturbances at the works of the British concessionaries on the Lena gold-fields, there is an unmistakable revival of Labour activities, long repressed. The officials responsible for the bloodshed are brought to trial, and a young Labour member of the Duma, Alexander Kerensky, uses the opportunity of the prosecution to attack the régime. The number of strikers rises to nearly a million in a year, and in July 1914 labour disturbances become gravely menacing.

1910. This renewal of Labour demonstrations coincides with a period which we have already described as one of prosperity, at least for some, with foreign capital entering Russia in ever-increasing volume, and the accompanying symptoms of boom. In the meanwhile, the police have been continuously active, and a legal state of emergency has been continuously in force in the greater part of the Empire. If Witte's gall is not too much for his veracity, the letters even of the Dowager Empress are being intercepted and copies of them transferred to the appropriate *dossier.* Hardly have the Field-Courts-Martial brought their operations to a close when the British Ambassador, Sir George Buchanan, is writing of political difficulties, particularly in the Universities and High Schools, with Professors delivering their lectures under police protection. The Duma thunders against exceptional laws and administrative exile, and its Chairman, the conservative Octobrist, Alexander Guchkov, resigns the chair. The conservative reconstructor, Stolypin, is murdered. In 1912 Buchanan tells us of political strikes, of mutinies in the Baltic and Black Sea Fleets and among the troops at Tashkent. In 1913 the fourth Duma, with its Octobrist majority gradually taking up an attitude less and less friendly to Government, censures the Ministry for the continuance of a state of exceptional law: and Guchkov tells Buchanan that there has never been a time when Russia was so deeply permeated by the revolutionary spirit. It has been suggested that one of the considerations which took the Government into war was the wish to escape from revolution at home.

How are we to account for the existence of this menacing unrest in the Russian people, despite "prosperity" and a respectable and efficient Duma, before the war and the attendant maladministration had brought hunger and destroyed confidence in the capacity and even in the good will of the rulers?

There is a school of thought which denies that anything was wrong, or at least that anything was *so* wrong as to call for cure by a drastic operation. The autocracy was, in essentials, like every other Government which is concerned with the defence of property: it had abolished it in its most obviously objectionable form, of property in men and women: and had secured to the emancipated a proportion of the land which amounted, from the first, to half of the whole, and was steadily advancing by purchase. It was doubtful whether any other system would have ventured so far to ignore vested interests or to achieve so much. It had shown itself conspicuously of the best European quality in Catherine the Great's offer of an asylum to the Jesuits, in Alexander I's contribution to the European settlement of 1815, a far wiser one than that of a century later; and in the initiation of the Hague Court of Arbitration for international disputes. It had established peace and the primary essentials of good government over vast areas of Asia, and had ended the raids of the man-stealing Turkman, as at an earlier date those of the Krim Tartar. It had suffered the birth of a literature of world-wide appeal, at the very moment when its assertion of discipline over its subjects was most uncompromising. Since the remission of the redemption-dues, its imposts on the peasantry were no longer excessive. Its courts were modernised, the jury was at work in them, and, whatever might happen in the repression of revolt, its normal jurisprudence was the mildest in Europe. The industrial revolution was still at an early stage: and there had been similar abuses in that stage in all the industrialised countries. Elective organs for the consultation of public opinion had been brought into existence, and were producing administrative reforms. If all was not well, at least it was as well as in the rest of Europe, with its slums and work-houses and prisons for one section of its peoples, and its palaces for another.

Russians—thus the argument continues—are dreamers. The peasants hear of a country of warm streams, as in Tolstoi's *War and Peace,* or of a Land of Truth, such as that of which Gorky's wanderer tells us in *Down and Out:* and at once leave their homes to seek for it. They are no wiser when they are educated, and Utopian theories exercise an irresistible attraction for them. Liberal concessions only set their imaginations off in riot, and make them greedy for more. There are no rigid traditions, no respect for history, no sense of reality, to keep them from harnessing the Winged Horse. They are incorrigible talkers, and the talk intoxicates them. They are not concerned with the dull routine of cause and consequence, and even their interests do not make a determining appeal to them. They claim the impossible from life, and are the natural and very easy prey of revolutionary propaganda. With such a people the fatal error, for a Government, lies in the first beginning of concession. It was the slackening of discipline, not in 1917, but at an earlier date (some seem to suggest, even as far back as the Emancipation), which made the Revolution.

I might go further, and point to hysterical and sadist traits upon which some observers have dwelt, and quote the lady who informed M. Paléologue that what appealed to Russians in time of revolution was, not the political or social ideas, but the excitement, the processions, the bloodshed, and the red of the conflagrations. But I have my suspicions that a good deal of this was due to the influence of Dostoievsky, in his morbid phases, upon the neurasthenics of educated society, and that the creatures of his imagination reproduced themselves, as such things will, in the minds of his readers, while the laborious mass was too busy in getting daily bread to have lodging space for this particular visitation of devils. However, this may be, the meritorious and experienced officials who were convinced that there was still much to be said for the knout, must have argued somewhat on the lines which I have suggested. I will only note that a good deal of it is true of human nature in general. Many of us would be far safer under lock and key. But—*quis custodiet?*

There was plenty of discipline in the Russian empire, but it was not an even discipline, with laws intelligible to all, and it was not equally applied. I will not say that there was one law for the rich and one for the poor: but there was certainly one administration for the rich and another for the poor. It seems nearly certain that, to the vast mass of the Russian people, then *and perhaps now*, autocracy was the only conceivable form of government, in everything, outside of the routine of village life, where the tradition was truly democratic. If anything was wrong with the autocracy, anything, that is, which could not be cured by the well-tried method of a palace revolution, and a change of the person of the autocrat, it was that the autocrat had in some measure ceased to be the *leveller* which public opinion expected him to be: that, in the words of Pobiedonostsev already cited, "wealth, acquired by rapine, overmastered power itself"; that the true tyrant was not the Tsar himself, but the exploiters who sheltered behind him and mastered his governing machine.

The increase of wealth and its uneven distribution, the development of the cash-nexus, the rise of the money-lender of all types, squire, merchant, churchman, and peasant, the power of the industrialist, and the harsh conditions which he enforced upon the worker, with the frequent co-operation of the police, had ended the old patriarchal supremacy of the Tsar, and made obvious the existence of gross and oppressive inequalities which his power did not avail, even if he desired, to level. The fancy that the Tsar, if you could reach him, would always do justice, was long in dying. Perhaps it died finally when the Grand Duke Vladimir fired on the crowd outside the Winter Palace on Bloody Sunday, and the participants in the demonstration were expelled from the capital, to spread the news over thousands of villages. Even the Constitution, particularly in the form which was given to it by the restrictive electoral law, seemed to create political privilege (as perhaps most constitutions do): for some were to be consulted, and many not: a very wide departure from the dream of equal *accessibility* for all, never realised in practice, but always surviving in tradition. It may be that the rule of a hereditary autocrat, with its periodical accident of ineptitude, and the rare emergence of great ability, could not for long have outlived the primitive conditions in which it had originated. Perhaps the appropriate cure was a different way of choosing the autocrat, with more exacting tests of his capacity for the tasks of a superman, and the Revolution has hit upon this: the substitution of a ruler for a *fainéant* (sluggard).

But we anticipate something with which this preliminary

study does not deal. On the policy of the War there was from
the outset a radical difference of opinion in governing circles.
Not only was Germany the main support of the autocracy,
and her overthrow by the western democracies a likely prel-
ude to the further liberalisation of Russia, but she was the
principal source of supply for machinery and for the half-
manufactured articles which were completed for the market
in Russia. Many, like Witte, must clearly have foreseen the
economic consequences of the closing of Russia's frontiers
and western and southern outlets, have hoped for an early
settlement, and been half-hearted or sceptical over the measures necessary for the prosecution of such a struggle to victory.
Suspicion, if not of German leanings, at least of luke-warm-
ness to the war and of animosity to the Russian Commander-
in-Chief, attached from an early date to General Sukhomlinov,
the Minister for War. At a conference, at which the Emperor
was present, he had reported sufficient reserves of small arms
and ammunition, and he gave the French ambassador an assurance to the same effect. The catastrophe of the Galician retreat, partly due to the losses of artillery in East Prussia,
threw an odious glare upon his responsibility: and a letter of
the Empress makes an unexplained reference to the bribing
of his wife. He was removed from the Ministry, and the Duma
demanded that he be put on his trial. But obstacles were placed
in the way of disposal of the case, and the Empress interceded
with her husband to hush it up. The lack of munitions was
discovered in December 1914, the Minister was removed
from office in June 1915, the court-martial procedure was in-
terrupted for him to be taken to hospital in July 1916. In
December 1916 the Empress is still interceding, and referring
mysteriously to stories which may bring disgrace upon important personages if the trial takes place. Among these personages is a famous dancer, in whom Nicolas II was interested in his bachelor days, and there was at least one Grand
Duke who protected her later on. The Empress's letters convey,
in connection with this scandal, messages from "Our Friend",
upon whom she always bestows initial capitals, and who is no
other than Gregory Rasputin.

Rasputin (the name signifies debauchee, and acquaints us with the bearer's reputation in his native Siberian village) was neither priest nor monk, nor in any sort of religious orders, but a wandering "man of God". He was lucky enough to exhibit curative or mesmeric powers over the precious and only son, who wrung his mother's heart by being a sufferer from haemophilia. Then he became something for which our western experiences have no parallel, but readers of Dostoievsky may recognise in the part which he plays with the Empress, some resemblance to the *Elder,* to whom Alyosha Karamazov entrusts his spiritual life. The devoted wife and mother, grand-daughter of Queen Victoria, and of life not less strict than her grandmother, surrenders her soul to the guidance of this religious adventurer and presses all his political counsels upon her Imperial husband.

Rasputin is something of an enigma, because he started with a few simple and great ideas which multitudes must have shared with him: an immense sympathy with his fellow-peasants and their sufferings, a religious devotion to the autocracy as the hope of Russia, and a passion for peace. He foresaw (perhaps he had no need of exceptional qualities for this perception) the confusion which would come upon Russia during or after the war. Kerensky (no friend of his) speaks of his "wonderful intuition" and it is evident that he possessed some sort of animal magnetism. Those who are aware of the wilder orbits of the Russian spirit may not be surprised that he regarded sin as necessary to salvation, because without sin there is no repentance. Some highly-placed ladies lent themselves to his orgies, religious and other, or visited him to intercede for their husbands. Probably his head was turned by the enormous influence which he found himself to possess. In the later stages of his life at Court, a knot of financiers provided him with money and gave him a weekly dinner, at which he generally became drunk. It cannot be said that the Empress was blind to all of this. On one occasion she writes to her husband: "Our Friend was very gay after dinner: *not tipsy.*" The italics are mine. When he was tipsy, he talked, and what was said by him was used for the Stock Exchange, or reported to Berlin.

He had not the brains to carry through any systematic in-
trigue, but he easily became an instrument for the intrigues
of others, and he had plenty of cunning to protect his own
interests. A final and particularly effective device was to convince the Empress that his departure would be followed by
the death of the Tsarevitch and the fall of the dynasty.

In April 1915 he got very drunk at a dinner party, and
boasted to his fellow guests, with obscene gestures, that he
did what he liked with "the old woman". The horror-stricken
police reported this at Court, and one might have supposed
that it would have ended his career. But the Empress only
thought that the Devil had set a snare for the holy man, she
complained of the Commandant of Gendarmerie who had
given the information, and used all her powers of persuasion
to forestall any opportunity of interpellation about the scandal
in the Duma. On this occasion, Guchkov, the head of the
Octobrist party, figures as her particular *bête noire*, no doubt
because he had already exposed Rasputin in 1912. She asks
angrily: "Cannot Guchkov be hanged?" We get the full significance of this interjection when we recall that, at the March
Revolution, Guchkov was prominent among those who strug-
gled for the monarchical principle against Kerensky and the
republicans. When it is a question of giving effect to the
promise of autonomy in Poland, she tells her husband: "Our
Friend begs you to wait. . . . His love to you and Russia is so
intense and God has sent Him to be your help and guide."
When a comrade of Rasputin's, who had been foisted into a
Bishopric, wants to have a certain person canonised, so as to
attract pilgrims and their money, and the Procurator of the
Holy Synod, a man of great weight in Orthodox and conservative circles, stands firm against the trick, the Empress writes
indignant letters, the Procurator is displaced from his lay
headship of the Church, and—*the false Saint is duly canonised.*

The Commander-in-Chief, the Grand Duke Nicolas, was
suspected by the Empress of intending to use his influence
with the troops to secure his own position (possibly as Regent), in the event of the death or removal of the Emperor.
She talks of "the game for which the Left wanted to use

Nikolasha", the depreciatory nickname by which she described the bluff soldier. There is a blank in the letters from July 11th, 1915, because the Emperor was at this time with his family: but we soon discover how the time was being spent. On September 3rd, the Empress writes a paean on the "great decision" which the Emperor has taken, and two days later he assumes the supreme command of all the forces of the sea and land armies operating in the theatre of war, with General Alexéev as Chief of his Staff.

What the armies thought of the new High Command we learn from Major-General Knox, the military attaché of the British Embassy. Misgiving was almost universal. It was felt that the change would give advancement to Court favourites, and that few would be able to resist the temptation of intriguing to catch the Imperial eye. The Foreign Minister Sazonov said: "The only way out is to go and drown ourselves." It was not only the military situation which was prejudiced. Henceforth, and more particularly after Stürmer became President of the Council of Ministers in February 1916, the Empress was in control of the civil government of the rear, and distrust of authority permeated all classes.

Nicolas II was jealous of his authority, jealous of it even against the encroachments of his own wife: and he did not always yield to her insistence. Paradoxical though it may appear, his judgment was good. It was not on every occasion that he showed lack of will-power. Rather it would seem that he was the victim of a sort of morbid apathy, perhaps the result of fatalism. He felt himself born for suffering, a feeling which presently deepened into a sense of being a destined sacrifice. M. Paléologue, the French Ambassador, has left us an account of a conversation of 1909 in which Nicolas told Stolypin that his birthday was the day of the Patriarch Job, and quoted the despairing words: "Let the day perish wherein I was born, and the night wherein it was said there is a man-child conceived." There is a figure in Tennyson's *Princess*, who, in moments of crisis, at grips with enemies of flesh and blood, has the hallucination of fighting with shadows, and collapses before them. Some such morbid neurosis affected the life of Nicolas.

Dec. 1916. He was not, like his wife, under the direct influence of Rasputin, and it has been suggested that the murder of the latter came to him as something of a relief. The three persons who carried it out were Prince Yusupov (who married the Emperor's niece), the Grand Duke Dimitry, son of the Grand Duke Paul, and Purishkevich, prominent in the reactionary *Union of the Russian People*—all men of the Court and of the extreme Right. There was joy in Petrograd because Rasputin met his death by drowning (the drowned cannot be canonised), and the Churches were filled with candles, burning before the icons of St. Dimitry, in honour of the Grand Duke's namesake. But, lest we should forget the contradictions in Russian life, the murdered Man of God became a martyr for the peasants. "He caused the Tsar to hear the voice of the people"—doubtless because he spoke for peace.

The murder did not end the influences which were carrying the dynasty to ruin. Rasputin had had his predecessors in the function of fooling the Imperial pair: some other would have stepped into the place if he had ceased to fill it; and, when he was dead, the Court or its satellites were busy raising his ghost to consult him, up to the very night of Revolution. It seems that decaying monarchies must have their Cagliostros. A cynical old gentleman told M. Paléologue that things would be worse without Rasputin: who—*entre deux fornications*—gave to his Imperial patrons advice for their salvation and the government of the empire. He was their amusement, their plaything, their fetish: and worse follies might be expected when they had been upset by his removal.

Alongside of steady Socialist propaganda among soldiers and workmen, it had long been known that members of the Romanov family contemplated the deposition of the Tsar and the removal of the Tsaritsa to a convent. There was another plot for the deposition of the Tsar only and the appointment of the Tsaritsa as regent for her infant son: and yet a third for the removal of the Tsaritsa only: the former designed to facilitate a separate peace with Germany, the latter to make possible a more vigorous prosecution of the war. Palace conspiracies, or the talk of them, continued after the murder of Rasputin. The odium of Russian defeats and of Russian sufferings was concentrated largely on Alexandra Feodorovna, whose sobriquet, "the German woman", recalls "L'autrichienne", the name by which Marie Antoinette was known to Paris when the Austrian armies were advancing against France. There was an attempt on her life in January 1917 by an officer in the Imperial Hospital at Tsarskoye Selo. She was naturally in correspondence with her German relatives, was grieved at mob attacks upon Germans, protested against the changing of German place-names, of which Petrograd itself was an instance, and against a foolish proposal of the Holy Synod in 1914 to prohibit the German custom of the Christmas tree: sympathised with German prisoners of war, and urged the Tsar to allow Americans to inspect the prison camps. The suggestion of treachery to the country of her adoption is without foundation. But that she became an instrument in the hands of men who sought to bring about a separate peace with Germany, is probable.

In February 1916, one Stürmer, described by Buchanan as a second-rate man and a sycophant, but having the support of Rasputin, was appointed President of the Council of Ministers. This man together with the Empress, visited the Emperor at Army Headquarters, where they secured the destruction of a scheme of autonomy for Poland, and the dismissal of the Foreign Minister Sazonov whose portfolio was entrusted to Stürmer. It was not long before they had obtained the dismissal of an effective War Minister, Polivanov, on the ground of his co-operation with the unofficial War Munitions Committee, and his replacement by a man of inferior capacity.

The assistance given in the prosecution of the war by Town and County Councils and by unofficial bodies, was always a cause of jealousy and suspicion to the Empress, as indeed to the official machine in general; and some of her most insistent letters urge the Emperor to "shut up that rotten War Industries Committee", or complain of the doctors and nurses emof one Protopopov, who was perhaps the worst selection even in this period of infatuation. He had been a member of the Duma but had recently visited Stockholm where he met a German agent, and had returned to Russia under the suspicion of secret negotiation with the enemy. His health—even his sanity—was doubtful, so that we find the Empress explaining in a letter, in which she asks the Emperor to put the food supply into his hands, that her protégé is *"not mad"*. Probably he was suffering from something like inchoate general paralysis of the insane. He was an accomplished necromancer and was the person who subsequently gave himself the pains of raising Rasputin's ghost. He at once set to work to reorganise the Black Hundreds for an attack upon the Duma, and to plan with the Empress a method of circumventing the bodies which were co-operating with the Government over military supply, but his courage failed him when he was asked to take the food and fuel supply into his own hands.

By this time economic conditions were reaching a crisis. Difficulties had made their appearance from the beginning of the war. Germany was blockaded in form as well as in fact, and, with her usual energy and efficiency, planned and executed compensatory measures. Russia was blockaded in fact, and soon she had lost Poland and with it a large part of such industry as she possessed. But compensatory measures were slow in coming, and, when they came, were hampered by a careful regard for the interests of grain-dealers and industrialists, whom the Government was unwilling to offend.

An unexpected feature of the economic troubles was the scarcity and dearness of foodstuffs. Out of a total cereal production of some eighty million tons, Russia had been exporting from twelve to fifteen per cent. It seemed that the stoppage of export should provide a margin for all requirements. In spite of the mobilisation of fifteen millions of men and two and a half million horses, there was hardly any reduction in cultivated area, doubtless because both man and ani-

mal power had been under-employe.
were increased by the contrast betwee.
ing and the low peace-time standard o.
wasteful army administration: while huge s.
doned or destroyed in the evacuation of Po.
western provinces. There was difficulty in carrying
able food and fodder, not, at this stage, because of the .sor-
ganisation of transport, but rather because of the inadequacy
of the railways. A railway map of the period shows, at a
glance, that the tracks were concentrated upon Poland and
the western portion of the Empire. East of the Petrograd—
Moscow–Kharkov–Sevastopol line, the lines had a capacity of
only one-third of those of the country to the west of it. As the
war rolled eastwards, railway facilities for the Russian armies
grew less.

There was another reason why food was scarce and dear.
Hitherto the peasants had cut down their consumption of food,
partly in order to pay their dues to the State and their rents
and interest to squires and moneylenders, partly to buy industrial goods, partly to indulge in vodka. By a generous self-
denying ordinance at the declaration of war, the Government
had prohibited, except for industrial purposes, the sale of spirit,
of which the State had a monopoly. M. Paléologue makes the
interesting suggestion that the deprivation of alcohol accounts
for the depression which is so evident in Russia during the
greater part of the war. However this may be, it went far to
cut off exchange between town and village. This tendency was
aggravated by the short supply and high price of industrial
goods. Many industries, especially those meeting military
needs, increased their output. But the production of agricultural machinery and implements went down to one-fifth of that
of the pre-war period. The villages suffered from the lack of
these, of textiles, iron-ware and leather goods: and the cities
and industrial centres were, by consequence, short of fuel,
flour, butter, eggs, milk and vegetables. The holders of diminished stocks of marketable foodstuffs effected a corner in them,
and raised prices to an unconscionable figure. Rationing began

in 1916 and was steadily extended till it covered all the more important articles of food.

The maximum prices fixed for grain and fodder were made ineffective by official and general corruption. The Government's own purchasing agents often paid more than the prescribed maximum. The British Ambassador told his Government in August 1916 that the civil population "had had enough of an administrative system which, in a country so rich as Russia . . . rendered it difficult for them to procure many of the first necessaries of life even at famine prices". Soon after, a further step was taken, by the compulsory acquisition of grain both for the army and the civil population, in the direction of the State monopoly of grain and of the requisitioning policy, which became the expedients of the Revolutionary Governments.

1914. The flush of enthusiasm which greeted the declaration of war faded into depression and suspicion after the disasters in East Prussia. There was a brief recovery during the Galician successes: to be succeeded in the summer of 1915 by a mood of tragic heroism, when munitions failed, and the slowly retreating troops offered their bare bodies to the cannonade of General Mackensen. But already the desertions, which afterwards assumed such catastrophic dimensions, had begun: and confidence in the military administration could not survive so severe a shock. The Government was now compelled to abandon its policy of excluding the rural Councils and other public organisations from co-operation in the tasks of military supply, and a magnificent effort to supply deficiencies was temporarily successful, so far as the direct object of fitting out the armies was concerned. In this effort it seems that the need of husbanding resources in machinery, plant, and means of transport, was overlooked.

In the meanwhile the working population of the towns was being subjected to an extraordinary strain by overwork and underfeeding, with severe penalties for every sign of resistance to the exaction of heavy tasks. The Government had been forced to raise wages and inflate the currency and so to set in motion the vicious succession of economic and financial evils which these measures entail. Trotsky has given us a picture of the conditions in the factories in the latter days which preceded the revolution: when nerves were in such a state of tension that an unexpected whistle might at any moment start a strike. The garrison of Petrograd, unduly large and demoralised by inaction, became restive and undisciplined. At the end of October 1916 there was a rising in the Viborg quarter of the city, where the great iron and steel works are situated. Infantry of the line fired on the police engaged in restoring order. Cossacks drove the infantry back to barracks, and a hundred and fifty soldiers were shot by the authorities—all very like an anticipation of the events of March 1917, except in the fidelity of the Cossacks and the consequent success of the repression.

A police officer in the capital about this time, sent to the Minister of the Interior a remarkable report on the conditions existing both in the city and the country. He spoke of the disintegration of the rear, as threatening to throw the country into anarchy, of the uncontrolled profiteering, of the unfair distribution of foodstuffs and articles of prime necessity, of the rapid increase in the cost of living and of the inadequacy of the sources of supply, of the extreme anxiety everywhere prevalent, and of exceptionally strong feelings of opposition and hostility to the Government in every section of the capital's population. "These hostile feelings have attained a power among the masses which is without precedent even in 1905–6 . . . complaints of the dishonesty of the administration, the unbearable burden of the war, the impossible conditions of everyday life. The inflammable statements of the radicals, that *one must first get rid of the Germans at home*, and then proceed against those abroad, are meeting with more and more approval. . . . Wholesale disturbances may arise anywhere . . . events of primary importance are approaching. . . . The peasants lease no more land because they feel sure that, after the war, land will be distributed to them free of charge. At the beginning of the war, the very idea of revolution seemed preposterous, but now everyone is sure that it is inevitable." Such was the situation, with an angry Duma about to meet, when Protopopov asked to be excused "for a fortnight" from undertaking the task of victualling.

Nov. 1916. The Duma met, and Professor Paul Miliukov (afterwards Minister of Foreign Affairs in the Provisional Government) launched a tremendous attack upon Stürmer and Protopopov. He charge Stürmer with treason, on account of the provocative action of the police in the strikes of the munition factories, of his secret correspondence with Germany, and of Protopopov's conversations with a German agent at Stockholm: and ended his speech by saying: We must struggle till we have ministers worthy of our confidence.

The Censorship—without warrant of law—forbade the publication of the whole text of this speech. But it is a testimonial to the effect of representative institutions, even in conditions such as those of Russia in November 1916, that the intriguers were thoroughly frightened by the publicity thus given to causes of public indignation. The Empress wrote to her husband that "both Protopopov and Our Friend" thought it would be wise for Stürmer to "go for a rest for three weeks". The Emperor removed Stürmer, but the Empress was able to save Protopopov from a similar fate. Her letters interceding for him, and begging that the Duma be not allowed to claim the success of expelling all the ministers, show morbid excitement. "Oh Lovey, you can trust me. I may not be clever enough, but I have a strong feeling, and that helps more than the brain often. . . . It's a hunt against wify. . . . I am fighting for your Reign and Baby's future." The same note reappears: "We must give a strong country to Baby . . . else he will have a yet harder reign, setting our faults to right." In the yearning for the preservation of the life of her son and of his full inheritance, we have the key to her infatuations. And what a revelation it is of the intimacies of that tenderly affectionate, yet fate-stricken household, when she writes: "Be Peter the Great, Ivan the Terrible, Emperor Paul—crush them all under you—*now don't you laugh, naughty one!"*

Jan.–Feb. 1917. Protopopov kept his post, had bogus telegrams despatched from the country daily to the Empress to confirm in her the illusion that she had the support of the

Army and the peasantry: gave occasion to Buchanan (who never minced his words) to tell the Emperor that his Minister of the Interior was bringing Russia to ruin; arrested the Workmen's group in the War Industries Committee, probably as loyal a lot as he could have found in the whole class; and fitted out the police of the capital with machine-guns, anticipating—some say, desiring to provoke and crush—a revolution from below.

The Duma had been summoned for the 27th February, and on that day, though the only crowds on the Petrograd streets were the food queues, a proclamation threatening the use of force against demonstrators was issued by the Commandant of the garrison. Then came a sudden reduction in the supply of bread. The bakers were dissatisfied with the officially fixed price, and were selling rye flour for horses' food. Some shops were ransacked, and some were closed by the owners.

The Cossacks riding through the streets went through all the apparent motions of suppressing riot. But a junior French diplomat took note of a trifling incident. He saw a Cossack wink to the rioters.

Chapter 5

Unity and Disunity in Russia

> "The Russians are a state-minded people, submissively giving themselves to be the material for founding a great empire, and yet, at the same time, inclined to revolt, to turbulence, to anarchy. . . . If the idea of the sacred anointing of authority was characteristic of the Russian, so also was the idea that all authority is evil and sinful."
>
> BERDYAEV, *Origins of Russian Communism*.

> " *'Tis thou that art monstrous,*
> *Thou that art fruitful,*
> *Thou that art mighty,*
> *Thou that art strengthless,*
> *Russia, dear mother."*
>
> N. A. NEKRASOV.

OUR AUTHORITIES ARE not at one in their opinion of the attitude of the peasant to the State. He is a natural anarchist: and he approves and demands an active Government. Gleb Uspensky exhibits to us his typical peasant, Ivan Ermolaevich, as one who has learned both obedience and the exercise of power, from the life of agriculture. The power which he exercises over his animals and over his family (the order is deliberate) is necessary if he is to conduct every operation in

127

its due season. He will not allow his sister to marry the preferred bachelor, because he must buy horses, and can't afford a dower. The swain tells the girl he must take someone else, whose father will give two hundred roubles with her. The money is necessary for the needs of farming. Both the lovers understand and obey—not a tyrant, but the power of the land, which demands the sacrifice. For the same reason the weak who cannot cultivate his lot must yield it up to the strong who can. The land demands it. In his turn, Ivan understands that the Tsar must have money to carry on the business of the State, and therefore the impost must be paid, and realises that the priest is necessary because the peasant has sins, for which neither the Elder, nor the tavern-keeper, nor even the Governor, can grant absolution. All is in its proper order, the product of an inevitable necessity springing out of the needs of life.

Another picture, this time a historical one, shows us, in the community of the Old Believers, an organised peasant culture with a permanent administrative Council, a number of institutions for mutual assistance, and—until Nicolas I confiscated the money—an exchequer of millions of roubles. For a long time a number of these institutions, including what we should now call a co-operative credit society—centred in a cemetery in Moscow: because a cemetery was the only form of common organisation which the authorities would allow. We are already familiar with the Village Meeting, springing out of the needs of an open-field agriculture, which for centuries discharged all the functions of local self-government at the base of rural life. That work was well done while peasant society was not complicated by economic change, and it was carried one tier higher by the canton meetings in which the spontaneous element was less: it went no further. That it might have gone further, if the next higher place had not been occupied by institutions having a different source, and descending from above downwards, we may suspect, but we cannot prove.

It is not only Gleb Uspensky, among the students of peasant life, who assures us that the peasant understands and approves the State. The writer of a later, and particularly convincing, monograph of the twentieth-century village, quotes his peasants as saying: We do not object to the State. The State is necessary to us. So much for one side of the story. Mr. Hindus, evidently describing the conditions at his own old home in White-Russia, quotes the local miller who "hated Government and regarded it as the source of all evil. Why, he asked, did not the Government leave the villages alone? Of what use was a Government to *his* village, anyway?" He was an anarchist, without understanding the word: and there were plenty such, as the history of Ukrain and of Siberia during the Civil War made manifest: men who hated the town, and the educated people, because they took so much and gave so little. A landlord of the Smolensk province, whom I have often had occasion to quote, is definite in saying: "the peasant thinks the administration is of no use either to the Tsar or to him. It it only for the masters. There cannot be, in his view, any improving of a useless institution." Note that the Tsar is not included in the repudiation. It is only the administrative machinery that is condemned: and this is probably very typical of the primitive peasant outlook. Above, a glorious figure, crowned and enthroned: and, grouped below him, the peasants in their communes, all having free access to the divine ruler, who keeps all equal.

It may be that the peasants could have built a State, as the Old Believers built an organised community. But, in fact, as history presents itself to us, they stopped in the initial stages of organisation, and the upper storeys of the social edifice were added, not by their hands, but by the hands of others, out of materials strange to them: and the two parts of the work never formed a united whole. Something very like this has happened to other peoples too. At all events, different peoples, or peoples with differing histories, have actually exhibited widely different aptitudes for the development of social and political institutions. Some go further, and some less far, in the formation of social aggregations. Some stop for tens of centuries at the family, and some pass on to the clan or the caste, and find their limit for long periods at that stage, though military empires may bring them artificially together in much larger groups. Some have built the city-state, and some only the village community. We are familiar to-day with a number which have, ostensibly at all events, grown into nation-states. But this stage of growth is sometimes apparent or artificial only, and the organic unity which the nation-state should have attained is, in varying degrees, incomplete. The incompleteness may be only a local particularism demanding a federal instead of a unitary form of political government. Or the defect may be more radical than this, and may manifest itself in an obstinately fissiparous tendency. Even when organic unity seems to have been achieved, it may be unmade by new divisions of class or religion cutting across national limits.

The Great-Russian people found no difficulty in the formation of certain primitive aggregations: the patriarchal family: and communes of villages and even of larger units. Beyond these there was never an organic unity. In spite of a unity of language which varies very little over hundreds of leagues, it remained in essence a confederation of village communities governed by a common head, by means of an administrative system imposed from above. There are, in fact, two conflicting streams of tendency active at different levels. One, which may be loosely described as associational, brings the Russian people together to work out a common economic and social life, in the family, the Mir and the partnership of cultivators or artisans. The other—it might reasonably be called anarchical, in so far as it is inimical to the consolidation of the State—forces the primary units away from organic union. It is no accident that the most widely famous of Russian writers repudiates the State. He is giving literary expression to the subconscious conviction of the mass of his fellow countrymen.

Perhaps all humanity is, socially speaking, both centripetal and centrifugal. It needs its loves, and it needs its hates, or at all events cherishes both, and each seems necessary to the other. The difference, at different epochs, and among peoples with different histories, lies in the point at which attraction is replaced by repulsion: the limit of social aggregation at which it ceases to seem virtuous to give mutual aid and begins to seem virtuous to make mutual war. The British people—subject to certain incipient achievements of a higher order, such as the tenuous bond which unites the Empire, the attraction of the French Canadians and the Dutch Boers, and the inchoate, but much more doubtful, attachment of the Indian peoples— reaches its associational limit at the nation-state. But we do not forget the past existence of a narrower bond of attraction in the Heptarchy, and in the separate kingdoms of England and Scotland; and we still see international anarchy only slightly modified by a precarious agreement of peace and co-operation between nations. The Russian people ceased to be associa- tional, and began to be anarchical, before it had completely reached the state of the nation-state. Whether a difficulty in becoming a nation may make it easier to take the further step of forming an association which crosses national lines, we can only speculate. But the claim has been made: and made before the Revolutionaries of November set before themselves the definite ideal of a World-State.

The two agents which supplemented, or replaced, the organic growth of the Russian people towards nationhood were the Orthodox Church, in the first place, and the Autocracy as its defender and guardian. When the Church was divided by the Schism in the seventeenth century, unifying influences were gravely weakened. One of Lyeskov's stories shows us how real was the rift. We see a dissenting guild of bridge-builders griev- ing over their separation from the brotherhood, and ultimately returning to communion with the orthodox, because of the pain of this separation. The Tsar was the Orthodox Tsar, the people were, par excellence, Orthodox, and the fact that their religion seemed to consist only in the due performance of prescribed rites did not impair its character as the bond of nationhood. The identity of the religious with the national bond explains the efforts made to bring all within the religious fold. Dissenters were regarded as Orthodox who declined to perform their religious duties, and subjected to compulsion as such. Jews became Russians, immune from all disabilities, as soon as they became Orthodox. Uniats, who accepted Papal Supremacy while observing the Orthodox rite, were, from the State's point of view, as serious a stone of offence as the Roman Catholics, until they became Orthodox. Roman Catholics were the worst treated of all the unorthodox confessions, because they owned the supremacy of a foreign spiritual head, and therefore lacked the essential bond of Russian nationhood. All along the doubtful and shifting frontier between the Russian and Polish races, it was Orthodoxy or Roman Catholicism which in practice determined the question of race.

One of the consequences of the position, as I have described it, is that the Revolution, which made an end of the State Church as well as of the Tsar, left the new rulers with the task of creating a new bond of association. They found it first in class, and hoped to have made it international. The frustration of this expectation has now taken them back to the task of building a new nation.

If authorities differ regarding the attitude of the people of Russia to the State, they differ still more widely regarding the depth of their division into classes, and the degree of hostility between these classes. "Almost no trace of those class-hatreds which are conspicuous in Western Europe . . . very little caste-spirit or caste-prejudice," says Mackenzie Wallace. "My first impression was that of a conquered race and its foreign masters," says Dr. Dillon, ". . . a complete cultural separation of class from class . . . two classes, the masters and their workers, between whom yawned an abyss almost as wide as that between Spartan citizens and helots." "Distinctions of class never existed except on the surface," says Prince Cherkassky, one of the authors of the Emancipation Law, as quoted by Leroy Beaulieu. "If one scratches the soil one finds the old Slav stratum of equality and unity." "But," adds Leroy Beaulieu, "externally, Russian Society is the most completely divided into classes of any in Europe. The old classification, in orders or in estates, subsists in law, nominally, externally: in reality it has been singularly alleviated. All the reforms since the Emancipation tend to the lowering of the barriers of class." "A profound legal and cultural rift between peasants and masters," says Prince Mirsky in his Social History. Englehardt, the enlightened landlord, who tried to bring the intelligents into agriculture, says that he constantly came upon a hostile outlook on the part of the peasantry, not upon himself personally, at least upon him as a "gentleman". "The demand for arrears of tax, the demand for mending the roads, the demand for sending the children to school, the recruiting, the decisions of the Courts, the Law"—in short anything that is unpleasant to the peasant—"it's all from the gentry. He does not recognise the law: he reverences only something which he calls God's law. If he's caught stealing, and gets a blow, well and good. But as for the law awarding three and a half months' imprisonment for a couple of loads of hay, the gentry made it to harass the peasants." Mr. Chamberlin speaks of "the bitter hatred and envy which the poor, illiterate or semi-literate, of the Russian people felt for the educated minority . . . as undiscriminating as the *jacquerie* of Pugachev and Stenka Razin . . . an enormous and apparently inexhaustible reserve of class-hatred. . . ."

These are wide variations. Part may be due to differences of the time at which the opinions were expressed: part to differences of place. There is reason, for instance, for thinking that class-hatred was more bitter in Ukrain, where economic differences were accentuated by differences of race and religion, and where the townspeople were Jews or Poles or Great-Russians, while the country people were Ukranians, than in Great-Russia. In Latvia and Esthonia, where the masters were Germans and Lutherans, and the people Letts and Esthonians and largely Orthodox, the feeling was intense. Sir Bernard Pares tells us that the class-system, introduced by Peter the Great, was mainly operative in the country, and that the attempt to put people into categories was not successful in the towns.

The existence of the legal distinction between classes, made more definite by Peter the Great, is a fact. The institution of serfdom itself is the most glaring instance of the distinction. The questions which more particularly concern us are those of the survival or renewal of the distinction after the Emancipation of the serfs, and of the existence, after that reform, of hostility between the classes. Enough has been said in an earlier chapter to show how much of the old inferiority of the

peasant-status survived the reforms of Alexander II. It survived, in part because of the actual backwardness which no
legal ameliorations could amend, in part because the legal
changes were themselves incomplete, and because reaction took
away something out of what had been conceded. It continued
to survive after the Revolution of 1905 in spite of the improvements of status which were then made.

In spite of some fierce explosions of hatred such as the three
great rebellions of Bolotnikov, of Stenka Razin, and of
Pugachev, all of which seem to have the character of class-war,
I think that there was less hostility between classes, at all
events in Great-Russia, than in western Europe. A complete
system of occupational castes, some of which perform degrading duties, is capable of existing without more than sporadic
indications of hostility or discontent, so long as there exists a
general conviction that the various privileges and duties are
prescribed by an external authority, whether it be religious or
political. It is when the suspicion arises that the higher caste
is for its own purposes taking advantage of the lower that the
danger of internecine quarrel begins. The old placid acceptance
of an order imposed by the Deity or His viceregent on earth
then gives place to the notion that there is a quarrel to be
fought out. When Peter the Great established a hierarchy of
castes, and demanded varying services from each according
to his capacity, he was dealing, as the Roman Emperors were,
with a people of *"conservi"* all alike servants of the Imperial
power. If the serf owed duty to the squire, the squire too
was in his way a serf, bound similarly to work for his Tsar. It
was hard, but there was a kind of equality about it too. The
superior order in the hierarchy was not working merely for
itself, but had a function for the due performance of which
the collaboration of the lower was necessary. Moreover the
Autocrat could and did pick out, when he pleased and saw
fit, those who were capable of higher functions, and translated
them into the upper spheres of work.

1762. The system never found its logical completion, because successive autocrats declined to define the obligations of
the serf to his master: and, as a coherent whole, was destroyed

when Peter III emancipated the gentry from their obligations. But the idea of serfdom as something imposed from above, to meet the needs of the Tsar, not as something enforced by the master in his own interests, continued to colour popular conceptions. The peasants were a class apart, having their own duties, their own organisation and their own elected chiefs, and, according to their own conception at least, their own definite rights in the land, and a status of their own: not less than the masters, though different from them. Both were set in their places by an outside authority, and there was no room for envy or hatred between them as classes, whatever private grievance and private revenge might bring about between individuals. They had never fought out their grievances, as had so often happened between classes in western Europe, and there was no tradition of corporate hostility between them.

But there was a great and growing remoteness between the two, between *"people"* and *"persons"*: the one, bearded, long-smocked, occupied with manual labour, serving in the ranks, ignorant of books: the other, smooth-faced, breeched, having a smattering of foreign culture and language, serving in the commissioned ranks, military or civil: and the completeness of the separation was destined to produce misunderstanding and hostility, as soon as the peasant had tasted of the fruit of knowledge of good and evil.

The Emancipation and the reforms which followed it aimed at throwing down the barriers between the classes: we might even say, at unmaking the classes which earlier legislation had built up. They therefore put an end to the peasant's conception of his place in a hierarchy of classes, and revealed the naked fact of an economic rivalry between the man who tills the soil, on the one hand, and the squire and employer on the other. Such changes in traditional thought are not suddenly achieved. At least one whole generation is needed to bring them about, as the facts of daily life with slow strokes hammer conviction home. The peasant disturbances of the twentieth century are the unmistakable evidence that the new thought has passed through the period of gestation and come to birth.

I have emphasised elsewhere the fact that Alexander II

began a revolution which he did not complete. The new thought was embittered by a disappointment. The appetite comes with eating: and further reforms were too slow to keep up with the expectations which had been aroused. It was as though a new chemical element had been dipped into the crucible to mingle with its innocent contents, and had formed along with them a corrosive compound.

The writer's solution, then, of the contradiction between those who deny the existence of class-hatreds in pre-Revolution Russia and those who affirm it, is that they were long in developing, at all events in the Great-Russian core of Russia, but that they were coming into existence.

A patriarchal element in the relations of superior and inferior cannot have escaped the attention of those who knew pre-Revolution Russia. We see it represented in literature, where the serf who has just undergone a whipping boasts that "we don't whip for nothing in *our* household": and Turgeniev adds the observation: There's old Russia for you. But it was a survival and it was in the process of giving place to something different. The cleft was forming. It was worst, of course, where differences of religion and of race were added to differences of class, as they were in the western and south-western fringes. There it was already mutual hate. In Great-Russia it was a mutual aloofness and absence of sympathy, which will become something worse.

The writers who has left us a monograph of a village in the Valdai hills about the years 1920–25 says that the peasant greatly values the democratic side of the revolutionary order, and particularly the absence of "gentlemen" from posts of authority. Everywhere he finds his own people, "with whom he can exchange abuse and smoke". So his attitude is subconsciously sympathetic to the revolution, though there is plenty of criticism of those who administer, judge and collect taxes. Class-hatred is too strong an expression for feelings such as these. It is rather a liking for equality, and discomfort in the presence of those who claim to be superiors. Other descriptions suggest that the peasant looked down upon the "gentleman", as incapable of useful work: which the Russian "gentleman" often was. Tolstoi's Lévin, in *Anna Karenina*, finds that his peasant friend, a thriving farmer, not only grows wheat (in days when wheat was a novelty in that neighbourhood) but gets someone to hoe it for him. No landlord can get any weeding done. How is it managed? "Oh, we are all peasants together," says his acquaintance. "We cannot cheat one another. We cheat the gentleman because he is fair game, but there is no ill feeling." When the workmen in the factory wheel out the engineer or technician in a dirty wheel-barrow, as Mr. Monkhouse has described to us, we have reached a stage somewhere between the rough rude joke and the manifestation of hostility. But they did not hurt the expelled functionary, and sometimes they asked him to come back. This is not class war. We are nearer to it when Nil, in Gorky's *Townsmen*, bursts out with: "Honest men are commanded by swine, fools, thieves: but they will pass like boils from a healthy body."

Of the attitude of the superior to the inferior, to the "black" people, something has been said in an earlier chapter. One type of gentleman, inheriting a strain of madness from the old days of unrestrained power, was the stupid or savage practical joker, a sort of fifth-rate imitator of Peter the Great, who would cut off the clergyman's beard in a drunken freak, or lambaste a passing peasant, and then throw him half a rouble by way of consolation. Zlatovratsky's peasant jurors, on their way to the Assizes, are stopped on the road by a sort of Don Quixote landlord, who charges out of his courtyard on an ancient Rozinante, with a tagrag and bobtail of retainers. The peasants give him a gentle answer to his challenge, and snigger to one another: "God's landlord": evidently meaning a mad one. They understood the type. It is described again for us in one of Nekrasov's poems, where the peasants fool the dying squire (and comfort him), by pretending that serfdom has been restored. During the coronation festivities of the late Tsar at Moscow, the mismanagement of the arrangements for the distribution of the Emperor's gifts caused a destructive stampede. Children were saved by being passed out over the heads of the crowd, too tightly wedged together for them to fall: but the weaker, who could not escape in this way, were trodden under-foot. The Hodynkoye Polye north of Moscow, now the Airport, was like a battlefield. The city was filled with the carts carrying the dead, and the number of those killed was commonly reported to be about 2,000. Far larger numbers were injured. After the accident the festivities proceeded without a hitch, according to plan, as though nothing had been amiss. In conversation with a Russian lady, the present writer expressed surprise that there had been no suspension of the fireworks, or of the State Ball, fixed for the evening. "Oh!" said she, "but Russia has many, many millions. She can spare two thousand."

The governing class was bureaucratic in so far as it was not feudal, and—this trait was perhaps borrowed from Germany— it looked with contempt upon the merchants: stout, bearded worthies, wearing long kaftans, having their own manners and their own society, and living a life as completely apart as if they had been an endogamous caste. The plays of Ostrovsky have left us a picture of the merchant class. There was no class-hatred here, but there was a profound aloofness, another rift making a vertical division in the Russian people. Cosmopolitan finance was introducing another type of business man, and the barrier between this group and the governing class disappeared when the wealth was large, and the source of it decently veiled by an accumulation of stamped paper. It seems that the ancient contempt for the business of buying and selling has survived into the Bolshevik régime and caused embarrassment in the distributive function of the Government.

There was no sign in Russia of the inferior wanting to imitate the superior, or to win social recognition by deference to him, which is so marked a feature of British social conditions: perhaps because of the comparative ease with which the passage, or the illusion of the passage, from one class to another can be achieved. The cynic calls it snobbery: but the political student, passing no moral judgment, recognises in it an important asset of the conservative armoury. If there had been more of this type of snobs in Russia, the old order would have had more allies: but there was no use in pretending there, because no one could be taken in, and the virtue of snobbery was consequently absent.

When the social conscience awoke in Russia and the movement began for "going to the people", it was mainly to the broken link between the educated class and the peasantry that attention was directed. The former suddenly saw the gulf that was opening under their feet, and sought to close it by leaping in. As we gather from Turgeniev's *Virgin Soil*, most of these social missionaries did not know how to talk to the people when they reached them. One type is the Don Quixote type, a landlord fearless and outspoken. The peasants take him prisoner and deliver him over to the police as a preacher of dangerous doctrine. Another, somewhat of the Hamlet type, a bastard aristocrat, introspective and poetical, is merely ineffectual, and dies by suicide. These first attempts at filling up the gulf between the two nations of Russia, between *people* and *persons,* as the expressive distinction goes, were not wholly a failure, as they led to the study of realities and to the replacement of vague idealism by a body of verified facts. But already we see, in a figure which Turgeniev has drawn for us in the same story, a portent of a different type of intermediary, far closer to the people and having no illusions about them. It was not the gallant Curtius, who closed the gulf by his sacrifice: but a humbler person who took soundings, and carefully climbed down into it.

What we have seen thus far is a Russia which has advanced only part of the way towards complete nationhood, and is divided between classes by a rift which is still rather one of aloofness and contempt than of hatred, but begins to tend towards greater bitterness. I suggest that the comparative bloodlessness of the March Revolution, and of the November Revolution up to the crisis of the Civil War danger in July 1918, justifies this description, rather than the one which portrays an undiscriminating and inexhaustible class-hatred as existing from the start.

So far we have concentrated attention upon the Great-Russian kernel of the State, which constituted less than half of the population under the Tsars, but more than half after the loss of the western territories. In the pre-Revolution period, the non-Great-Russian peoples were numerically the more important, and they supplied forty-five per cent of the armies which fought for Russia during the Great War. They differed widely in history and conditions from Great-Russia, and one from another: and a picture which excluded them from view would give the impression of a closer approach to unity and less marked class divisions than actually existed in the Russian Empire.

To some extent, and generally in the west, the non-Great-Russian peoples were the inheritors of cultures superior to that of the Great-Russians, and were materially richer than the latter. This was very marked with the Finns, Germans, Poles, Armenians, and Georgians. The Ukrainian method of living was better than that of the Great-Russians, and the long association with Polish influences had introduced touches of western civilisation. The Mahommedan Khanates of Central Asia had an older culture, and a more advanced agriculture, with an immemorial system of irrigation. Except for the Caucasian mountaineers, the Mongolians, and the nomad tribes of the north, the Great-Russians were not governing their admitted inferiors: and there was little about Great-Russian culture of that attractiveness which sometimes explains an unexpected tolerance of unfamiliar influences. The Jews were so endowed by nature that it was not safe to admit them to open competition: Gorky tells us that most of the students of the St. Petersburg University were Germans, Poles, and Jews: and that, of the Russians, only the children of priests took the trouble to study.

The policy of the Tsars of the nineteenth century towards the nationalities had certain general characteristics. It disfavoured the non-orthodox confessions, particularly Roman Catholicism. It discouraged the use of the local languages for official business, for the press and for education. It tended to exclude the non-Great-Russian areas from the operation of certain beneficial legislation, for instance, of that which established rural Councils. But the policy of Russification, which meant, in general, Russia for the Great-Russians and for those willing to be assimilated to them by the adoption of the Orthodox Confession, began with Alexander III. Up to that time the policy of the Tsars is not to be regarded as always and everywhere unfavourable to the nationalities. On the contrary, the position of Poland under Alexander I, with her constitution and national army, was a reasonable ground of jealousy to Russia herself. Finland, a country populated by two and a half million Finns, and less than half a million Swedes, the descendants of the former conquerors, retained her "Constitutions", her Diet, language, and army, till the reign of Nicolas II. Up to that time Finnish soldiers had not been required to serve outside of Finland. Under military advice, Nicolas II insisted on general service. The resistance to this claim led to the abrogation of Finnish self-government, and to the obligatory use of the Russian language at post offices and on railways. A Russian Governor-General was killed in retaliation for these measures, and an armed insurrection took place. The autocracy, at that time in retreat, restored autonomy, but not the national army: and Finland became the refuge of Russian malcontents, and the meeting-place of revolutionaries, until the second abolition of self-government in 1909.

In the Baltic provinces there were internal contradictions, which put part of the population on the side of the Tsar when the others were not satisfied or actually hostile; and the Russion Government had improved, or attempted to improve, by its policy, the advantage which these contradictions gave. Broadly speaking the western appendages of Imperial Russia contained both a dominant and a plebeian nationality, and the Imperial policy was to support the plebeian against the dominant. The upper class is German or Polish, by race or tradition: the lower, Esthonian, Lettish, White-Russian, Ukrainian; the upper, Lutheran or Catholic: the lower, Uniat (that is to say worshipping according to the Orthodox rite but accepting the supremacy of the Pope) or Orthodox. In Esthonia, Livonia, and Kurland (now included in the two States of Esthonia and Latvia) the German descendants of the Knights of the Sword had been installed since the thirteenth century as conquerors and landlords among a subject population. The Hanseatic League had left indelible marks upon the towns, among which Riga and Reval were great cities and considerable ports. Peter the Great won these Baltic provinces by his long war with Sweden: and the German barons were faithful supporters of his dynasty and servants of the Tsarist administration. Their estates were like agricultural factories: Alexander I emancipated the serfs without giving them land: and the villages, like the towns, were largely populated by wage-earning labourers, were in fact, in the language of the Marxists, already proletarian. The Germans were only a small fraction of the population, not more than a twelfth, but they were its masters in virtue of arms, commerce, and culture, and they regarded Lett and Esthonian as something less than human. The clergy, first Catholic, then Lutheran, afterwards in part Orthodox, were on the side of the masters. The great ports were fortresses held by large bodies of troops alien to the country. The Letts hoped for an advantage by adopting Orthodoxy in considerable numbers, but the majority remained Lutheran.

Suspicion of the ambitions of the German Government, and the general policy of Russification, caused Alexander III to introduce Russian administration and Russian schools, and to persecute the local languages. The proletarian conditions made the Baltic provinces receptive to revolutionary propaganda, and a Lettish Social Democratic party was formed, which used the churches as its meeting-places. During the first revolution there was an armed insurrection on a large scale. The cities were held down by the Russian garrisons, but in the rural tracts three hundred country houses were taken and burned and many Lutheran pastors killed. The German squires fought their own battles, with the support of Russian dragoons, and exacted severe reprisals. We are told by a Bolshevik historian that ten thousand Letts and Esthonians perished in the pacification. It was a class-war of the bitterest kind, and he Letts became a source of strength to the Bolshevik party.

The part played in Tsarist Russia by the Germans, and in particular by the Balts of the maritime provinces, is a historical factor of immense importance. Though little more than one per cent of the total population, they occupied, towards the close of the nineteenth century, a very high proportion of the places in the upper ranks of the civil and military administration. Figures cited by Hans von Eckardt show that they held a third or more than a third of the administrative offices in the Imperial Council, the Senate, the Ministry of Foreign Affairs, the Ministries of Domains, Communications, Marine and War, and in the Posts and Telegraphs. Some of the names famous in the history of the Russian Army are those of Germans. Todleben, the defender of Sevastopol in 1855–56, is one of them. Germans were also very prominent in business and in estate management. The very name for a bookkeeper is German. The spirit of the Russian bureaucracy was more German than Russian, in a meticulous insistence upon detail, and in an inelastic conscientiousness, both of which appear to be foreign to the Russian nature. Some of the differences between St. Petersburg and Moscow, which attract frequent notice, are attributable to the large German element in the offices of Peter the Great's capital. Alexander III diminished the privileges enjoyed by Germans, in pursuance of his policy of Russification, and possibly did not improve the efficiency of his chancelleries in doing so.

The dynasty itself was German, and the Empresses and Grand Duchesses traced their origin in many cases to the petty courts of Germany. German policy thwarted Slavophil hopes at the Berlin Congress of 1878, after the Russian armies had arrived almost within sight of Constantinople. The history of Wilhelm II's relations with Nicolas II contains more than one example of the former's exploitation of the latter's mistakes, including the extortionate commercial treaty of 1904. The stage was evidently set for an outburst of anger against Germans within and without the Russian Empire: and, though the opinion of the ruling clique was profoundly divided, it came with violence in 1914.

The characteristic gifts and merits of the German people had done much for Russia: and the loss to her present rulers of the

German element in the Baltic provinces has involved a deprivation of valuable human material.

Russia has no physical boundaries in the west unless the
Pripet marshes can be so regarded, and no clearly ascertainable
racial limits in that direction. Between the Vistula and the
Dnieper, and even further east than the Dnieper, the ebb and
flow of Polish-Lithuanian and Roman Catholic influences
have confused history and complicated political and social
conditions. From the sixteenth century Poland and Lithuania
were politically one, and they carried Polish domination, and
an upper film of the Roman Catholic religion, over White-
Russia and Ukrain. In Ukrain the nobility and upper clergy
became Roman Catholic, while the population was Orthodox,
so that a difference of classes corresponded with a difference
of religions, and was intensified and embittered thereby. In
White-Russia the upper stratum was Polonised, and the Russian
serf stratum either became Roman Catholic, or accepted
spiritual subordination to the Papacy while retaining the
orthodox rite, that is to say, became Uniat. When the kingdom of Poland was disrupted, the Poles retained a historical
claim to provinces in which the facts of race, religion and
language, pointed, doubtfully, but predominantly, to a Russian
affiliation. During Poland's struggle for the restoration of
national existence, this doubtful claim has been the determining factor. Great-Russian sentiment was outraged by what
seemed an unjustified attempt to dominate Russian lands, and
gave vigorous support to the Tsarist policy of Russifying
Poland herself. In 1863 the Russian Government used the rift
between Polish gentry and peasantry to destroy unity in Poland,
and to bring the peasants of the territories, in which the
upper social strata had been Polonised by the long Polish
domination, into friendly relations with Russian troops operating against the Poles. It hurried the emancipation of the serfs
and gave them more than the Polish landowners had been
willing to give. Poland fell, or failed to rise, because her cause
appeared to be the claim of a selfish and oppressive class,
rather than a struggle for national rights, and because the
voices of Russian sympathisers were silenced by the outcry

against the Polish attempt to make the peasants of White-Russia and Ukrain participants in a Polish revolt.

For a few years after the repression of the revolt of 1863, Alexander II pursued the policy of weakening the Polish artistocracy and the Roman Catholic clergy without hurting Polish national feeling. But reactionary tendencies were growing in Russia herself, and, from 1866, a régime of intense Russification was established in Poland. It was accompanied by the attempt to convert the Uniats to the Orthodox Confession: and, since the ultimate line between Russian and Pole is drawn rather by religion than by race or language, the aim of Russification explains the law which prohibited the acquisition of land in the debatable area by any except the Orthodox.

1904. In the meanwhile, industrialisation in Russian Poland proceeded far more rapidly than in Russia. Wealth increased and factory labour became organised. A new middle-class party combined anti-socialism and anti-semitism with Polish nationalism. At the beginning of the twentieth century Russian Poland was far richer and further advanced than the dominant neighbour, with a much larger proportion of urban centres and of railway communications, and a more menacing clash between capital and labour. Alongside of Polish nationalism, there had arisen, particularly since the destruction by the Prussian victory of 1871 of the hope of French intervention, a movement of compromise and of reconciliation with the partitioning Powers. Russian Poland presented the phenomenon of a successful advocacy, of which Roman Dmowski was the protagonist, of collaboration between the Poles and the Russian Government. Nevertheless, resistance in Poland to mobilisation for the Japanese war was the beginning of the revolutionary movement in Russia. The Polish workers struck unanimously when the news arrived of Bloody Sunday in St. Petersburg: and martial law in Warsaw called forth the second general strike in Russia in November 1905. In terroristic outrage on the one hand, and in the activity of police repression on the other, Poland surpassed Russia. As elsewhere, the revolutionary movement of this period was the cause of the relaxation of the régime of Russification. But officers of Polish nationality were not allowed to serve in Poland: and the social composition of the Warsaw garrison was very like that of St. Petersburg, so that any movement among the troops would not, as a rule, get in touch with the local revolutionary organisation. In the counter-revolution Poland was almost continually under martial law. By far the most powerful element of discontent was nationalist, not socialist: though socialism also played its part.

In the second Imperial Duma the nationalist middle-class party of Poland supplied a particularly able group of members, headed by Roman Dmowski. Its nationalism did not extend to a demand for separation: and the later history suggests that the Tsarist Government would have been well advised if it had made this party one of its points of support. But nationalism, in any form, neutralised, from the point of view of that Government, the merits of a conservative attachment to property: and Peter Stolypin's revised electoral law, following his principle of diminishing the representation of the minority nationalities, cut down the number of Polish representatives in the Third Duma by more than half.

Whatever causes of complaint the Poles might have against Tsarist Russia, they were, as nationalists, far more afraid of German efficiency than of Russian unwillingness to make concessions. When, at the beginning of the Great War, an undefined self-government was promised to Poland by the Grand Duke Nicolas, the Poles of Russian Poland ranked themselves definitely on the Russian side of the quarrel. A movement led by the famous Pilsudski from Austrian Poland against the Russian armies was important mainly as a demonstration of Polish determination to take a military part in the war on behalf of the claim to Polish nationhood. The tide of war soon placed the fate of Poland beyond Russian reach, and destroyed the basis of Polish collaboration with Russia. The Poles had had their choice—and different sections favoured each solution, respectively—between the varying aims: of union under the comparatively mild suzerainty of the Hapsburg; of submission to the ruthless efficiency of Germany, which had already shown the desire to oust her Polish subjects from their lands; and of collaboration with Russia, suspect, but believed incapable of doing a fundamental injury to Polish nationalism. Except in a small measure for the first of the three, the Poles had no love for any of these Empires: and the collapse of all of them gave a welcome opportunity of cutting loose from all.

White-Russia, with a population of some seven millions of White-Russians, Great-Russians, Poles, Jews and Lithuanians, is a land of much bog and swamp, with a generally poor soil, within the boundaries of the old duchy of Lithuania, as constituted at the union of Lithuania with Poland. As political boundaries now go, it is partly in the territory of Poland, partly in that of the U.S.S.R., since it includes Vitebsk, Mogilev, Pinsk, Brest-Litovsk, Bialystok and Kovno. It has a language of its own, resembling the Ukrainian, but affected by Polish contacts. The separation between the three Russian nations, Great-Russian, White-Russian, and Ukrainian, appears to date from the time when Kiev lost the control of the Dnieper to advancing barbarians, and the Great Russians retired into the forests to mingle with the indigenous Finns. The marshes of the Pripet, as effective a separator of peoples as seas or high mountains, divide the White-Russians from the Ukranians to the south of them.

White-Russia has been unfortunate in her history as well as in her soil. The brutalities of serfdom were aggravated by the alien faith and spirit of proprietors who were either Poles or Polonised Russians and Lithuanians; and all non-agricultural pursuits were monopolised by Poles and Jews. The one bright spot was that the sale of serfs without land was never allowed as in Great-Russia. Under Tsarist rule, poverty and ignorance prevailed. Outside of the capital, Minsk, there was not a single hospital. The people were so crushed that they never expressed national aspirations: and when, at the Revolution, federal autonomy came, with the right of using the national language, it came almost as an unasked gift. We cannot hold that there was class-hatred here. There was not enough spirit surviving to cherish the growth of that poisonous weed.

If Poland lost something of its unity of sentiment by the partitions of the eighteenth century, Ukrain, "the frontier", has never been suffered to form a political unit. It has not even any linguistic or racial name of its own, but its language is sufficiently separate to be mostly unintelligible to the mere student of Russian. If the linguistic test be applied, it stretches from the neighbourhood of Lvov, in the present-day Poland, to Krasnodar, in the North Caucasus province of the U.S.S.R., and includes the present Carpatho-Ukrain and a former portion of the Roumanian kingdom, as well as Polish and Russian Ukrain. There is a recognisable common culture, much subdued and impoverished in Carpatho-Ukrain, formerly known as Ruthenia. Both in Poland and Russia the villages of Ukrain have a similar appearance, a brighter, more cheerful look, with white-washed adobé huts, trees and gardens, than those of the Great-Russians. The people seem happier. The women exchange chaff with the passing traveller. There is more of song and play and dance. Trifles, such as the existence of finger-posts on the roads, point to a greater interest in life, and more time and means to attend to it. On the other hand, the country slides easily into brigandage and anarchy. The raids of the Krim Tartars, and the life of the island stronghold of the Zaporozhian Cossacks, a centre of savage and war-like freedom, which held its own for generations against Pole and Turk, have left their mark. For centuries the "frontier" was the theatre of raid and counter-raid, and the alternate prey of different neighbours. A tremendous picture of a savage rising of Cossacks and Ukrainians against the Polish kingdom in 1648 is drawn by Sienkiewicz in his story *Fire and Sword*. The storm falls as fiercely upon Jews as upon Poles.

A counter-reformation at the end of the sixteenth century made the nobility and upper clergy Catholic, while the people remained Orthodox. A treaty of 1667 gave Kiev and all of Ukrain east of the Dnieper to Russia, while the rest, with all of White-Russia, went to Poland. Before that date, Poland held the territory on both sides of the Dnieper, and her influence, and that of the Roman Catholic religion which she professed, have brought a western infiltration. The Ukrainian outlook is to Galicia and the west. It was a Ukrainian Bishop who assisted Peter the Great with his reforms, when his own ecclesiastics looked glum upon them. The Ukrainian National Church was the product of an anti-Roman peasant movement and it was more popular and less authoritative than the Orthodox Church of Russia. There was more individualism than in Great-Russia, and the village Communes at an early date lost the right to redistribute the land, which thus became heritable household property. But the Ukrainians are a rural people, and the towns are almost monopolised by non-Ukrainians, Great-Russians, Jews and Poles.

1768, 1773. Ukrain to the west of the Dnieper was acquired by Russia under the Empresses Anne and Catherine the Great. The latter finally destroyed the famous stronghold of the Zaporozhian Cossacks, and introduced serfdom in Ukrain in 1783. The memories of freedom were thus much more recent than in Great-Russia, and the bitterness, due to the abrogation of it, correspondingly more intense. The great rebellion of the Haidamaks, celebrated by the Ukrainian poet, Taras Shevchenko, took place in then Polish territory on the west bank of the Dnieper, and in Galician Ukrain further to the west. It was a rising of Cossacks and peasantry against the oppression of Polish Roman Catholic landlords, and it furnished an incitement to the famous rebellion of Pugachev in Russia.

The poet Shevchenko was the mouthpiece through which the Ukrainian people found and expressed its soul. Born a serf, he showed a gift for drawing, and was set free by the generosity of a sympathetic artist. The chilly reception which the great critic Belinsky gave to his first volume of poems is typical of the Great-Russian attitude to Ukrain. The assertion of separate existence had in it something offensive. Why could he not use the Russian language, instead of trying to perpetuate a dialect? Russian had been good enough for the great Ukrainian Gogol, who was already becoming famous. Though Shevchenko subsequently came into favour with Great as well as with Little-Russians (the latter name would certainly give offence in Ukrain), he does not figure in the histories of Russian literature. It is as though a great London critic had spoken slightingly of Robert Burns, and the histories of English literature had omitted Gavin Douglas, Blind Harry, William Dunbar, Walter Scott, and Allan Ramsay from their pages.

Soon Shevchenko was in conflict with a more dangerous opponent than Belinksy. The names of the Saints Cyril and Methodius, the Christianisers of the Slavs, were assumed by a society which aimed at a general Slavonic federation, with liberation of the serfs, and popular education, and liberty to each member except in the matters of its basic laws, weights, measures, and currency. Authority took note of it. It was not proved that Shevchenko had participated in the meetings, but the proceedings drew attention to his poems: and they were reported dangerous, because they "expressed sorrow for the enslavement and sorrows of Ukrain, praised the Hetman's administration and the former freedom of the Cossacks, and, with unbelievable audacity, poured forth slanders against persons of the Imperial House". This was in 1847, and Nicolas I was not the man to pass over such errors. The poet was sent to Orenburg, to serve in a disciplinary corps, and prohibited from either writing or drawing, the two joys of his life. Later, he was found in possession of a Bible, a Shakespeare, the *Imitatio Christi*, a box of paints and portfolios for drawings, and civilian clothing: and the Emperor (still the same patriarchal martinet) ordered him under strict arrest, and sent him to a lonely fort on the desert steppe twenty miles from the Caspian Sea. There he spent seven years, seven years of torture to this sensitive soul: and was at length released, a martyr to drink, scurvy, and mental obsessions. It is said that, though he was only forty-three years old, women fled from him in terror when he made love.

He now published more poetry, which the Censorship, less rigorous than under Nicolas I, mangled but suffered to appear. This time the best Russian critics did not question his right to use his own language, and Dobroliubov, of whom there is something to say in a later chapter, declared that even Russia had not produced such a poet.

In the struggle which is depicted in his great poem, *The Haidamaks*, gentry, peasants, and Jews, play the leading parts in a sort of three-cornered class-war: the gentry all-powerful and unrestrainedly tyrannical: the Jews ostensibly humble, but despising the gentry in the full conviction of mental superiority, and exploiting the people as agents of the landlords, and through usury and the sale of alcohol: the peasants and the peasant Cossacks gallant fighters and thirsty for freedom and revenge. There is a savagery in the poem, a frank delight in blood and conflagration, which doubtless harmonises with the conditions of eighteenth-century Ukrain: and the poet, in a later composition, warns the gentry that the ideals of freedom and equality are still burning in his people. The doings of the anarchist Makhno in the Civil War, and the Ataman Grigoriev's threat to the Bolshevik governor of Odessa "to flay him and make a drum out of his skin", show that the old spirit is alive, and as savage as ever.

We cannot wonder that the Russian Government looked with some alarm upon Shevchenko. But he became a favourite poet with the intellectuals of socialist leanings, some of whom learned Ukrainian to be able to read his poetry in the original. His inspiration had been the passion of liberty for his people. He died on the eve of the Emancipation edict of 1861.

Shevchenko was embittered against Russia by the introduction of serfdom by Catherine the Great into the land "that was beguiled into a death-trap with a lie", and by her destruction of the Cossack fortress at the falls of the Dnieper, and by the brutal treatment meted out to himself. The Tsar made war upon the language and treated Ukrainian publications with great severity. As a result the Ukrainian movement took extreme revolutionary forms. The first Congress of the Social Democratic party of Russia took place at the instance of the Kiev fighting-union for the liberation of the working class. Kharkov, in 1901, was the scene of the first revolutionary procession. The first serious disturbance among the peasants took place in the area of small holdings and congestion in north-eastern Ukrain. The first general strike, that of 1903, was in Southern Russia, including Ukrain. In short, Ukrain was prominent in revolutionary enterprise, very largely because nationalist Ukrain feeling was outraged by Tsarist policy. The Russifiers could not leave their passion for religious unification

behind them: and when the Russian armies—coming as deliverers—occupied Galicia in 1915, the Grand Duke Nicolas,
who was commander-in-chief, was disgusted by the arrival of a
trainload of Orthodox clergy to convert the Uniats, when he
had hoped for munitions. But it does not appear that, except
in very limited circles, there was any desire in Russian Ukrain
for political separation, or any demand that local autonomy
and freedom of language would not have satisfied.

The Revolution of 1905 brought some alleviation to the
rigour of the anti-national administration of Ukrain. Publications appeared in Ukrainian and patriotic societies were
formed. In the first two Imperial Dumas Ukrainian deputies
organised national groups. After the amendment of the
electoral law the Ukrainian nationalists were not represented,
because the landlords, who were opposed to national autonomy, returned deputies of their own political colour.

The line of demarcation between Great-Russia and Ukrain
is difficult to draw. There is no clear division between the
two in the north; there are foreign colonies in the south-west,
sometimes called New Russia. The towns are almost entirely
populated by non-Ukrainians or by Russified Ukrainians. The
Donetz basin is filled with workers from outside, many of
them Asiatic in origin; Kharkov is alien in spirit to Ukrain.
It has been estimated that not more than half of those shown
in the statistics to be Ukrainians have any stable or convinced
sense of nationality. On the other hand there are Ukrainian
colonies outside of Ukrain, reaching as far as Vladivostok, and
the Japanese Foreign Office has recently taken considerable
interest in some of these. The interlacing of interests is even
more significant. Of the surplus-producing agricultural regions
of Russia, Ukrain makes up a third. The anthracite, iron, and
manganese of the Donetz basin constitute a large fraction of
the mineral supply of Russia. Except as the result of a ruinous
foreign war, compelling the abandonment of the south, the
acceptance by Russia of separation from Ukrain is unthink-
able. On the other side, when the irritation of interference is
not a grievance, Russia literature and the civilisation of the
cities exercises an attraction. It was a Ukrainian, Gogol, who

penned at the end of his story of Cossack life, the famous patriotic description of Russia as a swift troika rushing ever onward. During the War, the Germans were so sure of Ukrainian separatist sentiment, that they tried to organise Ukrainian legions out of the Ukrainian prisoners: but they were disappointed in the results.

The Jews of Russia are mainly residents of the south-west and west, for a historical reason. The Kings of Poland and the Dukes of Lithuania, who, between them or in combination, commanded, at one time and another, all of White-Russia and most of Ukrain, made it their policy to encourage the Jews. At the partition of Poland, these invaluable builders of commerce and the arts were allowed to remain in their old homes and in the Black Sea provinces conquered by Catherine the Great, but not to settle in the rest of Russian territory. This is the origin of the Jewish pale. Their treatment by the Tsars varied, but it must be understood that it was the religion, and not the race, which was placed under disability, and that the Jew who became orthodox was at once assimilated to the orthodox population. When the disabilities were in force, the pressure to accept conversion was strong. We hear of all Jews, in receipt of Government bursaries, being registered as Orthodox, and of converts obtaining free divorce from their Jewish wives. Alexander II gave them access to schools and professions and allowed them to settle outside the pale, but they remained ineligible for public service. Alexander III, in accordance with his general policy of Russification, limited them to towns within the pale, excluded them from the Bar and from technical schools, and restricted them to a maximum percentage in the Universities and Secondary Schools. They were not allowed to own land. The residential restriction did not apply to Jews with University degrees, to merchants paying a certain minimum tax, nor to craftsmen inscribed in a workers' fellowship. Readers of Trotsky's autobiography will recall that rich Jews, like his father, did well enough despite their disabilities. Those who administered the law made exceptions for those who could pay, and the severities recoiled upon the Government by making its officials corrupt, as well as by driving the Jews wholesale into the ranks of the revolutionaries. They were the first to form a Social Democratic organisation of their own, and they provided many leaders to the Bolsheviks: though the notion that the Bolsheviks are Jews is a myth.

The Russian public, in the mass, was with the Tsars in their repression of the Jews, and anti-semitism was particularly fierce in Ukrain where Jews were most numerous. In the towns at all events, it was always possible to bring together a mob for an attack upon them: and *pogroms*, non-official at the start, but becoming official or quasi-official in the Ministry of von Plehve, were numerous from the seventies on. Both Witte and Stolypin, statesmen who were capable of saving the autocracy or postponing its fall, stood for equal rights for the Jews: and the former is said to have ironically suggested to Nicolas II that a better course than persecution would be to collect them together and push them into the sea. The constitutionalists of the Duma took the line that anti-semitism was incompatible with constitutional government. Shortly before the beginning of the Great War, a Jew named Mendel Beylis was accused of ritual murder, a repetition of the immemorial story of "Little Hugh of Lincoln": and a public trial, of the "demonstration" type, was held. Strong feeling was aroused, but the case ended in an acquittal.

The devices employed by Jews to avoid military service were notorious; but two hundred and forty thousand of them were serving in the Russian armies during the Great War. This did not save the community from great suffering due to the spy mania which infected the Higher Command. The expulsions from the war zone in Poland were conducted with a reckless cruelty, and numerous deaths from starvation and disease were the consequence.

It does not seem that the unhappy experiences of this gifted people have made them generally haters of Russia. The Russian Jews in the United States told Witte, when he visited that country for the negotiations with the Japanese in 1905, that they did not love the régime, but that they loved Russia above all else. You may meet them now, returning after years of prosperity abroad, to their old homes, with the expectation that all will now be well.

This is not the place for considering the reasons of the popular dislike of Jews. Mr. Hindus, himself of Jewish descent, suggests one reason. There is much anti-gentilism, hatred or contempt of the *"goyim"* among Jews. There is a special irony in the persistence of anti-semitism in Russia because of the enormous influence which Judaism has had upon popular habits of thought. Possibly in consequence of the presence of the civilised tribe of the Khazars, who were Jewish converts, in southern Russia, Judaism greatly affected the Russian masses in the eleventh and twelfth centuries, and the Church was obliged to combat it, as it combated Catholicism in the thirteenth century. A Judaising sect was suppressed by Ivan III. In later times we find the doctrines of Count Leo Tolstoi far closer to Judaism than Christianity: and Rozanov, of whom we shall hear something in a later chapter, was powerfully influenced by the Old Testament outlook upon life.

The Cossacks were men of many races, having an origin, as communities, similar to the legendary origin of Rome. They were runaway slaves, runaway serfs, broken men and outlaws of every sort, who gathered together in asylums of which the Zaporozhian fastness on the Dnieper was the most famous. For long they were embodiments of anarchy, for ever seeking the weakest and least troublesome masters, if it was necessary to have a master at all; and their name gave to the Persian language its word for raiding. When Catherine the Great captured their settlement on the Dnieper she moved the Zaporozhians elsewhere. The modern groups are those of the Don, of the Ural, of the Kuban and of the Terek. Time and the policy of the Tsars have reversed their old function. From being frequent rebels they became the instruments of the autocracy for keeping the Russian people in order. They were organised in military colonies, holding their lands by a military tenure, and paying no taxes. On summons, they had to appear personally, bringing their own horses and equipment. Taken as a whole their lands were much in excess of those of the peasants. They were, and felt themselves to be, privileged persons and looked with contempt upon the peasants and workers and students, to whom they were called upon from time to time to apply their whips.

But there were internal contradictions in the status of the Cossacks. Since the sixties of the nineteenth century their officers held their lands by individual tenure: the rank and file held theirs by communal tenure. The officers' holdings were more, and the men's were less. These distinctions naturally drove a wedge between the classes. Another fact of importance is that their settlements were interspersed with those of non-Cossacks: and the non-Cossacks had far smaller holdings than theirs. On the Don, Kuban, and Terek, the Cossack populations of three millions held sixty-two million acres, while four and one-third millions of non-Cossacks held sixteen millions. It followed that there was envy and hostility between the two groups of the population. The famous Red Cavalry Commander Budyonny was a non-Cossack who lived among Cossacks. It was the traditional feud which took him to the Red Army.

The Caucasus, and the country south of it, was and is, a *macédoine*, out-balkanising the Balkans by its variety of faiths, languages, and races. In the post-revolutionary distribution of territories, which aims at the encouragement of local language and racial sentiment, the country north of the great range of mountains contains one autonomous republic, Daghestan, six autonomous regions, and one autonomous district (Circassian). In the mountains, and to the south of them, are three main republics, which, by the constitution of 1936, are elevated to the constituent status. These are Christian Georgia, Christian Armenia, and Mahommedan Azarbaijan. But, in Christian Georgia, Adzharians, who speak the Georgian language, have the Turkish culture and follow the Islamic confession. Adzhar and Abkhazia are autonomous Soviet Socialist republics included within the Georgian constituent republic. The Nakhichevan autonomous Soviet Socialist republic is included in the Azarbaijan constituent republic, and so is the Nagorno-Karabakh autonomous province. Under the administration of the Tsars there was no recognition of these distinctions, and the policy of Russification, thwarted by the inefficiency of its agents and the inaccessibility and recalcitrance of much of its material, aimed feebly at assimilation. But deadly quarrels prevailed between Georgians and Armenians; between Ossetians, Adzharians, and Abkhazians, and Armenians; and between Tartars, on the one hand, and Russians and Armenians on the other: and the aim of assimilation did not exclude the occasional utilisation of these quarrels to weaken opposition to the Government.

The trans-Caucasus territory is, for its size, immensely the most valuable part of Russian territory. The principal wealth is the oil of Baku, but other minerals, including manganese, are produced in Georgia, and the semi-tropical productiveness of the country, protected from the north by the mountains, gives to Russia grapes, lemons, tea, and the growths of more southern climates. The tract is also the seat of an old civilisation and an old intellectual life: and it contains in the great city of Baku, a kaleidoscope of races and an Americanised centre of business and proletarian life hardly inferior to Moscow and St. Petersburg themselves. In this territory the Tsarist Government figured as the protector of the Armenians against Turkey and Persia, controlled the appointment of the Armenian Katholikos and of his synod of Bishops and Archimandrites, and exercised, through this ecclesiastical organisation, a powerful influence on the Armenian race beyond the Russian border. The Armenians—traders before everything else—were grateful for the security which it brought, and were its convinced supporters, despite a dislike of the Russianising tendencies of their protectors. A cloud was cast upon these relations by the suspicion which arose in the reign of Alexander III that Armenian Church property was being used for separatist intrigues. The property was sequestrated, and only restored in 1906, when measures of Russification were relaxed by the first Revolution. An Armenian Terrorist Society which has existed for more than forty years was directed against the Turkish, rather than against the Russian Government, and Armenians and Mahommedans were in frequent collision.

Georgians have a proud and ancient history, and their nationalism is one which merely federal liberties do not satisfy.
But their country, of very great value in itself, is also necessary to Russia as the highway to the Baku oil. Georgia was
forced to accept Russian protection by the menace of the Ottoman Empire; and the Russification of the Georgian Church,
which was the intellectual centre of the country, at once began. A Russian ecclesiastic was put at the head of it, and
Church Slavonic was substituted for the native Georgian
language. Economic grievances were added to those of a
slighted national culture, and the competition of Georgian
with Great-Russian manufactures, which the local supply of
wool, cotton, silk and some minerals would have permitted,
was authoritatively discouraged. Eighty per cent of the people
were engaged in agriculture. Serfdom was abolished shortly
after the Emancipation in Russia, and with a similar distribution of land; that is to say, the peasants received allotments,
but not sufficient to save them from the necessity of leasing
more. They became socialists therefore, in spite of being
champions of property. There was a similar contradiction in
the position of the lords. The sense of slighted nationality
made them socialists, in spite of excellent reasons for not desiring subversive change: and they established an association
of the Lilac Cross, which had for its object the liberation of
Georgian Socialists from prison.

There were two proletariats in Georgia. One of these was
Oriental, living by the carrying trade and by odd jobs: what
we might call a *coolie* element. The other, largely Great-
Russian, the wage-earners in industry and the railway workers,
formed a sort of élite of labour, and naturally became a stronghold of democratic sentiment. Numerous Trade Unions were
formed during the Revolution of 1905: but were mercilessly
repressed during the reaction which followed. There was a
part brigand, part Georgian-patriot, part Social-Democrat,
movement, inspired by the name of Shamil, the Caucasian
patriot who, in the fifties of the nineteenth century, held the
Russians at bay for years. At the head of this was Joseph
Dzhugashvili, famous by the name of Stalin, "the man of

steel". His father was a Georgian of the trading class, his mother belonged to the small Ossetian mountain tribe. Trained in the theological seminary of Tiflis, and expelled from it for his interest in Marxian studies, his revolutionary activities in the later nineties were already enterprising, and he organised the first Caucasian workers' strike on the Tiflis tramways. His experience of the Caucasian *macédoine*, its mountain fastnesses, its city streets, and not least its jails, marked him out as the revolutionary expert on the question of nationalities. He made his first Marxian study of its intricacies as early as 1913, and then laid down the principles which have survived into the present-day practice of the Soviet Government.

The mountainous western portion of Georgia known as Guria, sent many workers to the docks and refineries of Batum. A strike in February 1902 scattered these men over the countryside and the consequence was a local revolution in 1904-5. The Gurians refused recruits and taxes, burned Government buildings, and drove out the police. For nine months Guria was a self-governing State, showing great enthusiasm for education. Then order was restored in the usual way.

Before the Revolution, Tiflis was the political capital of all the trans-Caucasus country. It was also an intellectual centre, which produced many political thinkers, mostly of the Menshevik complexion. Trotsky calls Georgia "the heart of the Menshevik Gironde". The Social-Democratic fraction of the Fourth Imperial Duma, which was sitting at the outbreak of the Great War, chose a Georgian Menshevik, Tchkeidze, as its leader. It voted against War Credits and Tchkeidze read the Zimmerwald manifesto for peace in the Duma. Tsereteli was another distiguished Georgian Menshevik who might have done great things—if moderation were a qualification for political success in times of Revolution. There was an elevation about these Georgian Socialists which gives a favourable impression of the national character: brave to a fault, large-hearted, songful, jovial: a little given to the drinking of wine.

1885. General Alikhanov, himself a Caucasian Mahommedan, who claimed that he had arranged the Russian attack upon the Afgans at Penjdeh (he was killed afterwards by an assassin's bomb, while engaged in the repression of the revolution) told the present writer the proverbial reputation of the leading peoples of the trans-Caucasus country. The Russians serve the State, the Armenians trade, the Georgians drink. It was a good epigram but it did not tell the whole truth. All three did more than the epigram credits to them. Some of the Armenians followed in the footsteps of Belisarius, and served the State in war and peace. General Loris Melikov, an Armenian, commanded an army in the war of 1877, and was afterwards the principal actor in the *Dictatorship of the Heart* which preceded the assassination of Alexander II. The Russians were not only officials. They also played a large part, though individually a less prominent one, in the cities and on the railways. Not only in the trans-Caucasus, but throughout the territories of the non-Russian nationalities, the proletarian élite in the towns and on the railways were not natives of the land. They were mainly Great-Russian, partly Germans, Poles and Jews, forming a sort of natural garrison for cities and communications, to which social forces gave an anti-national and pro-Russian unity and a spirit of Great-Russian chauvinism. This feature was very marked in Ukrain, where all or nearly all the Ukrainians were peasants, and the townspeople, with the exception of unskilled and casual labour, were of other races. In the oil city of Baku, a great metropolis set down in the heart of a Tartar country on the shores of the Caspian Sea, together with a transient population of unskilled workers from Persia and the Caucasus, there was a rich business community living the life of an American city, and a solid core of skilled Russian workers. In newly acquired Central Asia, the indigenous peoples continued to live in their own cities, and the "European" element occupied separate settlements alongside of these, as in the Cantonments and Civil Stations of British India: but the "European" element included more than officials, soldiers and well-to-do merchants. It is in the exportation of their wage-earning workers to dependencies and conquered territories that the Russians have followed a method different from that of Great Britain. In

Siberia the townspeople and the civilised elements generally have been Great-Russian: often political exiles respected for their high culture: and rarely having the desire for separation from Russia.

Towns exercise an immense influence upon the client countryside, and the presence of these quasi-garrisons, in key positions among the non-Great-Russian nationalities, tended to prevent the growth of effective separatist movements. A movement which is purely rural may be embarrassing, but it is not likely to be permanently disruptive while the towns hold. This factor would have exercised an even greater influence, if Great-Russian industrial jealousy, before the Revolution, had not stood in the way of the wider distribution of industries in the territories of the nationalities.

In Mahommedan Central Asia the Tsarist Government maintained the native Khans in their rule in Khiva and Bukhara, but "sat upon the head waters" of the rivers which supplied the means of agriculture and of life. As in the Caucasus, and on the Volga, Russians and Mahommedan towns were and are separate. There was no formal separation of the races on the railways: but the Russian guards did not allow natives to travel in the carriages where there were Europeans. In the areas of direct Russian rule, the Cadi and the Mufti continued to dispense Koranic law. The veil and the bride-price, and Islamic custom generally, were sacred. The official staffs and the official language were Russian, and even the names of the streets were written in Russian. But, if rules were strict, practice was judiciously neglectful. Schools were supposed to be Russified, but the pupils of the Koranic school continued to drone out the sacred texts to the supervising Mullah. The official missionary of Orthodoxy made his rounds, in all the dignity of pectoral cross and vestment: but the local administrator knew the danger of him, and kept him harmless.

In 1905 an Association of all-Russian Mahommedans was joined by Crimean Tartars and by Kirgiz and Turks of Turkestan. The Young Turk revolution in the Ottoman Empire encouraged the spirit of Mahommedan nationalism, always strong in Central Asia: and it seems likely that the desire for autonomy here comes nearer to a demand for separation than in any of the other non-Russian nationalities. There is a strong cultural movement among Mahommedans generally, and the Tartars on the Volga show a cultural superiority, particularly marked in their agriculture, to their Russian neighbours.

From the sketch which I have given of conditions in the non-Great-Russian nationalities of the Empire, before the Revolutions of 1917, it might naturally be inferred that Germans, Poles, and Jews, would be lacking in affection for Imperial Russia, while some of the plebeian nationalities, retaining grateful memories of anti-landlord legislation and administration, would be heartily loyal to it. There are no traces in the plebeian nationalities of gratitude to the Tsars. On the contrary the Letts were particularly vigorous in the revolutionary cause. The Russian Germans, on the other hand, though objects of suspicion and ill-treatment from the beginning of the Great War, acted as a genuinely patriotic element in the Russian State. It is one of the paradoxes of the Russian complex that the Russian Germans were of all others the people most likely to lose by German annexations, which would deprive them of an exceptional influence earned by qualities in which they surpassed their Russian fellow-subjects. The Poles of Russian Poland, fearing German efficiency and German land-settlement as worse enemies to Polish nationality than the less precise and less meticulous administration of the Russian Government, supported the latter, though they may have desired the equal exhaustion of both. Whether the Jews gained more by official venality than they lost by legal and administrative inequalities, must be a matter of conjecture. But, at the outbreak of war, their leading men were prominent in all branches of commerce and industry, and some of the wealthier were closely linked with the Russian bureaucracy. Whether or not some of them justified the suspicion of espionage, there is no ground for thinking that, as a body, they desired a German victory.

The material is now prepared for an answer to the question whether Russians were patriotic. At first sight, I seem to owe an apology for asking it. This people not patriotic, when for centuries we have seen it defending itself along undefined borders both on south and west: reversing the course of history by swallowing up in its snow-bound expanses the Grand Army of Napoleon: opposing to the artillery of General Mackensen the bare flesh of its gallant sons? What of the noble anger which inspired in Chaadaev his vituperative outbursts, or made Chernyshevsky cry: "A miserable nation, a nation of slaves!" if these were not the obverse of a love, outranged by the contrasts of hope and achievement?

Russian poetry abounds in hymns of patriotism: which, like all truly national literature, became familiar in the memories and mouths of thousands. When Europe sympathised with the Polish rebels of 1831 Pushkin addressed a splendid challenge to Russia's slanderers. It begins, like the second psalm, why do the heathen so furiously rage together and the people imagine a vain thing: declares that it is a strife of Slavs among themselves, not to be decided by strangers, for whom the Kremlin and Praga are voiceless of traditional memories: and arraigns the slanderers for hate to Russia.

> *"And why? Answer! Is it because*
> *On the ruins of smoking Moscow*
> *We did not bow to the insolent will*
> *Of him who made you tremble?*
> *Because we rolled into the abyss*
> *The idol which menaced your kingdoms:*
> *And with our blood redeemed*
> *The freedom, honour, and peace of Europe?"*

To this reminder of the fate of Napoleon, he adds a challenge to fight with deeds and not with words, and a picture of Russian warriors, from the cold cliffs of Finland to flaming Kolchis, ready again to meet the foe.

It is great: and we could set many other examples beside it, perhaps most eloquent those which come from the Panslavist poets, whose ideal was something larger and less tangible than Russia herself. Yet—how easily Russians forgot the German origin of Catherine the Great: how easily, it seems, did they even forget that Napoleon was an enemy. Baron Haxthausen, travelling in north-central Russia in 1843, found a portrait of Napoleon in every citizen's and in every substantial peasant's house, and said that he had now become the hero of popular story and that every trace of hatred had vanished. Leontiev, of whom there is something to be said in a later chapter, gives utterance to an eloquent misgiving about his own patriotism: "Great God! Am I a patriot? Do I despise, or love my country? I fear to say. It seems to me that I love her as a mother loves, and despise as one despises a drunken thing, a characterless fool."

Coming to a later date, we have Mr. Hindus's description of the conversation of his fellow travellers on the railway somewhere in White-Russia: "If only the Germans had not left when peace came. . . . *There* was a clever people. . . . Taxes would not be so high . . . salt would not be so dear . . . rye would not be so cheap . . . and trains would be where they ought to be. . . . Everyone had been against the peasant . . . even God . . . else why had not He kept the Germans in Russia?"

Change the names: and it is what you might hear from a casual collection of Indian railway passengers, if the British had left India, and commodities were too dear and the trains not running to time. A patriot might think such things, but hardly say them. But there have been signs, even in central and western Europe of the twentieth century, that the owners of property prefer a foreigner who will maintain order and defend property, to a native-born fellow-countryman whose attitude in these matters is less orthodox. The Roumanians were detested by the Hungarians: but when they put an end to the Bolshevik domination of Bela Kun, they were welcomed as deliverers. We are told that, in Germany herself, during the disturbed conditions immediately following the end of the War, the French occupation of certain areas was welcomed as the means of restoring order. A close and candid observer, even of Britain, in the doubtful days of 1938 and 1939, must have seen reason to question whether all political affiliations in the sphere of foreign policy were determined by patriotism or by class.

What is it that any of us actually love when we feel the sentiment which we call patriotism? What is it with us Britons for whom there is an ancient and very concrete unity to attach our affections? Very few of us know, still less love, classes other than our own: we are jarred and offended by trifling differences of speech and manner: often our overseas brethren are a trial to us. When we experience the feeling of love of country, do we call up before us its historic Head, the land and the features which it owes to nature and art, the white cliffs, the green meadows, the woods and the streams, the noble monuments and buildings lovely or familiar to our affections, the far-scattered sister-lands of the commonwealth: or a complex including all this and more, the history and the institutions and the glorious potentialities of betterment which they hold for the men and women who share their inheritance with us? A few, a very few of us, may have this wide vision, and these only in moments of exaltation. We must have the small change of the grand emotions; symbols to which we may attach our affection: the Union Jack: the map painted red: perhaps a calf-love for the figure of Britannia on a penny, surely loveliest of women, if anyone had time to look at her. Perhaps we must have something to hate, before we can love with single heart.

What, for the Russian, were the symbols of the grand emotion, for these are what make it possible for men in the mass to feel? The Church was difficult to visualise behind the somewhat gross figure of the parish priest: but some no doubt retained in memory the blue and gilded and star-spangled domes of some shrine, or the magic vision of Kiev seen from the eastern bank of the Dnieper. The Orthodox Tsar was the great emblem of unity, but the trust and love had somehow gone out of the picture which he presented to his people. The land meant much to poet and seer. For the mass, if she had a personality at all, it was that of a hard step-mother and task-mistress, under the long sameness of her robe of white, or the monotony of brown and grey: though veined with perennial rivers, decking herself like a bride at the sudden inspiration of spring, and wearing such glorious jewels as the city of Moscow seen from the Sparrow Hills. The rivers indeed awakened affection and had a personality of their own, Volga for all Great-Russians, Dnieper for Ukrain, Don for the Cossacks: and Moscow was a true centre and symbol.

But patriotism, if in the making, was still incompletely made: a weaker thing than the solidarity of class which the common life of the factory had developed in the city workers. There at least was a tangible and material unity. Elsewhere, if I read the signs aright, there was hardly even a common hate.

Chapter 6

The Orthodox Church and the Slavophils

"For where two or three are gathered together in My name, there am I in the midst of them."

Gospel according to St. Matthew.

"The soul of Orthodoxy is *sobornost*. . . . The Church, as truth, is not given to individuals, but to a unity in love and faith it reveals itself."

FATHER SERGIUS BULGAKOV,
The Orthodox Church.

"Simple peasants feel that their sufferings are, in part, an expiation of the universal sin, and they must bear it, as Christ bore His cross, to redeem all humanity . . . That does not prevent them from being brutal, lazy, liars, thieves, carnal, incestuous. . . ."

A Russian lady, quoted by
M. MAURICE PALÉOLOGUE.

"The holy words of the Scripture, in which we heard the voice of the Seven Thunders, sounded to them like catechism texts learned by heart."

D. S. MEREZHKOVSKY,
describing a meeting between
clerics and laymen in 1902.

I OFFER NO APOLOGY for the space which I shall devote to the Orthodox Church. In its strength it was a fundamental element in the life of the Russian people. It was the builder of the Moscow realm. In its weakness, we must seek the explanation of the facility with which—to all appearance—a people believed to be instinctively religious abandoned religion when the rulers ceased to support it. Both in its strength and in its weakness it has established habits of mind which profoundly affect the outlook and the actions of men and women who have repudiated all Religion, and are indignant of every suggestion that it continues to survive in them. It is in the history of the Orthodox Church and of its downfall, and of the revival of Orthodox thought in the twentieth century, that we must seek for light upon the question whether Religion is actually disappearing from Russia, or destined to reappear in new forms.

All the world-religions, and Christianity most of all, have taken different forms among different peoples and at different times, as emphasis happened to be laid upon one or another group of doctrines or practices. The variation of emphasis often depended upon profound differences of mental habit antecedent to Christianity. It has always issued in differences of what we call national character: It is not the only cause of such differences, but it is a potent one: and we shall be on the track of at least some distinguishing qualities of the Russian people if we are able to find the characteristic features of their religion.

To Eastern Orthodoxy the spirit in Man is a gift from outside, illuminating his darkness and creating in him the possibility of deification. But it is not a gift to the individual: it is a gift to all the faithful, a gift to the congregation, whether marked off by the acceptance of the sacraments or otherwise. It illuminates, and therefore it conveys the knowledge of Truth. The *consensus* of the congregation becomes the criterion of Truth. In virtue of the spirit which has been communicated to them, they reflect the ideas which are laid up, as patterns, in heaven. Since the faithful are not only the living faithful, but also the dead, the *consensus* tends to identify

itself with tradition. Thus conceived, it is a strongly conservative influence. But it is not always thus conceived. It has been
interpreted, again, as the *consensus* of the Bishops, as representatives of the whole body of the faithful, and in this form
explains the authority attaching to the decisions of the early
Councils of the Church. But those are not wanting who define
the Councils as declaratory organs, rather than authoritative
interpreters: and the claim to the rights of the laity, as those
upon whom, equally with the apostles, the spirit descended at
Pentecost, has been very vigorously asserted at different epochs
of Russian Church history.

The most significant feature in the gift of the spirit as conceived by Orthodox thought, and the one which has most
affected character and outlook, is that it is an undivided and
indivisible whole, present in the council or the congregation.
There is no room here for individual differences of opinion.
Truth, and along with truth, love, reside in the brethren: not
in any of them taken separately. For the individual, the gift
means will-less submission. By himself he is nothing: and, in
the words of a character of Dostoievsky's *all are responsible
for all*. The spirit is one, a part of the Godhead communicated
by the Word: and there is no distribution of it into a number
of separate inspirations. Nor does it express itself in the agreement of a majority: but only in the agreement of all. The
most that the individual can do is to interpret in humility: and
to submit.

More than this. The truth which is the reflection of a pattern laid up in heaven and is made visible by the gift of the
spirit, is an integral whole. It is one with righteousness. There
can be no valid distinction between spiritual and temporal.
The claim is upon the whole of life: by contrast with that
rationalistic fragmentariness which is characteristic of the
West. If the Russian Church seemed to have travelled away
from this conception, by the nineteenth and twentieth-century
claim of some of its members for the separation of Church
and State, the old totalitarian integrality has reappeared in
the Communist demand for the whole of man's allegiance: a

combination in a new form of the union of spiritual and temporal.

How much the Russian character owes to the conception of the undivided gift of the spirit to the congregation, I cannot attempt here to determine. Nothing less than a whole history would suffice. One obvious consequence is the idea of *sobornost*, of which I have more to say presently. Another, I think, is the worship of the plain folk, that "going to the people", as one would go to an oracle, to discover the truth which is in its keeping. Another is the merging of the individual in the mass, and the weakness of the individual will. Yet another is that absoluteness in Russian thought which brooks no compromise. He that is not with them is against them. To differ with the brotherhood—*even when the brotherhood has taken the form of the Party*—is to pass away into outer darkness, isolated both from truth and love. There are patterns laid up in heaven, to which the life of the congregation must conform, till it issues in the transfiguration of the world. It was for this that the transcendent and unapproachable Godhead sent His Word to dwell among men. Not atonement, the satisfaction of the justice of God, but love, seems to be the authentic note of this Eastern Christianity. If I may so put it, in my own unconventional language, He needed companions worthy of Himself and bestowed His spirit upon men that they might become so: but that they might become so not as individuals but as brethren. There is no presumption in suggesting that man is to be deified: for the spirit which is in him is already a part of the Godhead.

One of the patterns laid up for realisation was—from the fifteenth century onwards—the idea of the Third Rome: of a Messianic mission of the Russian people. Holy Russia was a God-bearer. The Church of Constantinople—so it seemed—had apostatised when, at the Council of Florence *(1439 A.D.)*, its representatives accepted reunion with the West under the supremacy of the Pope, and had been punished by the Turkish conquest. Ivan III of Moscow married the niece of the last Emperor of Constantinople, became the champion of the Orthodox Church, and claimed the new title of Sovereign of All

Russia. As the mystical successor of Constantine, the ruler of Moscow became identified with the Messianic mission of his people. He must be absolute because the spirit is integral. There was unity of Church and State, because the conception of a separation between the two had never come into existence. We learn from Nicolas Berdyaev that Ivan IV thought it part of a Tsar's duties to save souls. At least, it was his task to create and maintain an Orthodox society in which souls could be saved, or man raised to participation in divinity. A great icon, now in the Tretiakov gallery at Moscow, representing the triumph of Ivan the Terrible over the Tartars at Kazan in 1552, shows us the sixteenth-century conception of the Orthodox Tsar. Above, in the righ-hand corner, is a burning city. Opposite, on the left, is a representation of holy Moscow, surmounted by the Mother of God and the Divine Child. From right to left, across the picture, from burning Kazan towards Moscow, marches an army led by a young Commander. In front of him rides the Archangel Michael: behind him the Emperor Constantine. In the army are the Saints Vladimir, Boris, and Gleb. Above and below the earthly army is the Heavenly Host, surrounding and protecting the Orthodox warriors. The young Commander is the Tsar Ivan: his succession from the Emperor Constantine, and his alliance with Heaven, are symbolised by the scheme of the picture. To the theme of victory is added that of the inheritance of power, and the sanctity of the office of Tsar. It is the Third Rome triumphant: with its ruler, in whom the spiritual and temporal powers are indistinguishable, because they have never been conceived as separate entities.

The Churchmen were the servants of the Tsars. When they lifted up their voices against tyranny, and they sometimes risked and incurred the pains of martyrdom in doing so, it was as Elisha spoke to Ahab, as a dutiful servant, impelled by conscience or the spirit, speaks to an erring master, not as exercising the spiritual authority of a dominant Church. Monks, especially in the north and east, played a civilising and even a political part. Going out into the wilderness they founded and fortified monasteries which became centres of population and trade, served as outposts of Russian nationality, and sometimes as places of refuge for Russian princes. The Holy Sergei blessed the expedition of Dimitry of the Don against the Tartars, and so inspired in the army the hope which won the victory. Many monasteries were founded in the fourteenth century in the period of the Black Death, and one of these was the famous Troitsa Lavra, north of Moscow, a camp and a fortress as well as a shrine. But these movements were inspired rather by the nomadism which has been part of the Russian nature, or by the desire to escape from the world, than by any challenge to the authority of Russian rulers.

There was a period, in the seventeenth century, when it might have seemed that the Russian Church was about to enter upon a more ambitious rôle. Ivan the Terrible had destroyed his own line, anarchy loosed the bonds of the Russian State, the secular enemy, the Pole, established himself in Moscow. The Church inspired the armies of the Russian people which drove out the enemy, and the picture of the Redeemer, which long hung over the Saviour's Gate of the Moscow Kremlin, was carried at their head. Philaret Romanov, then Patriarch of the Russian Orthodox Church, might, it would seem, at that time have established a temporal power. But he claimed no power for the Church. His minor son Michael was elected Tsar, and the relations between the Patriarch father, and the Tsar son, became the Church's traditional ideal of the relations between Church and State: the secular power being with the son, while honour, reverence, and the obedience of affection, were given to the father.

There was life in the Orthodox Church at this time, and a reform party arose in it, conservative in rite but champions of a purer morality. The reformers were persecuted and the Moscow mob attacked their houses. But they had the support of the young Tsar Alexis, father of Peter the Great, and many of them rose to high place in the Church. When the Patriarchate fell vacant, a man was chosen for it who has left a mighty imprint upon Russian history. This was Nikon, a stiff-necked man, rough and overbearing, but a great one. In him we catch a glimpse of claims exceeding any made by other Russian

Patriarchs, and the beginning of a distinction between spiritual and temporal power. When he entered the city on Palm Sunday, the Tsar Alexis led his ass. He described the spiritual power as the Sun, and the temporal as the Moon, and he argued that the supremacy of the State was as apostasy from Christianity itself, vitiating the whole body of the Church. He sought to give life to the ceremonial observances and a moral direction to devotional feeling. He set himself to root out drunkenness. It was by his injunction that the Empress, hitherto secluded, appeared in Church: so that it was he who began the destruction of the seclusion of women which was completed by Peter the Great. Sacred pictures to which he thought idolatrous veneration was shown were taken away. It was he who first recognised as valid the Baptism of the Roman Church. He brought Church singers from Poland and Greece, and from the latter country manuscripts, not only of the Scriptures, but also of the great pre-Christian literature, of Homer, Hesiod, Aeschylus and Thucydides: and he revived preaching, at no time a strong point of the Orthodox Church. The serious consequences of his Patriarchate were not produced by any invasion of the temporal sphere, but by the favour which he was thought to show to the Greeks, and by his correction of the ritual in accordance with the Greek practice.

The Greek ecclesiastics became frequent visitors to Moscow after the fall of Constantinople, often with the object of obtaining alms for a Church which had fallen under subjection to the Turk *(1453* A.D.*)*. There was a good deal of imposition upon the simplicity and charity of the Russians, and also a good deal of criticism of changes which had found their way into the Russian liturgy. The Russians on their part did not feel sure of Greek Orthodoxy, since the apostasy which they held to be involved in the Greek surrender to the Roman Church *(1439* A.D.*)*. There was, in effect, a rivalry between the Orthodox Church in Russia and the Church of Constantinople, embittered by minor differences. The Greeks wore their hats in Church, smoked and talked, and grumbled at the length of the services.

Nikon was not the first to plan the correction of the liturgy, but he was the first to insist upon significant alterations. In his first epistle he ordered the use of three fingers instead of two in the blessing. The two fingers signified the two-fold nature of Christ, human and divine: whereas the three fingers typified the Trinity. The use of the three fingers was a Greek practice, not apparently of very ancient date. Apart from the religious questions involved in the symbolism, the adoption of the Greek practice involved the admission that the Greek way was the pure way, and the Russian way a corruption, it conceded a sort of superiority to the rival Church, and seemed like a negation of the Messianic mission of Moscow.

The correction of the liturgy aroused determined opposition, to which Nikon retaliated with persecution. The ablest of the clergy were exiled or unfrocked. Wives inspired husbands and followed them into exile. The example of martyrs spread resistance. Beginning with the questions of the shape of the cross and the mode of making the sign, of the direction of sacred processions, eastward or westward, of the spelling of the name of Jesus, of the number of wafers to be consecrated for the Eucharist, it made a deep rift in the Orthodox Church, on one side of which gathered all the obstinate reverence for the ancient symbolism, all the hatred of intruding foreign influences, and—a singular combination—all the surviving vestiges of primitive heresy and superstition. The Schism—Raskol—became a movement of rudimentary nationalism, or perhaps rather of xenophobia.

Its separation was consummated in 1666 when a Council at Moscow anathematised the old rites, and at the same time deposed the Patriarch, Nikon, on the charge of attempting to introduce the principle of Papacy into the Orthodox Church. The strength of the Schism lay among the most vigorous elements of the people: in the north, among the Cossacks, and along the Volga; and it has with good reason been described as a national peasant movement, having the germs of a national peasant culture. The persecution of Peter the Great could not kill it. Its mass-suicides by fire, when the oppressors were too strong for it, are typical of the Russian combination of resistance with submission: for the Russian sectary does not hold rebellion lawful. Its influence was nevertheless made manifest in the rebellion of Pugachev, who used its emblems and made its strongholds his rallying grounds. It gave an outlet to the peasant instinct for self-government in all those things which lie near to his hand: and when scope in other directions was denied to it, it organised itself round its cemeteries, with insurance and banking institutions: much as our own people might build self-government out of a co-operative burial club. In the nineteenth century, when peasant education was scarce, it was a rare thing to find a Schismatic who could not read or write: and the people ascribed to these Old Believers general wealth, doubtless because they did not drink and waste and idle, as too many of the Orthodox did. Avvakum, the protagonist of its beginnings, was also the first writer who expressed himself with force and clarity in the Russian vernacular tongue.

In the Schism are included remnants of heathenism, of Gnostic and Manichaean tendencies. But its force lies in the Old Believers who claim to be the true Orthodox. If we are right in thinking evil of prejudice—that strong defender of irrational man against dangers of which his reason does not warn him or fails to supply him with the will-power to resist—we must find the Old Believers at fault for the obstinacy of their prejudices. Against all the innovations of the seventeenth century they sturdily set their faces: against tobacco, of course, but even against potatoes, and against the adoption of the European calendar. The cutting of beards was anathema, and was one of the strongest reasons for regarding Peter the Great as the apocalyptic Anti-Christ. And all of the reforms, good and bad, which Peter forced upon his people were classed along with the cutting of the beards of the gentry.

The anti-foreign element in the Schism—far more important than the anti-innovating element—permeated Russia outside of the limited circle of the avowed schismatics, and we find frequent expression given to the idea that Orthodoxy is only a luke-warm and official faith, something half-baked, a compromise with the world, while the Schism is the true Christianity. The Church, which was sometimes tolerant, sometimes intolerant, of other faiths, according to the spirit of the temporal ruler, never recognised the Schism. It treated the Schismatic as an Orthodox who had neglected his religious duties, punished him for that neglect, enforced upon him the annual confession and communion, and made him take out the certificate of the latter, which was prescribed for all the Orthodox: refused to recognise his marriage outside of the Orthodox Church: and too often levied money upon him as a consideration for leaving him alone. One noticeable effect was produced upon the Church by the circumstances in which the Schism had taken place. Minute changes of ritual practice had been the occasion of it, though hardly its cause. Henceforth the Orthodox Church shrank in nervous timidity from all change. The notion that the other Eastern Churches, or the reconciled Uniats, would object, was sufficient to exclude the consideration of every new departure, however apparently harmless. "The Orthodox Church knows no development," said Seraphim, the Metropolitan of St. Petersburg, when condemning the Latin interpolation of the *Filioque* clause in the Creed.

Peter the Great handled the Church as he handled most other things, like a rough master. His knockabout tomfooleries with the mock Patriarch—of whom he made a sort of pantomime pantaloon—must have been a deliberate preparation for his ultimate abolition of the office. But it was a part of his policy with secular ministries to put them into commission: and the replacement of the Patriarch by a Holy Synod headed by a lay Procurator had nothing extraordinary about it, if once we take it for granted that there is no valid distinction between temporal and spiritual. Peter's successors were as little troubled as he, by any doubt of the right to use the Churches, Orthodox and other, as an instrument of temporal aims. But it was in the period of deliberate Russification that this policy became most intimately galling to the non-Orthodox.

There was no Ministry of Cults in Tsarist Russia. Each non-Orthodox confession—if it was recognised—had a governing body of its own, including civil representatives of the State, on the analogy of the Holy Synod which governed the Orthodox Church: and the Ministry of the Interior had the final control over all of them. Civil control of the Roman Catholic Church was particularly inimical to the principles of the Papacy. It was so exercised as to limit the supply of priests, to restrict the pastoral visitations of bishops, and to hamper communications with the Vatican. In Poland sermons had to pass the censor before delivery. In the west of the Russian empire, Roman Catholics were not allowed to acquire immovable property, and had great difficulty in obtaining employment in the schools or under the State, and the attempt was made to insist on the use of Russian in the Churches even where the mother-tongue of the congregation was Polish. The non-recognised Confessions were treated worse, for they, according to the theory of the State, were Orthodox who did not discharge their Orthodox duties. The so-called reconciliation of the Uniats with the Orthodox Church in 1874–75 was accompanied by persecution which stopped short only of capital punishment. The aim was to assimilate the nationalities by assimilating the religions, and the possibility that pressure might widen the separation does not appear to have presented itself.

In the Orthodox Church the clergy was divided into black and white: the black, celibate and exclusively eligible for high ecclesiastical office, the white, married and serving for the most part as parish priests. Some of the monasteries amassed great wealth in land and valuables, and sometimes used it in trading enterprise. The monks of Solovetsk on the White Sea for seven years resisted the troops sent by the Tsar Alexis to enforce upon them the reforms of the Patriarch Nikon. Wealth brought abuses and attracted those who had no religious vocation. Peter fell upon these abuses with his usual titanic heavy-handedness. A special police was employed to suppress the vagabondage of monks: and his daughter Elizabeth made use of corporal punishment to correct their excesses. But it was reserved for Catherine the Great to lay hands upon monastic property with which she dealt almost as drastically as did the English Henry VIII. All the land of the monasteries was confiscated, except a few acres round the palaces and country houses of the higher clergy, to whom fixed salaries were allotted, and their number was reduced to a fraction of the former figure. In spite of restrictions laid upon their acquisition of landed property and the prohibition of the gift or bequeathal to them of serfs, they gradually recovered a portion of what they had lost. But the Church property, which had been reckoned at one-third of the whole Moscow territory in the sixteenth century and was then growing at the expense of secular ownership, with hundreds of thousands of slaves or serfs, was less than three per cent of the Russian territories in 1905. The monasteries continued to receive large revenues from offerings and from the sale of objects of religious veneration. A single icon might make the fortune of a monastery and people paid large sums for graves in the cemeteries of the famous Lavras. But there is evidence pointing to the decay of monasticism, except as a channel for recruitment to high ecclesiastical office, which the monks, or the more highly educated among them, continued to the last to monopolise. It has been observed that a map of the monasteries of Russia would show them concentrated near the ancient centres of civilisation: whereas Roman Catholic institutions of recent date, both in the New World and the Old, are numerous, and new Roman monastic orders have made their appearance as late as the nineteenth century. Part of the monastic wealth was indeed expended on public benefactions or popular instruction: but the institutions which administered these funds were worked by laymen or White clergy, not by monks.

In thinking of Orthodox Monasticism we must dismiss from our minds ideas of beneficence, learning, and preaching, such as we attribute to the Benedictines, and of statecraft, energy and policy such as we find in the Jesuits, and we must realise that the East has not that rich variety of monastic orders, each created to meet a practical need, which exists in the West. There are no monuments of collective intellectual labour comparable with the "Acts" of the Benedictines. The spirit of Orthodox Monasticism was something quite other than this. Humility and purity of heart are the ideal Orthodox virtues, and it was these which the monks were cultivating.

1840–1841. When the Rev. William Palmer was seeking peace for his troubled conscience in a reconciliation of the Anglican with the Orthodox Church, and his own admission to the latter without a re-Baptism, which he felt to be a denial of his religious past, the Sergievsky monks told him that vermin have a use, to teach one patience. They wondered at the questions put to them by the eager seeker, and especially at his wish to turn some of the monasteries into working and learned communities. In reply they kept on repeating that prayer and holiness have more efficacy than learning or work of any kind. It is precisely what a Tibetan monk might say. The White clergy, they said, were all overburdened with work and families: and the academicians (meaning the higher monastic clergy whose ecclesiastical education had gone further than that of the monks) were equally taken up with work and instruction. The monasteries, they said, were little thought of by anyone, though they had more than once saved Russia— a reference to the splendid past of institutions such as the Troitsa Lavra. They added that the secular clergy were infected with Liberalism (a dangerous fault in the days of Nicolas I) and that they read Lutheran and other bad books. Wistfully they hinted a plea that some day or other the possessions which Catherine the Great had taken away might be restored to them. But for these last words we might fancy ourselves back in the Thebaid. But we must not misunderstand. The aim was to avoid all contact with bustling Martha, and to sit with Mary at the Master's feet: for which purpose a steady supply of the means of livelihood was naturally essential. To the statement of the objects of the Orthodox monks we ought in justice to add that, beside their personal salvation, the monks had in view—when they remembered it—the expiation of the sins of the age. Ideally, at least, the conception that each is responsible for all, and must expiate the sins of all, runs like a golden thread through all Russian religious thought, and sets the nobler spirits to their prayers for all.

The sub-procurator of the Holy Synod (the monks objected to him as a military man who wore spurs and practised dancing) told Palmer that the ritual offices of the Thebaid were imported entire into Russia. If they were all recited as they should be, Matins would take five or six hours, the Liturgy two, and Vespers three. They must not be changed or abbreviated—*there* would lie peril to the unity of Orthodoxy —*so they must be gabbled,* to the scandal of many. Certainly it might be well to change somewhat: but—with a shrug— *que voulez vous?*

Much of the "holiness" of the monks was not holiness at all: not merely because celibacy was required of men who had not the vocation to it, but because of the spirit prevailing in the higher ecclesiastical ranks. We hear of an archbishop who, finding women among the monks, rebuked the erring brethren with this observation: "The Church is the smithy in which we get our living. We have got to keep it in order." It was like a respectable merchant, finding his clerks at high jinks in the counting-house.

Konstantin Leontiev, seeker of salvation, of whom I shall have more to say presently, passed a judgment upon the monks of the famous Skyte of Optina Pustin, which shows the prevalence of a similar spirit. After a life spent in the exposition of Byzantine Christianity, he submitted himself to the guidance of an Elder—such an Elder as Father Zosima, in Dostoievsky's novel *The Brothers Karamazov.* Like the Indian *chela* with his *guru,* the disciple of the Elder discloses all his thoughts, and obeys implicitly all the Master's bidding, and the Master is, or should be, the perfect spiritual guide. Such Elders were a special feature of the post-Petrine period of the Church. When work on a great newspaper in St. Petersburg was offered to Leontiev, he submitted the case to his Elder, and the Elder told him to ask for better terms, more money and more amenities: thoroughly good worldly counsel, such as the family solicitor might give. The monks of Optina smiled at Dostoievsky's hopes of the earthly triumph of Christianity. Leontiev found among them "men of business, good, practical and wise, but all except Father Anatoly are traders by nature and spirit. And they don't elect Anatoly (to be their head) because he is too idealistic. They are honourable men and sincere monks in their special sphere. But they are concerned with economy and the management of the institution. They give no thought to the great historic part which Optina plays in nineteenth-century Russia, or to the importance of its influence for the laity. None of them has any idea of what is going on in the world about them." Be it observed that these criticisms come from a friend, not from an enemy. He did not find the spiritual food for which he hungered, or even the broad and understanding man, but rather the Bursary Committee of an Oxford or Cambridge College, very properly concerned with the management of the College Estates: a Bursary Committee, which had no intention of making the management anything more than an end in itself.

1865. The functions of the Church included the management of its internal affairs and the maintenance of discipline among its spiritual workers. In the nineteenth century it was much concerned over the poverty of the White parochial clergy, and with the degradation and corruption to which this poverty led: and for these evils it was unable to devise an effective remedy. On paper, at least, the education given to the candidates for ordination appears adequate. It began with eight years in a district clerical school, which was followed by six in the diocesan seminary, with an allowance, scanty in amount, from the clerical education fund for poor scholars. This course was heavy and it was difficult to finish it satisfactorily in the period allowed: and the seminaries, filled with hungry youths, became hot-beds of revolutionary thought. The clerical families (for they continued to constitute something very like a caste even after the law had abolished the recruitment of parish-priests by inheritance, and given to all Russians the right to join the secular clergy) contributed more than one famous fighter to the Socialist cause, and later on the theological training seems to have sharpened the wits of the budding priest for the discussion of Marxian problems. For the more gifted seminarists there were the four ecclesiastical academies at St. Petersburg, Moscow, Kiev and Kazan, with a four-years' course which opened the way to the Episcopate. The normal age for the monastic vows (for a man) was thirty, but the successful pupil of the Academy could take them at twenty-five, and had the opportunity of rapid advancement, leaving altogether behind him the rank and file of the monks, and retaining very little sympathy with them.

— In the reign of Alexander III, and under the influence of Konstantin Pobiedonostsev, an attempt was made to extend the functions of the priesthood into lay education, in order to combat the liberalising tendencies of the District Council schools. With a similar political motive, priests were required to disclose secrets of the confessional, where the interests of the State were touched. The Church exercised a judicial authority over ecclesiastics, and had its own prisons in which to carry out its sentences. Till 1767 it had powers of inflicting corporal punishment on ecclesiastical offenders. The Reverend Mr. Palmer tells us that if a secular priest married a second time after the death of his first wife, his Bishop would cut off his hair and secularise him: whereupon the lay authorities would send him for a soldier: a much dreaded punishment at the time when the soldier's term of service was twenty or twenty-five years. The ecclesiastical prisons were emptied in the period of reforms which accompanied the revolution of 1905. We are told that they were soon refilled, and that some of the new occupants were priests who had deserved ill of State and Church by their protests against the capital sentences inflicted by the Field-Courts-Martial set up in the reaction. This is not the only instance which we find a parish priests championing the dangerous doctrine of Liberalism, or risking their own livelihood to defend the innocent. There were many cases of interference to protect Jews in the *pogroms* which disgraced the later days of the Empire. But the higher clergy were not in general concerned with these things. "Serfdom and cruel punishment are not contrary to the spirit of Christianity," said a Bishop, "for physical suffering does not interfere with the salvation of the soul, which is our sole concern."

There was an ecclesiastical Censorship separate from the civil. It was a timidly nervous institution, which let nothing pass to which anyone could possibly object. How it dealt with some of the best and noblest work in theology even where no heresy was suspected, we shall see when we come to deal with the writings of the lay theologian Khomiakov. It was impossible for him to print anything in Russia, and communications to his address from abroad were intercepted and withheld. So he wrote in French, and published abroad, commenting upon his harassers with a Christian restraint. The Eparchial Consistory, the ecclesiastical Council of the Bishops, had jurisdiction in cases of clergy discipline, and of the marriage and divorce of the laity. Though the Bishops themselves had ordinarily a blameless reputation, these Courts, as well as the ecclesiastical offices through which the business of the Church passed, were commonly reputed corrupt as well as dilatory.

The Orthodox Church had a legal monopoly of conversion, and published official statistics of its achievements. The Rev. Mr. Palmer tells us of a priest who converted two thousand persons in the Aleutian Isles, and of the pectoral cross with which he was decorated for this service to Orthodoxy.

The close intermixture of politics and religion in the Russian State is shown by the history of the Lettish conversions to Orthodoxy in the reign of Nicolas I. A zealous Bishop converted seventy or eighty thousand Lutheran Letts, who hoped for protection against the oppression of their German Lutheran lords. The Lutheran lords and pastors complained to the Russian Government, which disapproved of such obvious sowing of dissension between lords and peasants. The Holy Synod removed the zealous Bishop to a monastery. But it sent, as his successor, another Bishop who went to work in a more tactful way, and the process of conversion continued wholesale. The procurator of the Holy Synod expressed his satisfaction at the movement, but made no bones of the worldly motives which lay behind it. In the Baltic provinces of Russia it was the policy of the Tsar to weaken the German overlords by creating divisions between them and the mass of the population.

Nicolas Lyeskov, who satirised Nihilists and Churchmen,

radicals and conservatives, alike, and was consequently kept out of his deserved literary fame for more than half a century, has left us a satire on the missionary enterprises of the Church. In his story the interference of the Holy Synod takes the form of a sudden order, due to a change of the policy towards indigenous religions, increasing the number of Buddhist temples and doubling the number of licensed Lamas. The Lamas spread the rumour that the Tsar and the Metropolitan had been converted to Buddhism. The Baptizers come back from the wilds, dirty and in tatters, the civil authorities protect the Lamas, and the people refuse supplies and transport to the discredited servants of Christianity.

But—as usual—headquarters speaks with two voices, perhaps with more than two. Pectoral crosses continue to be bestowed upon successful missionaries, and fashionable St. Petersburg society continues to give dances on behalf of mission funds. A young and energetic Bishop starts off on a sledge journey, first with reindeer and afterwards with dogs, to learn how a certain Baptizer achieves his successes in the mission-field, and hears some queer stories from his sledge-driver. It seems that the sledge-driver's brother is a professional convert, and accepts repeated Baptism on behalf of others who have scruples. But enough. The story is extant, and translated into choice English.

Under the Imperial law of 1857 the Emperor was the Supreme defender and guardian of the dogmas of the Orthodox Faith, and the preserver of Orthodoxy and of all good order in the Holy Church. In this sense, and properly speaking in this sense only, he was the Head of the Church. In the Government of the Church the autocratic power acted through the most holy Synod, of which the Procurator was a layman (and occasionally a soldier, if circumstances made a military appointment convenient). The Procurator sat at a separate table, away from the ecclesiastical members of the Synod, and he had no vote in their deliberations: but he was a nominee of the Emperor and the channel of communication with him: and, as a smiling monk observed to Mr. Palmer, he had very great influence. The Holy Synod enjoyed along with the Senate (before the creation of the Imperial Duma) the right to initiate projects of law, but the final decision was that of the Autocrat.

The position of the Autocrat as Head of the Church did not give him authority to define or modify dogma. But the apparent domination of the Church by the State, and in particular the exercise of that domination through a Synod with a lay head, was a cause of offence to tender consciences, as soon as the notion of the separateness of temporal power had arrived, and the struggle for the restoration of the Patriarchate appears at intervals during the last century of the Empire's existence. In principle, said Khomiakov, the Orthodox Church is free; but owing to the weakness of Churchmen, her actual position is one of dependence. George Samarin, another of the Slavophil Church reformers, said bitterly that if the Emperor were to assert a doctrinal infallibility such as that of Rome, only a few laymen would protest, not a Bishop, monk, or priest, would say a word. When, in 1885, an official document of the Russian Government declared that the Eastern Church had renounced its power, and placed it in the hands of the Tsar, only one protest was made (by Vladimir Soloviev) and that—perhaps by reason of the ecclesiastical censorship—was made anonymously.

What the power of the State actually was, in the latter days, and how little Churchmen were able or willing to resist, we have seen clearly enough amid the gross scandals of Rasputin's day, when an unworthy claimant to the honours of sainthood received canonisation, to favour one of "Our Friend's" protégés. There is, of course, an important distinction to be drawn. The sentiment of the masses was not outraged by the canonisation of an impostor, any more than by the favour shown to Rasputin himself: because the masses could be made to believe that both were deserving and holy persons. But if the Emperor had made a change in the smallest particular of customary ritual, not to mention dogma, embarrassing results might have followed. Nothing less than an oecumenical Council of the Eastern Churches could define or modify dogma. It was a Council of the Eastern Patriarchs, meeting at Moscow, which degraded the Patriarch Nikon: and the oecumenical Patriarch had approved of the abolition of the Patriarchate by Peter, and was asked to approve its restoration by the Provisional Government after the March Revolution. But it was not till after the Bolshevik Revolution that anyone in Russia had the enterprise to propose the summoning of a full oecumenical Council of all the Orthodox Churches, the first after an interval of centuries. The plan broke down owing to diplomatic difficulties: but its initiation in the post-revolutionary atmosphere is instructive.

For a picture of the White clergy in their lives and work during the first half of the nineteenth century, the reader should turn to another story, by the Nicolas Lyeskov whom I have already cited, called *Cathedral Folk*. We see them in a country town happy with their families, indulging innocent foibles, the best of them conscience-stricken when they play cards or smoke, the less scrupulous drinking more than is good for them. Humility, charity, brotherly kindness, are their evident qualities, and there is no pride in them. They are very poor, and, the region being one in which schismatics abound, we see them occasionally replenishing the family funds by levies on these undesirables, "in order that I might not have to dress my wife like a chanter's wife". A priest is reproved by his Bishop for a sermon in which he points a moral at the expense of the local officials, since "the higher they are in station the more sacred they are". The Church servitors petition the Bishop to relieve their poverty, and he, good easy man, points out to them that Our Lord had not where to lay His head, and recommends the perusal of the *Imitatio Christi*. There is a description—it is dated May 9th, 1836—of the destruction, by the orders of authority, of a Schismatic chapel: the people gather about the place, with the Schismatic and the Orthodox clergy, and, as the demolition proceeds, consciences are touched, all lift up their voices and weep, and at last they all —Schismatics and Orthodox—embrace and seek union together. A typical Russian scene. But, later, the Schismatics bring out a lamp and begin to pray over the broken stones, whereupon the police turn a hose over them: against which the priest—he calls it an impudent arrangement—protests in vain.

An eccentric noble-woman (these are the days of serfdom and she keeps dwarfs and wants to breed from them) makes a present to the priest. This arouses the jealousy of the arch-priest, who talks about Achan, and about "something kept back from the Church". This jealousy gets the priest into trouble. His chanter-sexton has sold to the Schismatics an ancient psalter. The priest is placed under ecclesiastical censure, and transferred *to the Brewery Department,* to brew *kvas* for the seminarists, while the chanter-sexton is sent to a hermitage for two years. The use of the hermitage for a house of correction is suggestive.

The Governor, a haughty person, apparently of German origin, talks in Church, and the Bishop sends his crozier-bearer to ask him to be quiet. The Governor continues his talk. The Bishop proclaims from the pulpit that he will hold his peace till the Governor has finished. *They decline to call on one another*. The Bishop rebukes the Governor's daughter for coming in her gloves to receive the blessing. The squabble ends with the transfer of the Bishop to a less desirable diocese.

The priest himself gets into fresh trouble when he gets back from the ecclesiastical brewing business, because he tells the Governor that landlords make their serfs work on Sundays: and "even on the twelve great Feast Days". The Governor is angry, and the priest gives him lip. This time he is degraded from his inspecting office, and says that he was lucky not to be unfrocked. He is in trouble again for objecting when some Polish (perhaps he means Roman Catholic, for the words are used almost as synonyms) officials make fun of the Requiem Service.

There is a long gap in the priest's diary from 1850 to 1857, at the end of which period he notes that he has gone through a severe course of schooling, and no longer cares to kick against the pricks. He now receives a purple velvet cap of honour and the cross of St. Anna, recommended—here is a characteristic touch—*by the local Police Commissioner*.

His troubles are not over, for his impulsive temper leads him into preaching a sermon about Rehoboam, with unmistakable allusions to a Tsar misled by evil servants. This time the police take him off to the provincial capital, where he is put into an unordained dress and made reader to the Bishop. But we have already been seduced into telling too much of the tale—which has been excellently translated into English. Let us add only this much, that in the last page the good Father forgives all his enemies, "but, in observing the dead letter of the law, they are ruining the work of God here".

The Orthodox Church of Russia in its unthinking days (and these were prolonged) was alternatively swayed by Roman and by Protestant influences, and a Protestant tinge was imparted to the teaching of the ecclesiastical Academies in the second half of the eighteenth and the first half of the nineteenth centuries, with emphasis upon the study of the Scriptures. On the other hand more than one Russian religious thinker has found virtues in Catholicism, to the loss of which he has attributed some of Russia's failings. One of these was Peter Chaadaev, an isolated thinker, a sort of scholar Diogenes, who, from the recesses of a somewhat misanthropic tub, ventured to reject offers of Imperial favour, and for long enjoyed an amused tolerance as a "character". He is believed to have been the original of Chatsky, the hero of *Wit works Woe*, in which Griboyedov satirised the society of the capital. Some of his mordant sayings passed from mouth to mouth, and people told one another, with a snigger, how he had described Moscow as the city with a great cannon that never was fired, and a great bell which fell down and broke as soon as it was put up. But he said other things, about persons, which were not so easily forgiven. He was a friend of the poet Pushkin, who left an epigram on his portrait:

By the high might of Heaven
Chained to the service of the Tsar:
Might have been Brutus in Rome and Pericles in Athens:
With us, a Hussar officer.

Great men appreciated him, and we catch glimpses of him

in the intellectual society where he was at home, sitting all
night with Khomiakov and Bakunin—strange combination as
it seems to those who know the later stories of the two men,
Slavophil theologian and anarchist firebrand—over the never-
ending samovar. He stands at the beginning of the movement
by which thought in nineteenth-century Russia came to ma-
turity. He wrote in torment and anxiety, a dark and tragically
afflicted figure, and was in the same line with Tolstoi and
Dostoievsky, seekers of salvation, thirsters for expiation.

For some years his essays in French on the philosophy of
Russian history had been handed about in manuscript. The
head of the terrible Third Section certainly knew of them, and
perhaps Nicolas himself, the barrack-master martinet, had
august cognisance of his ideas as well as of his personality.
The author was what was soon to be called a Westerniser in
his sympathies, and his theme was the duty of Russia to assimilate what the creative genius of other peoples had made
available to her. But alongside of this he emphasised her isolation, and its advantages, as enabling her to accept the good
and reject the bad: and he foretold the rapidity of her ultimate
advance, when she would become the teacher of her present
masters. His desire, as Merezhkovsky sums it up, was the
Kingdom of God on earth as well as in heaven: and as a
means, the preservation of the liberty of the Church in the
world. The French manuscript, or one form of it, declared
that political changes were not necessary, and that an indefinite liberty was not an indispensable condition, and it
praised the judicious attitude of the Emperor.

In an evil hour for themselves, Chaadaev and the Editor of
the *Telescope* periodical, who hoped to rehabilitate his dwin-
dling sales by a sensation, decided to translate the French
manuscript into Russian, and publish it in the Review in the
form of a series of philosophical letters *To a Lady*. It was in
the year 1836, the year of the great outburst of laughter (in
which Nicolas himself joined) over the publication of the
Inspector General, in which Gogol satirised the Russian bureaucracy. One of these letters appeared, omitting the praise
of Nicolas (possibly only postponing it): attacking the empti-

ness of Russian life and civilization: and—worst of all—attributing its defects to the absence of the vivifying influence of Roman Catholicism, "the active, impressive, social form of Christianity".

An onslaught, it seemed, on the Orthodox Church, the very heart and brain of Holy Russia, and therefore on the Autocrat, its Head and Defender!

The indignation which Chaadaev's sharp witticisms had been storing up for years past, found an outlet. Society was furious: and society consisted of the whole body of high officials, ecclesiastical and lay, and of everyone who counted. The Church suggested solitude, fasting, and prayer, for this wandering sheep. The *Telescope* was suppressed. The censor (in spite of his plea that he passed the offending article when engaged in a game of whist with some lady friends) was dismissed and deprived of his pension. As for Chaadaev, the Chief of the Third Section expressed sympathy with the unhappy man, who was "evidently mad", and gave instructions that he should *receive medical attention and be protected against the raw cold air* of November until he should recover. This must have been the grim joke of the pewtery-eyed Nicolas himself, who desired to make the punishment fit the crime in his own fashion. For a whole year the medical régime continued, with a drunken certifying doctor, who was not too polite, and monthly reports to the Emperor on the state of the patient's health. Poor Diogenes suffered cruelly from this intrusion on the cynic dignity of his tub, and from the damage done by police perquisitions among his papers. But all his "irascible pride", as the Emperor called it, did not prevent an abject submission, and he wrote the *Apology of a Madman,* by which he tried to remove the causes of Imperial and ecclesiastical offence.

All society was agog with curiosity and laughter over the story, and Peter Chaadaev's disparagement of Holy Russia and the Orthodox Church set the lists for the controversy between Slavophils and Westerners which divided Russian opinion for many decades.

At the heart of Slavophilism is Russian Orthodoxy and the

Orthodox mysticism which is the essence of all Christian culture in the East. The first Slavophils were men of the ancestral life, typical Russian landlords, racy of the soil, who had sucked along with their mother's milk their living convictions. They were bred in the ideas of the old Orthodox way of living, of the Christian peasant commune, and of the Christian patriarchal State, in which all things are framed, in ideal at least, to the pattern of father with children. In their Orthodoxy there was something of the spirit of the Schism and of the Old Believers, the same convictions of Russian Messianism which began with the idea of Moscow as the Third Rome, and was so deeply outraged when Tsar Alexis and the Patriarch Nikon adopted the Greek tradition in the liturgy, and again when Peter the Great established an upstart capital in a non-Russian land. It was expressed in Konstantin Aksakov's apostrophe to Peter: "Thou hast despised Russia and all her past. Therefore a seal of malediction is imprinted on all thy senseless work. Pitilessly thou hast repudiated Moscow and hast gone out to build apart from thy people, a solitary city. For thou and they could no longer live together."

In the reverence of the Slavophils for the patriarchal head of the Russian community there was mingled a dislike for intruding Byzantine and German elements, and in particular for the bureaucracy and the machinery of State which Peter had imported. They had their ears attuned to the Liberty Bell of Novgorod the Great, and their eyes fixed on the parliament of Kiev, or on the independent Communes, and the free assembly of the Zaporozhian Cossacks writing their outrageous letters of challenge to the Sultan of Turkey. They idealised the life of the people, of the plain folk. They held that they should return to the people and be made whole by them on the soil of a common faith. They were the first of the worshippers of the people, of the *Narod*, as the Russians call, not the nation, but the plain folk: and, anti-revolutionary themselves and upholders of a patriarchal autocracy, they were first to institute that "going to the people" which played so large a part in subsequent revolutionary movements. In Moscow, always alien in spirit from Peter's capital, the reaction towards antiquity took extravagant forms. Leading Slavophils put their trousers inside their high boots, and wore the shirt with the collar fastened at the side, or masqueraded in robes which caused the gaping peasants to take them for Persian merchants. Pan-slavonic patriotism ran riot and it became a pose to adopt popular superstitions and sacrifice reason to antiquarian sentiments. At a certain dinner-party a Slavophil poet recited verses in which he declared that he would drink the blood of the Germans and the Magyar. Fortunately a humorous person was at the table. He picked up his silver fruit-knife and said: "Excuse me, gentlemen, I have just remembered that my piano-tuner is a German. I'll just slit his throat and be back with you in time for the walnuts." For that occasion at least, laughter cured folly. But we need not be surprised that the fanatical nationalism, not a nationalism of Russia but of all Slavdom, degenerated into a Chauvinism which led Russia into dangerous adventures.

The most characteristic feature of the Slavophils, in their first and best inspiration, was their religion. In the face of an ecclesiastical censorship which made it impossible to publish anything for Russians in the Russian language, a retired officer of Hussars made a simple but far-reaching revival of the thought of the Orthodox Church. This was the doctrine of *sobornost*, "congregationalism", apparently in no way schismatic, and certainly not new, but rather a rediscovery, in the Slavophil spirit, of a fundamental conception which had been overlaid with later accretions of ecclesiastical habit. Put in its simplest form, the idea was that the Church consists of all its members, lay and clerical, gathered together in mutual love, and that truth is to be found there where love is. The Prayer of St. Chrysostom: "where two or three are gathered together in Thy name Thou wilt grant their requests," seems to breathe the same spirit.

Britons, with their tendency to state all things in terms of politics and administration, might express this idea in the language of self-government. This, no doubt, was one of the implications, and the close connection, in the thought of the Slavophils, between religion and civil affairs, must have tended to extend the self-government into what we should regard as the political sphere. It is not surprising that the authorities (who instinctively disliked and suspected all thought) looked with distrust upon the Slavophils in their earlier phase. The Governor-General of Moscow, speaking of the Petrashevsky affair of 1849, in which Dostoievsky was sentenced to death, said that all the Moscow Slavophils were in it, but "so devilish sly you can't put salt on their tails". We know what Nicolas I, the martinet, thought of Hussar-Captain Aleksei Khomiakov's essays in theology. We must remember that, with Nicolas, the word *liberal* was not a laudatory one. He said: "In what Khomiakov says about the Church he is very *liberal:* but in what he says about its relations with the temporal authority he is quite right."

Some of the things which the retired Hussar-Captain said about the relations of the Church with the temporal authority were these. "It would be better if we had less of official, political, religion, and if the Government could be convinced that Christian truth is not in need of perpetual patronage, and that excessive preoccupation with it weakens, rather than strengthens." "We do not regard the Emperor as an oracle moved by unseen power, as the Latins regard the Bishop of Rome. We think that, being free, the Emperor, like every man, may fall into error: and that, if this should happen, which God forbid, despite the constant prayers of the sons of the Church, he would not lose any of his rights to the obedience of his subjects in temporal affairs. . . . There would be one Christian the less in the bosom of the Church: that is all." "However high a man stand on the social ladder, be he our Magistrate, or even our Emperor, if he is not from the Church (that is from the Church as Khomiakov conceived it, the body of the faithful in mutual love), then, in the matter of faith, he can only be our disciple, not our equal nor our fellow-worker in the task of preaching. He can in that case do us only one service: to listen." "When the people elected Michael Romanov to be their Tsar, they transferred all their powers to him, ecclesiastical and civil, and he has only the powers which they transferred. Not he, but Christ, is the Head of the Church."

Those who know most of the pewtery-eyed Nicolas will wonder whether he had read these passages when he made his tolerant comments. There was nothing anti-monarchical or intentionally revolutionary in what Khomiakov wrote: and yet here (as in much professedly anti-revolutionary Russian thought) we cannot but hear the distant rattle of the tumbrils. At a later stage in the development of Russian religious thought, the free attitude of the Slavophils towards the Tsardom gave place to a mystical conception of the Autocracy, which played its part in political reaction. In the meanwhile, an anarchical tendency in the Slavophil doctrines has justly been noticed. It is but one step from the federation of free communes to the State which is not a State. Konstantin Aksakov said: "The lie is not in this or in the other form of State, but in the State itself as such."

The first use of the word *soborny,* which we have translated by "congregational", is by way of distinction from "catholic" in the description of the Western Church, now separated and out of communion. The Latin translation *"conciliaris"* would naturally mean "based upon the oecumenical councils." The word *sobornost* has often been translated by "conciliarity". The idea reappears in the nineteenth century in the reply of the Eastern Patriarchs to the Encyclical of Pope Piux IX to the address of the Eastern Churches. They disclaim all control over the dogmas of Orthodoxy. "We have no sort of worldly inspectorship, or, as His Holiness calls it, sacred direction, but are united only by the bond of love and zeal for our common Mother in the unity of the faith. . . . With us neither Patriarch nor Councils *(sic)* could ever introduce anything new, inasmuch as with us the body itself of the Church is the guardian of Orthodoxy."

It was Khomiakov's task to rediscover and interpret further this fundamental idea in its application to the Orthodox Church of Russia. He tells Mr. Palmer that the gift of truth is separated from the hierarchical functions, is attributed not to individuals but to the totality of the Church, is considered as the corollary of the moral principle of mutual love and he draws the distinction between the position of Orthodoxy on the one hand and Romanism and Protestantism on the other, in a passage of singular clarity and eloquence: "Romanism is an unnatural tyranny. Protestantism is an unprincipled revolt. Neither of them can be accepted. But where is unity without tyranny? Where is freedom without revolt? They are both to be found in the ancient, continuous, unadulterated tradition of the Church. There a unity is to be found more authoritative than the despotism of the Vatican, for it is based upon the strength of mutual love. There a liberty is to be found more free than the licence of Protestantism, for it is regulated by the humility of mutual love. There is the Rock and the Refuge." And again, in an address of the year 1855 to the German Churches: "Romanism has a man, Protestantism has a book. Replace these by the whole Church, as in the doctrine of the Orthodox, and you have the whole difference of Life against Death."

Some of us, recalling unpleasant facts, may feel doubtful about the truth of this picture. But a Church must be judged by its ideals as well as by its practice: and here surely we have the ideal at its noblest. As expressed by a recent historian of the Russian Church, the function of the laymen was a reality. He says they had at all times refused to the hierarchs the sole right to represent the Church and her doctrine. Laity and ecclesiastics possessed, *and should exercise*—note the *should*— an equal right to participation in the internal life of the Church, in her teachings and the maintenance of her doctrine and her canons, and in her glory and her universal triumph. Only when the people took a "counselling"[1] part in the affairs of the Church, could that Church become truly the Church of Christ. Perhaps the writer is doing what many Russians have done and still do, mix up their wish with its fulfillment.

From the "congregational" or "conciliar" character of the Church, Khomiakov deduces the consequence that there is no

[1] This is the same word which I have translated "congregational". From *The Russian Church* by Nicolas Brianchaninov.

division, similar to that in the Western Churches, between the teaching Church and the Church of the disciples. There is no teaching Church in the true Church: which means, no doubt, that the clergy have no monopoly of teaching, and explains why the Slavophil theologians and the later religious thinkers of whom they were forerunners, were laymen. All the World-Religions had their origin outside of the official representatives of older cults, and, in Asia at least, almost all the great reformers of religious thought, were not priests or of priestly caste. In this respect the Slavophils, and the later theologians of the Orthodox revival, were of the Asiatic tradition, with Sakyamuni and Zoroaster and Confucius, with the authors of the Upanishads, with Jesus and Paul and Mahommed and Guru Nanak.

Khomiakov was a historian as well as a theologian, but there is much of religion in his history. As he saw history, the idea of legal right lay at the foundation of the thought of Rome, which passed it on to the Germanic conquerors, not only in the life of the state but in the life of religion. It was this which, in the Roman Catholic Church, gave to the relations of man with God the character of a perpetual law-suit, or as we should perhaps put it, of a perpetual running-account, in which good deeds and bad figured with meticulous accuracy on either side of the ledger. Orthodox Russia, on the other hand, preserved freedom of the spirit, attaching little importance to the material, the formal, the judicial. She had not that pre-Christian culture which prevented the West from becoming truly Christian, but received her civilisation along with her Christianity. The aristocratic spirit which came along with the conquerors to the West was alien to her. The communal spirit exists in the Russian people from the beginning. They are organically Christian. Power to them is a burden and a duty, not a right. They reject power as they rejected it (according to legend) when they invited the Varangians to rule over them. Equally they reject formal guarantees of their liberty. Such things are needed in the relations only of conqueror and conquered. When the power of the State is organic, popular in origin, there is no need of a Constitution.

None of the Slavophils were constitutionalists and Konstantin Aksakov declared that the fullness of power and action was for the Government, while the people should have the fullness of thought, and freedom of the spiritual life. But we find the Slavophils prominent in the struggle for the emancipation of the serfs, and for its accompaniment by the allotment of land and the retention of the Mir, their palladium. Khomiakov himself was in trouble with the authorities for a poem in which he declared that Russia's sins, among them the institution of serfdom, made her unworthy of the task of setting free her sister nations.

> *"O thou unworthy of choice*
> *Thou art chosen. Be swift and lave*
> *Thyself with water of repentance,*
> *That the storm of two-fold punishment light not on thee."*

In another noble poem, Khomiakov called upon the Russian Eagle to remember the brother Eagles on the Alps, the Carpathians and the Balkans, and on the Danube. It is significant of the profound "Orthodoxy" of the Slavophils, that Poland, the Roman Catholic, was counted out from the full Slavonic brotherhood. When Tyutchev, a greater Slavophil poet, sang of Poland among the other Slav peoples, it was to anathematise the Poles.

> "Only he has escaped from disgrace, and been spared from the enmity (of western Europe) who has been foremost in ill-doing to his own. Only our Judas is honoured by their kiss."

And when he addressed the Czechs, it was on the anniversary of Huss, to recall the memory of a Protestant martyr to persecuting Romanism: and he used the occasion to call upon them to break the chains binding them to Rome.

Tyutchev was a diplomatist, as Khomiakov was an army-officer. He has left, in poetry of a lofty inspiration, a running commentary on the affairs of Europe from the revolutions of

1848–49 to the fall of Napoleon III and the establishment of the German Empire. In 1854, when the Crimean War is beginning, he has a vision of midnight and moonlight, in which, over the walls of Istanbul—the Tsargrad of Slavophil dreams —he sees the shield of Oleg gleaming. It is a call to the Slavs to win back Imperial Byzantium. Sometimes he bursts into the language of a purer patriotism, nearer home. Here is the authentic note of the love of the much-enduring, for ever tormented, people of Russia—

> *"Over the dark crowd of this unawakened people*
> *When wilt thou rise, O Freedom?*
> *When wilt thy golden light gleam over them?*
> *Thy light will gleam and make alive,*
> *And the sun will drive away the clouds,*
> *But the old festering wounds,*
> *The scars of outrage and insult,*
> *The corruption and emptiness of souls,*
> *That gnaw the mind and ache in the heart,*
> *Who shall cure these, who shall cover them?*
> *Thou, pure vestment of Christ."*

It is no mere Liberal emancipation of which the Slavophils dream when they talk of Freedom.

Generally it is something outside of Russia, some event in the field of ecclesiastical or State politics which awakens Tyutchev's muse, and often it awakens her to the glorification of the Orthodox Tsar. In December 1866: "the East is smoking with fresh blood: out upon our evil age. Yet one mighty refuge remains, one holy altar for Truth. In thy soul it is, our Orthodox, our glorious, Russian Tsar."

A later poem describes the triumphal feast of the Padshah at Tsargrad, while, somewhere in the shadows, millions of his Christian victims are bleeding to death.

At the formation of the dual Austro-Hungarian Monarchy in 1867, by which the Austrian Slavs were divided between the Austrian Empire and the Hungarian kingdom, there is an angry outburst against the Austrian minister. He had said that

Austria must pin the Slavs to the wall: and Tyutchev replies: "the wall to which the Slavs will be pinned is Russia herself: a wall in which every stone is alive." He is no less bitter on the declaration of the Papal infallibility, which touches his Orthodox Russian soul to the quick. He prophesies an end of the dream of the new God-man: for "the Vatican Dalai Lama will not be recognised as the vice-regent of Christ". Britain, the opponent of Russian designs in the East, comes in for the lash:

"Why is the British leopard so wroth with us, why lashes he his tail, why roars so furiously . . . our northern Bear, our all-Russian peasant, will not give up his right to defend himself, nay sometimes to snarl back. . . ."

Already, in Tyutchev, there is a note of something cruder and more flamboyant than the pure Slavophil music. Dostoievsky's excursion into imperialist politics, in the concluding portion of his address on the Pushkin anniversary, made that note yet harsher. We begin to see that mere jingoism is no impossible issue from patriotism of this kind. We hear it still louder in N. Y. Danilevsky, the complete Pan-Slavonic theorist, whose *Russia in Europe,* a catechism of the Pan-Slav ideal, was sold out in one year. In advance of Otto Spengler, his thesis is that all civilisations have their day and cease to be, and the Slav race must have its own, rejecting the elements of individualism and of violence which disfigure the Western. For every Slav—after God and Holy Church, be it noted—Slavism must be the highest ideal, *higher than liberty, science, and education.* The disease of Russia is the tendency to Europeanise herself. The reforms of Alexander II—not excepting the abolition of serfdom, it would seem—are condemned as "European". We are nearer here to the racialism of Nazi Germany than we were in the early phase of Slavophilism.

There must be, say Danilevsky, a generally Slav federation, *without Poland,* but including Greeks, Roumanians and Hungarians, "whose historical destinies have attached them by indestructible bonds to the Slav world"—in other words for the sake of a scientific frontier. There must be *a war between Slavism and Europe which will fill a whole period of history:*

and Constantinople must be won: but it must not be the capital of Russia—doubtless because Moscow is the centre of the dream.

By this time we are very close in spirit to that very able journalist Katkov, a conservative and nationalist of the Western type, who reproached a too lenient Government for its decision to try strikers by jury: the true Nemesis of Slavophilism, as V. Soloviev described him. But we must break off here to follow, for the present, another line of growth.

Chapter 7

The Intelligentsia and the Worship of the Plain Folk

"The whole history of the Intelligentsia was a preparation for Communism. Into Communism there entered the well-known traits of the Intelligentsia—thirst for social righteousness and equality, a recognition of the working classes as the highest type of humanity, aversion to capitalism and the bourgeoisie, the striving after an integrated outlook, and an integrated relation to life, sectarian intolerance. . . ."

> BERDYAEV, *The Origin of Russian Communism.*

"He clacked away about something or other: wanted to stretch his tongue a bit. Of course he's a gentleman: what does he understand?"

> TURGENIEV, *Fathers and Sons.*
> The peasant's comment on the Nihilist, Bazarov.

"The peasants have seen in us only strangers. We have avoided them with contempt. A terrifying abyss separated us from them."

> The cholera doctor, beaten to death by villagers, in Veresaev's story.

ONE OF DOSTOIEVSKY'S minor figures says that if he were a writer of romance he would take his characters from the Russian hereditary nobility: for there alone is the really perfected product, something that rests the eye and gives peace: *not the perpetual demolition and the flying chips and the scraps and fragments from which for the past two hundred years it has been impossible to escape.* He expresses the dislike of normal good-humoured inertia for those who cannot leave things alone but are for ever pulling down and reconstructing the comfortable home. Peter the Great began the process in Russia with his opening of windows upon Europe. Catherine extended the premises, and put into the heads of her subjects the idea of extensive social change. Alexander I planned, if he did not execute. By this time every traveller and reader was disturbing the minds of the peaceful residents. Even the Slavophils had antiquarian plans of their own for altering the layout and superstructure in accordance with ancient models.

The English and French do not ask themselves the place of their country in the world. They are happily convinced (or were till very recently) that it is at the summit. They do not question fundamentals. They accept them. It was otherwise in Russia, at least among the intellectuals.

1813–1825. It was contrast which set these restless minds to work: contrast between the promises and the performance of rulers: contrast between conditions in Russia and the West. A victorious war took the Russian armies into Poland and Germany and France. They saw constitutions established or reestablished by the help of their arms, and civilisation among the vanquished superior to their own: and came back to Russia to serfdom, barbarism, and schemes of reinforced repression. The once liberal Alexander was ordering the teachers of mathematics to start their lectures from the eternal triangle of the Holy Trinity, and setting up military colonies for the preservation of the virtues which accommodate themselves to autocracy. Some of the officers conspired to set up a constitution, but did nothing to prepare for popular support of the movement. One of them, Colonel Pestel, was a Socialist in advance of Socialism, who sought, as did the Revolutionaries of half a century later, to attain social reform by political means: and all the leaders, though not in agreement in all their aims, desired the abolition of serfdom and the endowment with land of the emancipated serf. Nicolas I, the "pewtery-eyed", neither so brave nor so unfeeling, perhaps, as he has sometimes been portrayed, crushed the ill-planned insurrection without serious difficulty, but not without some days of anxiety, and was confirmed by the experience in a reactionary determination. That did not prevent him from doing more for the peasants than his liberal brother had done, or from earning from the anarchist Bakunin—no friend to autocrats—the commendation of being more of a man than "that mad calf Alexander", who preceded him.

Neither did he tell the children pretty stories, as the poet Pushkin, in a comparison between Russia and a child put to bed by his mother on Christmas eve, says that Alexander I did. His thirty years of rule were severely partiarchal, growing more repressive as Europe became more revolutionary, till the climax of repression was reached after the revolutions of 1848–49; and the general spirit of the reign is expressed in the sage counsel of a character in *Wit works Woe*, who advises Government to wait till the evil is ripe and then get all the books and burn them. Paradoxically enough, this period was perhaps the richest in the history of Russian literature. It is distinguished by the names of Pushkin, Lermontov, Gogol, and the first utterances of Leo Tolstoi: it sets the stage of the controversy of Slavophils and Westernisers, and it incubated, however unwillingly, that idealistic thought of the thirties and forties which continued to leaven ideas till the period of the twentieth-century revolutions.

1826. It was in the University of Moscow that the ferment began to work. The Government, instinctively aware of the perils of Philosophy, but unaware of the Prussian remedy of employing a philosopher with principles favourable to the autocratic state, abolished the chair of that study. Whereupon the Professor of Physics used his lectures to satisfy the young men's thirst for the forbidden subject, and Physics became unprecedentedly popular. The rest of the academic body was

more orthodox and less interesting, and a student, who afterwards became a famous Slavophil, tells us that "the sun of
truth enlightened us in a dull and chilly fashion". But there
was still much freedom in the University and, in the relations
of the students, a remarkable disregard of social position and
wealth. Discussion circles sprang up, to which the thinking
élite of all Moscow brought its contribution of thought: and
in these circles we first see grouped together the men of the
type to which the label of *Intelligentsia* afterwards attached
itself. They were of all classes, but their ideas and interests
were not those of a class. They were the Hamlets and the
Quixotes, the men of sensitive conscience and of injured pride,
men of compassion "without audacity and malice", agonising
over the problem of the justification of suffering, and convinced
of Russia's mission to all mankind; capable of a lofty heroism;
with heads full of cursed questions, and often in direct conflict
with art and aesthetics, because art and aesthetics were a dis-
traction from the task of social reform; planning revolution on
behalf of a people which was to reject them when revolution
was achieved. George Plekhanov, the first interpreter of
Marxism to Russia, says we must regard the Intelligentsia as an
intellectual proletariat, bound to earn its own living; weak in
foreign languages because of early poverty, and knowing foreign literature only at second hand, having a rough and ready
literary style and sometimes neglectful of grammar. From the
philological standpoint, their label should apply equally to
Khomiakov and Dostoievsky, even to Leo Tolstoi. Actually, the
religious thinkers are by usage excluded from the class. The
"Intelligents" are agnostic, materialist, positivist, anything but
formally religious: until in the first decade of the twentieth
century, religion finds itself for the first time associated with
liberalism, and with even more advanced forms of political
thought.

We have said that they are not religious; and yet the influence of religious tradition and habit upon their whole moral
and mental make-up is unmistakable. There is the sick conscience, the sense of sin and the passion for expiation, the

moral austerity, the readiness for martyrdom—all surviving the belief in God and the hope of immortality.

They had their faults: and one of these was a contempt for manual labour or at any rate a feeling that manual labour was not their task. Perhaps there was a physical softness: encouraged by sedentary occupations and too much of midnight conversation round the samovar. One landlord, who was convinced that agriculture would never prosper while the intelligents were work-shy and the workers were ignorant, has left us a picture of his attempt to turn intelligents into agricultural labourers. He was a sort of Cato: and the advertisement in which he invited the intelligents to join him on his farm deserves quotation. The workers "live in" with the employer and this is what they are to expect:

> "Strict hours, strict discipline, labour on holidays when necessary, benches to sleep on, hut or shed for sleeping in, food at the common table, Cabbage soup, beetroot soup, porridge, rye bread, coarse groats, potatoes; bacon fat on holidays; hemp oil on fast days; *wages three roubles a month till he learns to work:* do his own washing; keep his own implements in condition; pay for damage to horses or tools. No smoking in barns or stables. Keep the police informed of his way of living when they ask for information (as they often did, being nervous of eccentric people who left their own jobs). No pupils taken: only workers. There is never beef in the summer: milk, generally in the form of curds, only in July. Fish on fast days, if there is any. Tea on holidays. Weigh all this; and, *if you feel enough strength of will in you for such a life,* we shall be glad to see you."

The passage regarding women "intelligent" workers is even more discouraging.

> "The women work in the cattle-yard, in the vegetable garden, and on women's field-work. They get up at sunrise for the milking. They are not advised to come before May 15th, *when it is warm and one can sleep anywhere.*"

Let us hasten to add that some of them did come. One young gentleman, who arrived with such shattered nerves that he wept when the midges bit him, went away at the end of his year with rosy cheeks.

But let there be no misapprehension. Weak people, who resolve to be strong, may become stronger than the strongest. The annals of the revolutionary Intelligentsia abound in records of an iron heroism. We see this heroism, in the making, in Chernyshevsky's picture of the "rigorist", Rakhmetev. He abstains from alcohol and from indulgence of the natural appetites, sleeps on a straw bed studded with nails, rations himself as to conversation (that sweet sin of Russia), studies deeply and travels widely. It is a new and non-Christian form of the religious hermit training his will for some great task— what we are not told. But this was written in 1863: and we can guess.

In the early thirties, the two most interesting of the Moscow circles represented two different intellectual tendencies, and at first looked askance at one another as "Germans" and "French" respectively. The "French" circle discussed history and the social sciences. The leading figure here was Alexander Herzen, destined at a later date to edge his way past the censor, and to influence, though not to conquer, Imperial and official opinion. The social sciences were dangerous ground, and Herzen and others were exiled in 1835. The "German", or philosophical, circle included many names afterwards of note: among them K. S. Aksakov, the Slavophil, Vissarion Belinsky, and Michael Bakunin, the anarchist, at this time known as a quixotic young army-officer with a turn for philosophy. Literature, particularly poetry and the drama, as well as philosophy and philosophy in its application to literary criticism, occupied this group of ardent seekers. Sometimes they met in the house of Peter Chaadaev, Nicolas I's "madman", who deserves a book to himself.

Vissarion Belinsky, brought up in poverty and unkindness, ill-looking, dyspeptic, awkward in person and manners, shy till the passion of talk enveloped him in its blaze, always in extremes, a fierce flame in a cellar gas-jet fed by uneven pressure, was the moral enthusiast of the philosophical circle. They named him Orlando Furioso and "the raging Vissarion". He had been expelled from the Gymnasium, and was soon to be expelled from the University too, for an invincible irregularity and one-sidedness of mental habit, and an unwillingness to humour academic dignity. From the start he was a worshipper of Peter the Great, and (if we may anticipate the name), was never anything but a Westerniser. He loved literature, and had a natural gift of ruthless logic, as well as a passionate devotion to truth as, from time to time, he saw it. He was no linguist, and no great reader even in his own language. The descriptions of him suggest the ideal journalist, raised to the nth power, catching thought on the wing, and compelling it to his purposes for the discussion of the moment. He got his philosophy by word of mouth, in the heat of conversation; for his literature he was largely indebted to the current journals, which were active in the translation of foreign masterpieces. The falcon-like pounce, which a school-inspector had noticed in him as a boy, gave what he lacked in industrious study. He differed from the older generation of literary critics in that he applied a philosophy to his criticism. He never wrote a book, after the tragedy which was his first boyish effort. His writings are to be sought in his correspondence and his reviews.

Belinsky's circle was sympathetic with Chaadaev's condemnation of backward Russia: but it had no politics: and his own inclination at that time was towards a conservative quietism deduced from first studies of Hegelian philosophy. He changed: and it is certain that, like his intellectual descendants, he was never a profound philosopher. Rather, he took from philosophy what harmonised with his moral instincts, and changed both opinions and the friends who preached them, when the ardent life within him burst the bonds in which abstractions had enmeshed it. The successive changes were preceded and accompanied by an internal struggle, whose bitterness testifies to the sincerity of his passion for truth. The change which has permanent interest for the study of Russian thought was consummated when he turned his back on Moscow and went to St. Petersburg to take up the editorship first of the *Sketches of the Fatherland*, and afterwards of *The Contemporary*, reviews. From the conservative who came near to holding (as did Hegel himself in his defence of the Prussian monarchy) that whatever is is right, or at all events that the actual is the reasonable, he becomes the reformer: from the champion of art for art's sake and of the self-regarding development of human personality, he becomes the protagonist of social usefulness in literature: a claim carried so far that he has been charged with an undue disregard for form. He becomes a complete humanist—an anthropologist as he himself called it, in the language of the day: curses his previous "reconciliation with odious reality" and declares that there has grown in him "a sort of fanatical love for freedom and the independence of human personality, possible only in a society based on truth and virtue". In a passage which anticipates Ivan Karamazov's famous challenge to the Almighty on behalf of innocently suffering humanity, he declares that if he could climb to the highest rung of self-perfection, he would call from that height upon his old idol Hegel to answer to him for all the victims of life and history. Otherwise he would throw himself down headlong from the ladder. He does not desire happiness, even gratuitously, unless he can be at peace for each and all of his brethren. It is difficult to believe that Dostoievsky had not this declaration in mind when he made his Ivan Karamazov respectfully decline his ticket to Paradise, unless he could be satisfied of juctice done to all his fellow-men. Here the religious and the irreligious thinkers meet, on a height above that attainable to ordinary mortals.

Nature could hardly have designed a more complete example of the Russian Intelligentsia, and it is easy to understand why Belinsky has been called the father of it. In him we have the westernising, the humanism (which he called anthropology), the idolisation of science, the attraction to the doctrines of Socialism, not always very clearly defined, the replacement of orthodox Christianity by a sort of idolatry of the popular masses, the sublimation of the monastic sense of sin into a spirit of repentance and expiation for past wrongs to this collective human deity, the tendency to philosophise without a

profound study of philosophy and to find in every philosophy
only material for the moral passion, the depreciation of mere
aesthetics, the utilitarian criterion applied to the work of writers
and artists, the ascetic surrender of personal joys, the exaltation of moral and political duty over the religious or cultural
development of the personality: all the qualities and ideas
which are characteristic of the Intelligentsia for the next six
decades.

The permanent interest of the change in Belinsky lies in its
close correspondence with the change then taking place in the
"westernising" portion of the Russian public. Belinsky found
himself the mouthpiece of a movement, and his journal became
the home of much that was best in a literature of increasing
significance. It may be an exaggeration to call him the founder
of Russian Realism, of those pictures of life which, for six
decades, were to hold the mirror up to nature, and to show the
true face of Russia to her sons. But he was the embodiment
of the demand and the encourager of the task. He and his
friends greeted with delight the first timid attempts of literature
to probe the sore of serfdom, and encouraged the new studies
of Russian economic and social life. From the first his falcon
eye detected genius in the early stories of Gogol, when the
high-brow critics of St. Petersburg were sneering at the new
writer as a vulgar *farceur*.

When Belinsky had passed completely out of the phase of
old Hegelian conservatism, he and his friends found themselves
naturally fused into a new circle which began to be called by
the name of the Westernisers, in contradistinction to the
Slavophils, and he plunged into the fray with that enthusiasm
for extremes which earned him his friendly epithet in the days
of the Moscow circle. But there was something of the Slavophil
in him too: for he was convinced that Russia was better qualified than western Europe for dealing with the social problem.

Herzen, less extreme, and indeed powerfully attracted by
certain aspects of the Slavophil doctrine, travelled between the
two camps, and tried to moderate the passions of this battle
of the books, persuading Belinsky to drop his violent talk of
"the nationality of birchbark sandals and peasant smocks".

But when the quarrel reached its crisis in 1844—characteristically enough it was a series of lectures on the history of the Middle Ages which topped the climax—even Herzen had to give up some of his friendships on the Slavophil side of the fence.

Those were days—even before the intensified repression which followed on the European revolutions of 1848—when poets and literary men lived a precarious life, under a system half bureaucratic, half paternal, which did not spare the rod. Society, which combined a large part of the wealth of the country with the whole of the ecclesiastical, official, and court influence, had a tremendous solidarity, and was able to take care of its friends and to avenge effectively all invasions of its dignity and authority.

Judged in the light of freer and more outspoken days, Belinsky, cautious of the censor and careful to avoid the expression of opinions on the practical issues of politics, seems the most innocent of journalists. But some of his Slavophil opponents had friends in high places, and it is evident that he ran risks. There is a story of the Governor of the Peter and Paul fortress, in which political prisoners were detained, meeting him on the Quay, and, pointing across the river to the fortress, saying, with a hospitable grin: "When are you coming to *us*? I have a nice warm cell ready for you."

Belinsky had not that special form of bigotry which is the result of the possession of a rival body of systematic doctrine. Rather, to borrow the words of Herzen about him and his friends, they opposed to the Slavophil idolatries of the past "a lively sympathy for all which agitated contemporary man, a love of freedom of thought and a hate of all that limited it". These were the contributions to the Russian mind of the men of the forties: largely destructive and tending towards that complete denial of authority which later on received the name of Nihilism. It was a true instinct which caused Nicolas, when Belinsky died, to prohibit all literary references to his memory. He supplied the solvent which began the process of eating away the foundations of the old order. He also laid a foundation-stone of his own in the encouragement of a realistic literature.

This literature prepared the way for social changes, by under-mining the moral position of the gentry, whose virtues would not bear a too lively description.

Alexander Herzen, the illegitimate son of a noble whose wealth he inherited, was one of those men "of no class in particular", to whom, along with the "conscience-stricken gen-tlemen" ashamed of their privileges, has been attributed the creation of nineteenth-century revolutionary ferment. It was he who introduced Socialism into Russian thought, and the cause of woman's emancipation made a particular appeal to him. From the Slavophils he took his admiration of the Russian village Mir and the Russian co-operative workers' fellowship, and his ideal of the Russian people, which assumed for him the form of the Plain Folk, distinct from the nation. His dislike of the modern formalised State must have come to him from the same source. He compared it to Chingiz Khan, plus the telegraph, and thought the military camp of the fighting Cos-sacks, the Zaporozhian Syech, the most suitable form of State for the Slavonic peoples. In particular he despised the political forms of western Europe, as an inheritance from a Roman religion of property and legalism, involving the swallowing up of personality by society, and he put aside the demand for constitutional reforms. As with the Slavophils, there was not a little of anarchism in his political, or anti-political, thought: and he expressed this clearly enough when he wrote that it was "time for man to challenge republic, legislation, representa-tion, and all the ideas regarding the citizen in his relation to the State".

His early discussions with Belinsky led him to German philosophy, where he soon discovered that "double-facedness" in Hegel, which made some of his disciples into conservatives and others into reformers. Out of all these elements, together with a culture wider than that of Belinsky or the Slavophils, he wove a system of his own which supplied the Populists of the seventies and the Social Revolutionaries of a later date with their staple ideas. It was that synthesis of Westernism and Slavophilism which went by the name of Populism with its idolisation of the Plain Folk, principally of the Peasant, and its

plans of agrarian socialism based upon the Mir, to which the
progress of rural capitalism pitilessly gave the lie. The attitude
to the Mir was Slavophil, with a difference: for the Slavophils
emphasised the ethical, the Populists the economic, aspect of
the Mir.

He conceived Russia as a federation of free communes into
which the Romanovs had introduced serfdom and a noblesse,
and, later, a bureaucracy, radically foreign to the people and
their institutions. All but Tsar, peasants, and clergy, are strange
and unassimilable elements. Liberalism is an exotic flower. All
that is necessary is for Russia to throw off serfdom, noblesse,
bureaucracy and the Byzantinised Church, and, basing herself
upon the Mir and the Workers' partnership, to achieve her free
and peaceful revolution. The West has a heavy task of construction before it: Russia has only to clear away mischievous
accretions upon her original structure. In the final words of his
History of Revolutionary Ideas, he appeals to the Slavophils
to join with the Westernisers in clearing these away. The task,
it will be observed, is one of destruction.

The reforms of Peter the Great are always a touchstone of
Russian opinion. Herzen, true to the broad outlook which
makes him a sharer equally in Slavophil and Westernising
ideals, sees two sides to these reforms. Peter broke away from
the Byzantine conception of the Tsar as a remote and mysterious figure, and made his people (and himself with them) a
nation of workers. He destroyed the prestige of the Byzantinised Church, which has never had any hold on the people,
except through their ignorance—so says Herzen—and at that
time threatened the creation of a State within the State. He let
in the light and forced the Boyars' ladies out of their oriental
seclusion. But he detached the nobility from the people, and
made two nations, the bearded and the beardless, serfs and
masters, and added a German bureaucracy to the structure of
the State. Since that time the history of Russia is the history of
Tsar and noblesse—with only parasites and officials between
the two. Only the Mir and the Workers' fellowship resisted
these changes. Otherwise the people disappeared from history
except for the brief moment of national upheaval at the Napo-

leonic invasion. The division, he continues, accounts for a profound *malaise* in Russian life. Europeanised Russia desires one thing: old Russia desires another. Hence the prevalence in literature of the "superfluous man", the hopelessness of the poet Lermontov, and the ineffectiveness of much of Russian character. The Decembrist revolt was unsupported because the nation knew nothing of what its self-appointed champions hoped to attain.

He goes on to the revival of the mind brought about by Belinsky's championship of the freedom of thought, and the outburst of wholesome laughter provoked by Gogol; but brings down the clouds again in 1848, when European reaction caused Nicolas to drop his project of emancipation and to substitute for it the regimentation of the Universities, a severer censorship and the closure of the frontiers against travel. This was written in 1853, and Herzen seeks to frighten Europe with a picture of a world dominated by an irresistible Russian empire absorbing the mediatised princes and the petty sovereigns.

1854 to 1856. Perhaps the bugbear really caused some alarm. If so, it was only one of a long series of miscalculations of the military power of Russia, based on the destruction of Napoleon's *Grande Armée*. Within two years, the scandals and the humiliation of the Crimean War had disclosed the feet of clay in the Imperial image. With all the mediaevalism of serfdom, and the choking of thought, the Tsar could not win his country's battles against the free and more industrialised West.

His successor relaxed the reins, and Russia's Troika, held too long and too tightly, broke into what looked for a time like a runaway gallop. There was a rush to the Universities, no longer restricted. Journalism came into its own, and, in close harmony with educated opinion, began to express itself with a new freedom. Beside the central question of serfdom and emancipation, every kind of project was debated by an eager public. We are told that a drama was written in defence of free trade, and a poem in defence of a method of taxation: and proposals (which the Bolsheviks have since carried out) were put forward for the elimination of unneeded letters from the Russian alphabet.

A picture of a St. Petersburg salon in Dostoievsky's novel *The Possessed* may be taken as depicting the excitement of these days. "They talked of the abolition of the censorship, and of phonetic spelling, of the substitution of the Latin characters for the Russian alphabet . . . of splitting Russia into nationalities united in a free federation: of the abolition of the army and navy, of the restoration of Poland as far as the Dnieper, of the peasant reforms and of the manifestoes, of the abolition of the hereditary principle and of the family, of children, of priests, of women's rights." When a strong-minded and enterprising lady, anxious to feel herself in the swim with all these men of the moment, proposes to found a magazine to give utterance to their thoughts, "charges of being a capitalist and an exploiter were showered upon her to her face", from which we gather that Socialism was fashionable, and that capitalists were out of favour in advanced society. From abroad Herzen was sending his magazine *The Bell* into Russia, and seeking to convert the Emperor himself and his leading officials to his own principles of reform. In rural areas there was a movement for temperance—not normally popular with the Russian peasantry. Nominal marriages, to secure the freedom of the girls from parental control without involving conjugal obligations, became common. Count Tolstoi, who had met Froebel on his European travels, was establishing his school at Yasnaya Polyana on the principle of freedom for the young. A writer famous in Russia was publishing his picture of an indolent and inefficient Russian gentleman, which has passed into the language of proverb; and Turgeniev was depicting in *Fathers and Sons* the gulf between the older and younger generations, the pathos, from the elders' standpoint, of the children's crusade, and the appearance of the new type of Nihilist.

1828 to 1889. N. S. Chernyshevsky shared with his comrade and pendant Dobroliubov—a pair of Radical Saints they have been called—the kingdom of criticism in this new epoch. The first-named was the son of an Archpriest, who had been brought up in an old-fashioned family, where the servants were serfs of good birth and good conduct, and he had been educated in an ecclesiastical seminary among comrades even poorer than himself. He joined the St. Petersburg University when the reputation of Belinsky was at its height. It was a typical training for a member of the old Intelligentsia, and he brought a typical moral fervour into his work. Within twelve years from his graduation he was the recognised head of the extreme party, with the conservative press denouncing him as a Nihilist and a supporter of the rebellious Poles; and a few months later he was in prison, whence he only emerged a broken man.

He was an original thinker of powerful calibre, not to be classified under a particular label. He was indeed a Westerniser, a follower of Belinsky, and an agnostic. But he was no Populist, for he did not idealise the Plain Folk, regarded the peasants as barbarians and expected little or nothing from the proletariat. In the friendliness of his attitude to the Slavonic peoples, he went in one respect beyond the Slavophils: for the Slavophils had no love for Roman Catholic Poland, and Chernyshevsky regarded the Polish influence on Russia as one of enlightenment, and was—if all tales be true—prepared to co-operate with the Poles when they revolted. Unlike Belinsky, whose harsh criticism of the Ukrainian poet Shevchenko, written in the uncompromising Great-Russian spirit, was a blot upon his reputation for literary acumen, he was sympathetic to the Ukrainians when they set up an organ to defend the national cause in the period of the relaxation of the censorship. On the other hand he opposed the Slavophil ideal of an asylum for all the Slavs under the wings of the Russian eagle. He valued the Mir for the sake of the spirit of association which it represented, but was not one of its unconditional devotees. The Slavophils supported the Galician Ruthenes in their struggle against the Poles. But Chernyshevsky saw that they were playing into the hands of the common enemy, and sought to bring all the Austrian Slavs together in combined opposition to Austria.

The temptation to classify thought in definite categories has led to the division of Socialist thinkers into the Utopian and the Scientific, the Scientific being those who hope only for that of which the course of historical development appears to guarantee the attainability. Marx is the leading example of the so-called Scientific type. Chernyshevsky is remarkable among the Russian Socialists for having in him something of the Scientific as well as of the Utopian element. Unlike Marx, he did not ask himself whether the objective environment guaranteed the attainment of the ideal, but only whether the ideal was good. Unlike Marx he believed, at least for a time, that fundamental changes in economic relations could be brought about without violent revolution by the demonstration of their utilitarian value, and he was prepared to co-operate with the Imperial power, and hoped that one of the old parties would make peace with Socialism. Unlike Marx, he had no thought of any effective initiative by the urban proletariat, or indeed of any section of the common people, and along with the other idealists, believed that the world was ruled by ideas and that the small circle of the "best" people would guide the mass. He compares history to a river, forcing its way to the sea, says that circumstances divert it, this way and that, and alter the speed of the flow, that these circumstances are accidental, and that the appearance of great personalities is one of them. If he had held that the circumstances are not accidental, but dependent on the economic milieu, he would have been anticipating Marx.

It is interesting to note the points upon which he does anticipate Marx, of whose works, except by hearsay, he can have known little before his imprisonment. Like Marx, he saw that a Socialist society could not be based merely upon a revised distribution of wealth but demanded the fuller development of the means of production which technical resources have placed at the disposal of man, and looked hopefully to the machine and the factory and all the devices of capitalism, when the Russian Socialists were still expecting Utopia from the wooden plough and the handiwork of little groups of co-operative workmen. This was perhaps the most important seminal idea which the Bolsheviks took from Marx, and it has before it a future of immense significance. Like Marx, again, he took a lively interest in the possibilities of politics, and thought in terms of the State when the Utopians were planning voluntary colonies, supported by private means and embracing only groups of enthusiastic individuals, and rejecting the political weapon as unsuited to their aims. Like Marx, he had no expectation of human altruism and defended Socialism as a product of economic necessity. In short, as the first Russian expositor of Marxism put it a generation later, he was a Socialist with a method: he was "travelling on the right road though he had not time to get there"; and the Marxians are nearer to him in spirit than are his own fancied followers.

For years Chernyshevsky was a skilled evader of the censorship, concealing a meaning, easily recognised by the adept, behind apologies and examples drawn from foreign history. Yet sometimes the *Contemporary Review,* in his hands and those of Dobroliubov surprised the reformers by its outspokenness. The novelist, Ivan Turgeniev, said to him, "You are a simple snake, but Dobroliubov is a cobra". Herzen, who had a pretty wit, dubbed the pair the *zhëlchniki,* the bilious ones, much as Thomas Carlyle called a French revolutionary "the sea-green incorruptible".

These men of the sixties spoke on the whole more plainly than the men of the forties had dared to speak, and there was one article of Chernyshevsky which might have awakened the most somnolent of censors. It shows how literary or learned criticism was used as the vehicle of political suggestion. Reviewing the work of an American economist, the writer suddenly passes to the slaying of Holofernes:

"The road of history is not the pavement of the Nevsky Prospect. It passes over fields of dust or mud, over marshes, over rubbish. He who fears dirty boots must not occupy himself with public activity. True, you may take another view of ethical obligation. Some, for instance, may hold that *Judith did not make herself unclean. . . ."* The italics are mine.

It reads like a call to tyrannicide, the first from a Russian publicist.

1861. Chernyshevsky had fought for a solution of the Emancipation problem which would give land as well as liberty to the serf, without pecuniary obligation. The article was published a month before the Emancipation Decree, when it was already evident that the peasants would be burdened for an indefinite term with large redemption payments. The cup of bitterness for the "bilious ones" was full. The publication of the decree was followed by disturbances among the students and the imposition of restrictions upon them. Chernyshevsky attacked, in a fierce polemic, the action of the Government as deliberately designed to impede education. Somewhat later he was using the subject of the abortive reforms, drafted under the imperial ægis in the two preceding reigns, to ridicule all calculations based upon the goodwill of Governments. Even if there had been no suspicion of his complicity in an abortive plot for a rising on the Volga, he could hardly have escaped the wrath of authority. Governments must either abdicate, or preserve their existence; and the lightning descended.

There is nothing surprising in the imprisonment of Chernyshevsky, or in the later suggestion of the police that he was responsible for the attempt on the life of the Emperor in 1866. What is surprising—it illustrates the unevenness of Russian administration and policy—is that he was able to publish, *from prison*, a work which affected behaviour and ideals for a whole decade. The ideas put forward in his novel, *What is to be Done?* are not original. They are all to be found in Owen, Fourier, George Sand, Godwin or John Stuart Mill. Florence Nightingale had recently given, in her own activities, an example of one side of them. The Rochdale Pioneers, and their successors in Co-operation, had been at work for nearly twenty years. Belinsky had been talking of some of these ideas in the forties, and Herzen's "Circle" had been deeply absorbed in others. Nor was there anything remarkable in the literary presentation, in regard to which the critics express themselves with coldness. But something in the book, aided perhaps by the personality of the author and his recent misfortune, caught and fixed popular attention. Henceforth all the original young men were emulating the husband who shot himself to make room for a friend in his wife's affections. All the advanced young couples were emulating the companionate marriage, in which each has his or her own sanctum, and each treats the other with all the respect of a stranger. All the girls were planning to earn their own living and to form Co-operative Producers' Associations, and the Swiss Medical Colleges were filled with Russian women studying medicine, "like Vera"—till the Government ordered them home; on moral grounds, of course.

The Fourierist features of the book show themselves in one of Vera's dreams, where we see the community of the "phalanstery" living in a palace of aluminum and glass (it is impossible to resist the suspicion that the Exhibition of 1851 and the Crystal Palace have something to do with this picture, for Chernyshevsky is a great Anglo-maniac), and Russia converted into a paradise of fertility, beauty and healthfulness, by the subjection of nature to the needs of man—a glimpse of Socialism as a systematic development of productive resources, which anticipates the Bolsheviks.

Lenin's widow tells us that the works of Chernyshevsky were among her husband's favourite books. He was very plainly a forerunner of the Bolsheviks, he was inspired by English Utilitarianism, and hardly, if at all, in the regular Populist succession.

Nihilism—not a new word when Turgeniev applied it to his famous hero Bazarov—was the natural revulsion, carried to the extreme, from the authoritarianism of Nicolas I. He had set up the brazen image of authority and called upon all the people to bow down to it. The Nihilists denied all authority—of the State, of Religion, of the Family, even of Science: for there were particular sciences, no doubt, but no Science in general. Pisarev, the successor of Chernyshevsky in the leadership of the Intelligentsia, called himself and his followers "thinking Realists" but he was quite willing to accept Bazarov as his prototype. Among the things denied was the existence of any valid canons of art (on the ground that everyone has his individual notion of beauty, and no science can reduce this variety to unity) and of any inspiration in poetry not accessible to the ordinary man; and education was condemned as an outrage upon personality.

These negative convictions did not prevent Pisarev from appreciating the poet who writes "with the blood of his heart and the juice of his nerves": a class in which he included Heine, Goethe and Shakespeare. But after being in prison in 1863 he attacked aesthetics in general: none but a philistine and aesthete can allow himself personal pleasure from art while the hungry and unclothed are with us. It is the frequently recurring strain in Russian thought which—long before the Bolsheviks—demands social value from art and condemns art for art's sake.

Pisarev denied the existence of any valid science of history, because it is inevitably a theoretical justification of the historian's personal convictions. This denial, by a singular irony, has earned for him the title of the Father of the Subjective method, of which he probably never dreamed. The Subjective method, practised by Mikhailovsky and the later Populists, was a frank acknowledgment that the only way of describing man as a social being was to give up the pretence of objective detachment, and to feel as a man feels, suffer with his pain and weep with his tears.

If there was some extravagance in Pisarev, it was carried very much further by his followers. They launched a campaign against verse, which all but drove Russian poetry from the bookstalls. They denied the distinction between good and evil, and, as is hinted in Dostoievsky's novel *The Possessed*, some of them were sexual perverts. The elders were naturally shocked: and, of course, employed the term "Nihilist" as a label for everything which they did not like, including young ladies with bobbed hair who lived in communal boarding houses and tried to earn their own living. Katkov—once a member of one of the "Circles" and thereafter a journalist of liberal sympathies—went completely over to the reactionaries. The Slavophils found themselves allied with the Government against their own aspirations to liberty and were drawn towards Byzantinism. One side talked of a Katkovshchina, the other side talked of a Pisarevshchina, as we might talk of a Garvindom, a Beaverbrookery, or a Kingsley Martinate; and, as Nicolas made the Nihilists, so the Nihilists made the reaction.

1863. The Government of Alexander II did not abandon its policy of reform: but a reactionary influence inevitably gained an ascendancy with the Polish Revolt and with subsequent attempts on the life of the Tsar. In its educational policy it adopted the device of substituting classical for scientific studies. The publication in 1859 of Darwin's *Origin of Species* was doubtless regarded as one of the causes of the movement against traditional authority. But it is strange that the Classics, which were a standard of revolution for the eighteenth-century French, should have become the criterion of the "well-intentioned" in nineteenth-century Russia. Presumably the professors had instructions to avoid the subjects of Harmodios and Aristogeiton and of the Ides of March.

A more active revolutionary than any of the thinkers hitherto mentioned was Michael Bakunin, one of the "conscience-stricken gentlemen", who inevitably spent all of his mature life in Siberia or out of Russia.

After a few months as an officer and a gentleman, he left the army and passed into the circle of philosophical undergraduates of the Moscow University. Belinsky described him as a profound, unique, lion-like nature, but said that his pretensions made friendship with him impossible. "He loves ideas, not people: desires to exercise his authority but does not love." And again: "Bakunim has many faults and sins. But there is something in him which outweighs his defects: the *perpetuum mobile* in his soul." Associated with Richard Wagner in the German revolutions of 1848–49, he was probably the original of the musician's Siegfried, destroyer of gods. But his earlier life seemed to prognosticate for him a very different future. Converted from early leanings towards French philosophy, he became an ardent, but not very penetrating, student of the Germans, particularly of Hegel, was convinced that all reality is reasonable, and thus acquired philosophically conservative opinions. In this intellectual attitude he continued for a whole decade, but the Young Hegelians of Berlin converted him about 1842. He had the reputation of an acute logician, seeing all life through a prism of abstractions, and able to deal with facts only after they had been fused into an idea. An element of abnormality was contributed to his personality by the fact, stated upon apparently good authority, that he was sexually impotent, in spite of his powerful physique. When we look at what came afterwards it is difficult to believe that we are not dealing with two different men whose biographies have been accidentally confused. From 1848 or thereabouts what we see in Bakunin is a Russian giant of enormous vitality, who roared and swore, and rushed about Europe, devising conspiracies against Russia, against Austria, against the German and Italian rulers, setting the police on their guard by sheer inability to restrain himself, telling everyone that the first thing in every outbreak is to set fire to the townhall, advising the Communards of Paris to destroy half the city. This second personality is suggestive of a huge will-o'-the-wisp, that not only blazes but buzzes. But the fire which he carried was a real fire, and no mere marsh vapour, and did its work on combustible hearts: and he established a school of insurrectionary action which at times had the upper hand of the school of propaganda, and contributed an important influence to the policies of Lenin. It was impossible to ignore such a portentous firework, and among his own associates he was the subject of many descriptive witticisms. A Frenchman, who had seen him at work in Paris, said he was a treasure on the first day of a revolution, but *"bon à fusiller"* on the second. Herzen, the most delightful of commentators, said he had a way of mistaking the second month of gestation for the ninth, and that he enjoyed all the preliminary bustle of the Polish revolt "as though he were getting ready a Christmas tree". The reactionaries called him the Old Man of the Mountain, after the famous head of the Assassin sect, who inspired terror and agitation from Cordova to Bactria. *"C'est un brave garçon,"* said Nicolas, "but we must keep him locked up." In essence the method which he advocated was for a small body of conspirators to seize and hold power till the mass of the people should be drawn into revolution, not into political revolution, for that is superfluous, but into the destruction of the State, and the substitution for it of a purely economic organisation. He was for making a clean sweep of existing institutions, as Siegfried destroys Wotan and Valhalla. He may have got his Anarchism from Weitling or Proudhon, if he did not get it from something very deep down in Russian nature or history, something which reveals itself as clearly in Count Tolstoi as in the most ardent of avowed revolutionaries. Something he took from the Slavophils, the hatred of the foreign brand—Byzantine, Tartar, German, or Holstein-Tartar as Herzen called it—upon the Russian State. His aspiration was for a free Slav federation—to include Poland, which the Slavophils excluded: even though it should involve war to the knife with all Germans, Magyars and Turks, after the Government of Russia herself had been transformed to an appropriate amorphism: a somewhat highly spiced dish for the foreign offices, not to mention the ministries of home affairs. Like more than one of the nineteenth-century revolutionaries, and like all of the early Slavophils, he hated the apparatus of government much more than he hated the personal autocrat. It is this which explains the abject confession which he made to Nicolas, and his subsequent declaration that he "would gladly follow Romanov, if Romanov would transform himself from Petersburg Emperor to National Tsar".

He made enormous mistakes and sometimes acknowledged them. He never understood, or did not understand in time, that the Polish malcontents had the mentality of the aristocrat and the landed proprietor, that they desired the extension of the Polish frontiers into Russian lands, and that co-operation with Russian revolutionaries was impossible to them. He ruined the circulation of Herzen's *Bell*, by his collaboration over the Polish question, when all sections of Russian opinion had turned against the Poles. Herzen told him frankly that he did not know Russia, either before his imprisonment or after his exile, and that he had lived for half a century in a world of ghosts and dreams. Herzen's brother editor begs him "to conquer the enthusiasm which carries you away, and even bring yourself to make a preparatory study" of the subject, before hurling his mighty bulk upon the Russia agrarian question. He knew how to answer back: for he vigorously criticised Herzen's attempt to conciliate Alexander II and the reactionaries around him: and he found a powerful phrase in which to crystallise his rebuke: "Cease to be Erasmus, and become Luther!" he said.

His official jailors in Siberia, who went to work to make him talk, must have smiled at his easy illusion that the Governor-

General there was a revolutionary at heart, and only awaited a suitable opportunity to bring about portentous changes, including the general war on behalf of the suffering Slavs. But his most colossal error—this was one that he himself discovered—was his surrender to Nechayev, a sort of Jesuit of the Revolution, to whom all means were lawful. At that time Bakunin was attracted by the power and vitality of the Society of Jesus, which he attributed to the complete effacement of the personal will of the individual and the perfection of the collective organisation, and he was ready to abdicate his own personality for the sake of such a force in the revolutionary field. Nechayev's plan—it gave to Dostoievsky the material for his account of the conspiratorial five in *The Possessed*—was to create a small circle bound to a rigid discipline by mutual fear and the possession of one another's secrets, to strengthen the hold upon each member by seductions and other measures of intrusion into private life, and to enforce loyalty and obedience by murder. In pursuance of this design, he actually arranged, in Russia, for the murder of a student who was suspected of the intention to turn informer, and carried off a mass of papers belonging to Bakunin and others, with the apparent aim of using them for purposes of blackmail. Bakunin, a generous, even noble, character, with something of the boy eternal in him, repented of his delusion, which incidentally gave to the political police an opportunity of claiming from foreign Governments the extradition of political offenders as common criminals.

One feature of permanent interest in Bakunin's career was his origination of the first conception of an institution which played a prominent part in later history. When at Naples in 1865–67, he founded a secret society called the International Brotherhood: divided into two categories, to be known respectively as the International Family and the National Families. The former was to be the directing organ, with members bound to strict discipline, and engaged both in open propaganda and in secret revolutionary preparations. How much of this design was realised at the time is doubtful: but, somewhat later, we find Bakunin establishing an International Social Democratic

Alliance, for the training of propagandists, apostles, and finally of organisers. He intended this organisation to be a secret one: and, in idea at all events, it seems to have contained the germ of the future Social Democratic, or Communist, Party, in the select and disciplined form conceived by Lenin.

This International Social Democratic Alliance, or certain of its branches, was designed by Bakunin to be incorporated in the International organisation of Karl Marx, without losing its own separate identity. In other words, he desired to enter the International at the head of his own following. Defeated in this design, he continued to pursue the aims of securing for himself a dominating position in the International, and of forcing upon it the adoption of his own principles of policy. The difference between these and the principles of Marx was radical. Bakunin regarded the State as something to be destroyed, and his strategy was of the conspiratorial and insurrectionary type. A small minority should destroy the power of the State, in full assurance that the people would give their support to the successful conspirators. He entirely despised the political weapon and regarded the political revolution, except in the sense of the destruction of the State, as superfluous. Still less did he conceive that change was dependent upon a gradual ripening of social conditions for it, and that the revolutionist's share in it was no more than the discovery and seizure of the appropriate opportunity. In these matters he was at the opposite pole from Marx. There was an additional cause of difference. For Bakunin, the German was the eternal oppressor of the Slav. Marx thought that the German school was a good one for the backward fragments of the scattered Slavonic race, who had neither a common language nor a civilisation comparable to the German. The controversy was fought out upon charges against Bakunin in connection with his association with Nechayev, of fraud and intimidation, and he was expelled from the International.

Russian Revolutionaries were divided at this time between allegiance to the conspiratorial and insurrectionist Bakunin and to Peter Lavrov, who by his *Historical Letters* published in 1868–69, sent the élite of Russian youth into the villages to teach and help and awaken the peasant masses of Russia. Lavrov's is a trumpet call, to the few who are endowed with the capacity for thought, to take their part in the realisation of an ideal of progress. Progress for him means two things: the physical, moral and intellectual development of the individual: and the realisation of truth and justice in social institutions: the two being so balanced one with the other as to be in perfect equilibrium, so that neither individualism nor socialism may prevail. Ideas rule the world, and the society which suppresses the few who have the faculty of criticism dooms itself to immobility. This leaven was to become operative in the Russia of the seventies by that process of "going to the people" by the intellectuals, which assumed the proportions of an Intelligentsia's Crusade in 1872. In order to give perfect freedom for the work of those who possess this faculty of critical thought, the rôle of the State as a coercive authority must be reduced to a minimum: so that we arrive at an ideal of political anarchy, regulated by a reciprocal exchange of contractual obligations, and guided by a natural aristocracy of the intellect. The many, who lack the gift of critical thought, must recognise that their subordination to the few that have it is the price of their progress: and upon the few rests the sacred duty of diminishing the cost, and increasing the progress attained in return for it, in the greatest degree possible. Nothing like the dictatorship of a gifted minority was contemplated. As Editor of the *Forward* in 1874, Lavrov argued that dictatorship spoils the best of men, that only a second revolution can tear power from a dictator, and that power belongs to the people and the people only.

Lavrov was from the beginning a revolutionist, but he stood for preparatory propaganda and the gradual ripening of ideas, as opposed to the abrupt methods of the insurrectionary school of Bakunin. For a time he was the editor of the magazine *People's Will*, which stood for terrorism. The distinction between the two schools is not between revolution and terrorism on the one hand, and peaceful persuasion on the other. Both were revolutionary, and both were terrorist, the propagandists directing their attention to a sort of punitive terrorism against oppressive and unpopular officials. Both stood for action by individuals, whether propagandist or insurrectionist, whether terrorist, educational or agitational, and did not contemplate mass action of the kind which involved prior organisation, such as the Bolsheviks practised later.

The contrast is between propaganda for ultimate revolution, on one side, and agitation for insurrection, whenever possible, on the other. The Lavrovist held that the revolution must come from the instruction of the plain folk by the intelligentsia: the Bakuninist, that the revolutionist is not to teach the people, who already know better than he, and have an instinctive appreciation of the methods of Socialism: he is to combine isolated protests into united action, and find occasions for action, and the people will join him spontaneously. The one expected delay in the revolution: the other thought it might come at any time with luck and courage.

Little though Russians at this time knew about Marx, the fact that the nickname for the Lavrovist party was "Marxists" shows that the Marxist teaching was at this time recognised to be propagandist and gradualist.

1871. In spite of the failure of the Commune in Paris, the fact that it had established, and maintained for several weeks, an actual Workers' Government, greatly encouraged the Insurrectionist section in Russia, and profoundly influenced the plans of the Revolutionaries both in December 1905 and in November 1917. As early as 1869, Breshkovskaya's Co-operative Bank and School had been closed by authority with the cynical observation: "We want no apostles here." This was a fair example of the attitude of the Russian police, and since many, if not all, of these intellectual missionaries had aims ultimately, if not immediately, subversive, we cannot affect surprise. The "going to the people" without the subversive accompaniment, has its parallel, in England at a somewhat later date, in the University Settlements in the poor quarters of cities; in the fashionable craze for slumming; in "Darkest England"; in Bernard Shaw as a vestryman; and in Charles Booth's study of London; followed by the work of the Webbs. What happened in Russia has been depicted in Turgeniev's

Virgin Soil. Rural Russia could make nothing of its missionaries, did not understand what either insurrectionists or propagandists were aiming at; probably connected them with Antichrist; and often delivered them to the police. But there is a figure in *Virgin Soil* of a new and significant type. This is the engineer-manager, Solòmin, who has succeeded in setting up a little school and a little hospital, very much against the wishes of the owner of the mill, and is occupied in organising the men. The literary critics depreciate Solòmin as a literary creation, and call him a wooden and unconvincing figure. The Maximalist Socialists despise him as a gradualist and a man of little deeds. He is a portent, for all that: a quiet man who really knows the workers, and knows the job, and is a forerunner of Bolshevik organisers.

Organisation, as distinct from either propaganda or insurrectionism, began with Zaslavsky, an intellectual, who in 1875 drew up a statute for the Southern Union of Workers. Stepan Khalturin, very like a Solòmin come to life, did similar work for the Northern Union in 1878–79. He was a joiner, who started chain-libraries and circulated books among the workers, deprecated terrorism and looked forward to a revolution to be brought about by a general strike—a plan which was realised in 1905. His comment upon the activities of the intellectuals is interesting. "As soon as we have started something going, bang!—the intellectuals have killed somebody, and the police are on us. Why don't they give us a chance to organise?"

The police broke up his union, he became a terrorist, and was executed in 1882. So much for propagandist gradualism!

In the meanwhile work of a very different kind was being done by a group of Populists who aimed at depicting the lives of the Plain Folk, for whose emancipation the revolutionaries were risking life and liberty. They centred in *Notes of the Fatherland,* one of those periodicals which have played so great a part in the expression of Russian thought. The "Letters from the Country" of Englehardt, former military officer and agricultural professor, which I have more than once had occasion to quote, were published first in *Notes of the Fatherland* which continued and developed further the ideas of Chernyshevsky's

Contemporary. The *Notes* were the instrument for the creation of that conception of the peasant which was the characteristic basis of Russian Populism. In the sixties, the editorial group of the *Notes* included the poet Nekrasov, Saltikov-Schedrin, author of *The Golovlev Family,* a picture of the life of poor provincial squires, and Mikhailovsky, the maker of the later Populist philosophy, which was inherited by the Social Revolutionaries of the twentieth century. Nekrasov had been writing poetry since 1838, when he received encouragement from the king of critics, Belinsky, and devoted himself in particular to poems of peasant life. *Who can be happy and free in Russia?* is an account of the wanderings of seven peasants, who put the question to all and sundry. The Censor's hand was heavy on the poem, but there is enough of it to give us a distressing picture. Most poignant of all is the answer of the old woman who after narrating the cruel sorrows by which she has been visited, says:—

> *"The keys to the welfare*
> *And freedom of women*
> *Have long been mislaid:*
> *God Himself has mislaid them.*
>
> *And which fish has swallowed*
> *Those treasures so priceless:*
> *In which sea it swims:*
> *God Himself has forgotten."*

In 1868 the literary group of the *Notes* was joined by Gleb Uspensky, who is typical of the realistic portrait-painters of the humbler Russian life, starting with the country town, the inn, and the posting station, and finally concentrating on the peasant. He was neither a Populist nor a Socialist, when he first contributed to the *Notes,* but he deliberately set himself to study the people in their daily lives, beginning on a friend's estate in the Samara province in 1877, passing on to a village in the neighbourhood of Novgorod the Great, and afterwards travelling extensively for thirteen years both in Russia and abroad.

He was no idoliser of the peasant as were so many of the Populists, but sought to describe him as he was: without any of that magic which transfigures Turgeniev's *Sketches of a Sportsman*, and rarely rising to the heights of great literature. The title of one of his own tales, *Figures come to Life*, suggests the function which he sought to fulfil. He filled out the jejune outline of the statistical tables, and showed what manner of man he was of whom the averages and the decimal points and the column of remarks recorded the skeleton. But he did it with the vision and the sympathy of one who might have been an artist if he had been content to be less of a publicist. His was one of those cases of sick conscience, so common in the Intelligentsia, and the period of his activities was one of disequilibrium in social ideas. Most of the older men and women had been brought up in the traditions of serfdom. The former serf-owners had not forgotten their privileges and had not yet learned to "drink beer and keep accounts" or to adjust themselves to the conditions of a less ample life. The former serfs were free, and yet not free, economically dependent on their former masters, or on the new men (Uspensky describes one who had kept a *maison tolérée* in St. Petersburg) whose money had won them the succession. The new cash-nexus and the heavy demands for redemption payments, for poll tax, and for other imposts, have set all the peasants plotting and planning to find money: flattering the holiday sportsman from town who has roubles to spend: admiring the clever rogue who has grown rich, no matter how. The old type of official, who had supposed that it was sufficient to be polite to his superiors and have his gaiters brightly polished, is disconcerted by the discovery that "honest earnings"—the charming euphemism of happier days—are no longer permissible: and still more by the further discovery that there are peasants who will not offer them. The times are out of joint. And Uspensky yearns for the restoration of a harmony even though it be a barbarous one.

The truth was that the equalitarian Mir was a Populist ideal, and that it was perishing before the eyes of this Populist investigator. The agricultural banks and the cottage industries, beloved of Uspensky and the Populists, could not stop the devouring progress of capitalism. Now and again we hear from him a cry of the heart: as when he has a sudden vision of his loved villages passing under the yoke of a German master. This vision came to him because he had realised the weaknesses of his people, or the compelling power of the life of agricultural toil, which determined the form of every institution and dictated every action. In a powerful simile, he describes them moving all together, like fish into the net: and he makes one of his characters say that they "live without will of their own, without thought of their own, live only in obedience to the will of their work: only do the tasks which the work lays upon them". In such a life the thought of man sleeps a deep sleep: and, in place of it, the objective logic of facts, and the conditions fixed upon him by nature and her economics work out their own way, whether to crush or support him. It is a life in which there is no room for the growth of human personality.

This sense of sacrifice to an inexorable fate was expressed in poetical form by his friend and colleague Nekrasov, when he wrote of the "eternal repetition of that cruel way of life, in which generations live and perish without trace, and leave no lesson to their sons".

There was, of course, another way of regarding the life of the farmer: and another peasant poet, Koltsov, puts a happy song into the mouth of his ploughman. But the "cursed questions" were not so insistent when Koltsov piped his bird-songs. It is the sense of contrast that makes the sadness, contrast between east and west, contrast between what might be and what is.

The idealist must always be in despair. He is debarred from optimism, as soon as he finds a gulf between his own ideas and those of others, by the belief that ideas rule the world. The Marxist finds the hope of a remedy in the knowledge that not ideas, but the relations of production, determine the course of events. He knows that there is at all events a possibility of putting things right. This is what a Marxist critic of Gleb Uspensky said: and the observation has the merit of suggesting one way in which the arrival of Marx changed the current of Russian thought: by putting optimism in the place of pessimism: even for those who cannot be content with existing realities. He taught that man can make his own history.

The sick conscience found a satisfaction in expiation, and the character who takes this sort of pleasure in suffering, is almost as much of a favourite with Uspensky as with Dostoievsky. One character is the brighter in soul, the more he is humiliated, and the worse he suffers from cold and hunger. Another, in the *Power of the Earth,* is happy after the beating which the magistrate orders for him. If Uspensky has these bonds of union with Dostoievsky, he has also bonds with Tolstoi. There is work which is good for a man and there is work which is bad. The work in the field, wringing subsistence straight from nature, is the good. The work of civilised life, and especially the work of the official, which is done merely to earn the means of living, is the bad. Here we are in company with the simplifiers and the natural anarchists, of whose thought Tolstoi gave us the supreme expression. And yet the peasant, as described in Uspensky's most elaborately drawn figure of Ivan Ermolaevich, is the very reverse of an anarchist. Rather he is the convinced conservative and individualist, taught by nature and by the agricultural life to obey and to command. Nature is to be obeyed, and obeyed under penalty of starvation and death. But to obey nature and do her work, Ivan must rule his family, and his animals, the human and the non-human agents of toil, with an absolute rule. When his daughter-in-law falls ill, he and his family treat her harshly. The needs of the farm are too urgent: and he can't spare a single hand from work. These things teach him to understand the Tsar, and to regard the revolutionaries as of Antichrist. He will not listen to Uspensky's well-meant efforts to persuade him that co-operative effort would cure the troubles of the peasantry. A good manager will never lend his horse to a stranger. As to putting a stop to the depredations of a one-armed horse-thief by combining with others to give him an honest job, "I should do better to break his other arm, so that he shouldn't steal." He is even inclined to leave the Mir, for "I once made a clearing, and, as soon as I had done it, they made a fresh distribution of the land". To every suggestion of changing anything he has one answer only: "We can't do without it." Religion is part of the necessary order: and Ivan teaches his son to pray in a jargon of half-remembered scraps from the creed and the liturgy. That we have in Ivan Ermolaevich at least one type of the actual Russian peasant, and perhaps the type most frequent in the successful farmer, we cannot doubt: and Uspensky thinks Ivan would hand him over to the police as an agitator if he were less kind-hearted than he is.

One of the colleagues of Gleb Uspensky on the *Notes of the Fatherland* was N. Mikhailovsky, a worker true to the type of Vissarion Belinsky: not a profound philosopher, not a writer of books, after his first essay *What is Progress?* and not a systematic finisher of anything, a journalist and a reviewer, whose thoughts lie scattered over many volumes. A Marxian critic warns us that a not too high opinion of the works of Mikhailovsky is the beginning of wisdom: and yet his influence was prolonged and profound.

In the first edition of *The Leviathan* of Thomas Hobbes of Malmesbury there is a picture of a crowned giant, with a sword in his right and a crozier in his left hand, standing above a landscape of towns, villages, castles, and churches. All that part of the body which is visible is made up of innumerable minute figures, the clergy, it seems, filling the place of the heart. Below are representations of diadem and mitre, cannon and spiritual lightnings, battle-field and council-chamber. In his introduction Hobbes tells us that the Commonwealth is but an "artificial Man", the Sovereignty an "Artificial Soul", the Magistrates "Artificial Joints": Reward and Punishment are the Nerves: and so on: the conception of society as an organism being completed by the statement that Concord is Health, Sedition is "Sicknesse and Civill War, Death". The Brahmans had the same idea when they located their own origin in the mouth of the Deity, and the other castes in less honourable parts of Him: and Menenius Agrippa used it to explain to the Roman Plebs why, for their own sakes, they, the arms and legs, must continue to serve the Patricians, the Belly of the Organic Commonwealth. It was no better than a picturesque metaphor, which Bluntschli reduced to an absurdity when he located in the navel of the organism —the point of severance of child from mother—the function of capital punishment in the State, and made that a reason for the maintenance of the institution.

Our own Herbert Spencer put the conception of society as an organism into terms of Darwinian evolution, when he argued that evolution consisted in differentiation in the social as well as in the natural sphere. This meant that social evolution was the increasing division of labour, alloting progressively discriminated functions to the individuals. Herbert Spencer's works were being translated into Russian towards the end of the sixties, and Mikhailovsky, then a young man of twenty-seven, fell with hostile ardour upon the theory. It was the apotheosis of the factory system, which sets one man eternally on the performance of a single operation for the making of a pin's head: and so—it is argued—destroys his integral humanity. If it does not go so far as this, it at all events tends to divide men into those who work with their muscles and those who work with their brains, and has in it the makings of an Indian caste-system. Mikhailovsky argued that, though the English working man is on a higher plane of civilisation than the Russian peasant, the Russian has a higher type of civilisation because it presents to him a wider range of activities. He saw that the Mir was decaying under the impact of a growing capitalism. But the Mir and the Workers' Fellowship were precious to him, as to all the Populists, as a refuge for the individuality of the common man, fleeing from the menace of an industrial revolution. He therefore advocates the maintenance of the Mir by the action of the Government.

He wanted to save the treasure of individuality from the predatory host that threatened it, by substituting simple for complex co-operation. But he got into difficulties, and had to shift his ground, when he came to define what he meant by these expressions. At first he evidently meant that the desirable form of co-operation was that in which all the workers engage together in the doing of a common task: as in the common cultivation of a particular crop. But someone naturally asked whether he proposed to sacrifice all the triumphs which industry has attained by specialisation: and he found it necessary to adopt a different definition. Simple co-operation became for him henceforth the co-operation of equals: complex co-operation the co-operation of unequals. The military camp of Zaporozhian Cossacks on the Dnieper—always a favourite example—was a case of simple co-operation, despite the differentiated functions of its members, because there was equality. He seems therefore, to the present writer, to have abandoned his objection to the excessive specialisation which condemns a man to the eternal performance of a single contribution to the making of a pin's head: and to have adopted in lieu of principle, excellent in itself but irrelevant to the original aim—the principle of a classless society: in which the Marxists would heartily concur with him.

He missed the way out of the difficulty, which was suggested by a less well-known Populist colleague, who saw that the production of a surplus, by giving leisure to the workman, would solve the problem. A man may still continue to work at the single process which contributes to the making of a pin's head: but if he needs to work at it only for a limited number of hours, the rest of the day is available for the development of personality along more varied lines. This is the solution of the industrial division of labour; to which the Bolshevik attempt to achieve an immensely increased production points the way.

Progress, for Mikhailovsky, meant not an improvement in an imaginary social organism attained by the sacrifice of the personalities of the individuals who make it up, but a tendency to proceed from the simpler to the more complex in the development of the individual. The struggle for individuality was, for him, a universal principle, beginning in the inorganic and gradually penetrating the organic world. "Every whole, blindly, elementally, in virtue of the immanent laws of its being, strives to subordinate to itself its parts, to convert them to service for the fuller perfection of its existence." The Darwinians are right that man is not the centre of the universe and that Nature has no aims, is not teleological, as the jargon goes. But man can make himself the centre. He can say: Nature is pitiless to me and knows no distinction between me and the sparrow so far as right goes. But I will be pitiless to her, and by my blood and sweat will subdue her, and compel her to serve me. I am not the aim of Nature nor has she any other aim. But I have aims and I will attain them. This is how Ivanov Razumnik, of the Maximalist "Scythian" school of socialists, paraphrased the meaning of Mikhailovsky. It is the conception of creative evolution: of the primacy of personality in a socialist society, because man fights the brute law of competition by means of co-operation.

Mikhailovsky, and his Populist followers, had at heart the interests of human personality. Work was not only necessary but was also that which completed and ennobled personality. Therefore the interests of personality meant, more concretely, the interests of labour: and, more concretely still, those of the Plain Folk, and in particular, but not exclusively, those of the peasant.

They did not think of the urban worker as something separate from the peasant, as the Marxists did: and the idea of the proletariat, propertyless by definition, as the leader of labour, would have been repellent to Mikhailovsky, who looked upon property, or rights analogous to those of property such as the peasant had, as necessary to the completion of personality. The hegemony which the Populists envisaged was that of the men of ideas, of the intelligentsia.

If Mikhailovsky seems to us to involve his thought unnecessarily in abstractions, to speak of simple and complex co-operation where we should speak of equality, of the development of personality where we should speak of freedom, let us remember that he was writing in Russia and that there was a Censor to be evaded: a Censor with a meritorious but not too penetrating staff, which might be deceived by a judicious publicist into missing the point of the lesson. Nothing is more remarkable in the history of the revolutionary thinkers than the vast amount of thought, dangerous to the existing order, which they succeeded in publishing: and nothing more strikingly illustrates the comparative efficiency of the present régime than the success with which subversive doctrines, as distinct from mere criticism of methods and details, are kept away from the public.

Unlike Herbert Spencer, Mikhailovsky, as an investigator of social conditions placed himself mentally in the position of the man whom he observed, suffered with his sorrows and wept with his tears, assumed or created an aim for man and society and passed moral judgments upon it; was subjectivist and teleological, as the learned say. He made no bones of it and called himself a subjectivist, denying that objective enquiry into such matters was fruitful or even possible. He recognised with the positivists, that only relative truth is accessible to man. He gets the elements of it through his five senses. If he had more than five, truth would present itself to him differently. The criterion of a scientific sociology must therefore be the same as the general criterion of truth, the ideas of a normal, integral all-round developed man, *totus, teres atque rotundus.* As this perfect rotundity is rare, as there is always a preconceived opinion, there is always a bias to the rolling of the ball. Tell me, he says, to what social union you belong, and I will tell you how you look upon things—a conclusion that is surprisingly near to the Marxian.

Mikhailovsky's popularity was at its height in the second half of the seventies, when revolutionism was at its apex. Even earlier he had been demanding the summoning of a constituent assembly, for he was one of the first to preach the combination of the political with the social struggle, an idea strange to the earlier Populists, but shared with the Marxists. In the *People's Will* magazine he appealed to the revolutionaries to support the demand for a constitution. "You fear the constitutional régime because it will bring with it the hated yoke of the bourgeoisie." (There was a fear that a constitution meant a middle-class domination as in England and

France.) "Look about you! That yoke already lies upon Russia. To the European bourgeoisie, autocracy was an obstacle: to our bourgeoisie, it is a support. By standing apart from the political struggle did you stay the growth of the bourgeoisie? No, you helped it on: because, the more autocratic the Police officer, the easier for the man of money to steal."

It has been convenient in this chapter to restrict our purview to the revolutionaries and their likes, but we must not forget the existence of a background of very different elements. The Rural Councils were busy, and they had been followed by bodies of a similar kind, but with a more restricted franchise, in the towns. The Government was remodeling the army on a theoretical basis of complete equality for all classes in the matter of military service. Leo Tolstoi, not yet "converted", was writing *Anna Karenina*. Dostoievsky was at work on *The Brothers Karamazov*, which was to contain the germs of a religious revival. Khiva had been stormed by Russian troops, and Britain and Russia were glaring at one another across a would-be scientific frontier. The Panslavonic enthusiasts had jealous eyes upon the Turk in the Balkan peninsula: Michael Katkov—high in favour with bureaucracy and nobility—was calling for a reversal of the engines of State. The reactionary novel, with the patriotic hero who fights the Poles and the Nihilists, was popular in the towns. A certain Evgeny Markov, of whom we know nothing else, was regretting the mistake of the Emancipation of the serfs, and remembering the good old times.

The prosecutions of 1874 had thinned the ranks of both the insurrectionist and the propagandist sections of the Populists, and in 1876 the surviving leaders united in a programme of "Land for the People", in an organisation which called itself *Land and Freedom*, after an earlier society of the same name in the sixties. This group seems to have included the northern Populists only: in the south the revolutionaries continued to wander, without plan or discipline, between Kiev, Kharkov and Odessa, till a skilful police officer used their disorganisation to effect captures which put an end to their activities, and incidentally taught the lesson of the necessity of discipline in a revolutionary party: which Lenin was to assimilate with notable consequences.

1877. In the meanwhile Russia was again at war, and at war in the Panslavist cause: and, as usual, war, or its result, was the occasion, for Russia, of intensified revolutionary ferment. Activity against the revolutionists increased, and thousands were put on their trial for political offences. The embarrassments of Government were increased by its diplomatic failure, and by the anger of its patriotic and orthodox supporters, who saw the fruit of Russian sacrifice enjoyed by Austria. The rejoicings which marked the acquittal of Vera Zasulich on the charge of shooting General Trepov, and her easy escape, show the half-convinced attitude of Russian Society in the struggle between Government and the revolutionaries. *The "Haves" were not sure of themselves and their rights*. A month after the Treaty of Berlin was signed, Stepnyak shot the Head of the Police in the capital, and Courts-Martial were set up to deal with attacks upon officials. The war was followed by a long crisis of unemployment, which sufficiently suggests the economic background of the years of revolutionary crisis.

Vera Figner, propagandist and revolutionist, has left us a record of the differences which now divided the revolutionists. The city members of *Land and Freedom* thought that those in the villages were doing nothing, because there was nothing to show. The Populists in the villages thought "that the city members were neglecting the real business of agrarian terror". One terrorist who had already attempted the life of the Tsar, is introduced as advocating his murder "as a means of producing greater activity in the movement". We shall clear away some misapprehension if we examine for a moment the different aims and methods of those whom we class together as terrorists. There were terrorists who stood for punitive or deterrent acts of terror against oppressive officials. This was what was meant by the Populists in the village when they talked of "agrarian terror". Entirely different aims were in the minds of those who demanded terroristic attacks on the Head of the State in order to secure political change.

1879. By this time almost all sections of revolutionaries were in agreement with Mikhailovsky that the aim must be a political constitution, as a preliminary and an instrument of social change. Even Tkachev, the successor of Bakunin in the conspiratorial and insurrectionary section, was convinced that it was necessary to seize and use the machinery of the State, not merely to destroy it. A new body, calling itself *The People's Will* was brought into existence to pursue the political aim. The dissentients, among them George Plekhanov, soon to stand forward as the champion of Marxist doctrines, formed a separate group called *Black Partition*. As usual, in times of distress or strain, the countryside was seething with wild rumours of a coming redistribution of land, of the coming of Antichrist, and of the Day of Judgment. *Black Partition* aimed at using the peasant's apocalyptic hopes to win his support for a social programme, and rejected the political weapon. It placed its trust in the workmen of the cities, was prepared to co-operate with the State, and founded groups for the study of Karl Marx. Zheliabov, the leader of *People's Will,* on the other hand, advocated the overthrow of Tsarism and the summoning of a constituent assembly. His programme included nationalisation of the land, but he deprecated present discussion of this or other economic questions, as likely to alienate the support of landlords and bourgeois liberals.

An inner ring of *People's Will* planned the murder of Alexander II, and achieved it on March 13th, 1881. The letter which was addressed to his successor demanded an amnesty for political crimes and a constitution in accordance with the findings of a free constituent assembly, and threatened "inevitable revolution" if these were not conceded. But the actual course of events was very different. The revolutionary parties were broken to pieces and revolution was reduced, as an able official boasted, "to a cottage industry". The heroism of the Terrorists, now killed or in exile, had behind it no popular resolve. Ivanov Razumnik, from the height of his Maximalism, calls the eighties the period of small deeds, and of political indifferentism erected into a principle, of a revolutionary intelligentsia which had decayed into renegades and *agents provocateurs*. Of this epoch, and its continuance into a later decade, Chekhov, with his pictures of aimlessness and futility, was the satirist. But it was as much an era of the birth of new forces as of the death or eclipse of old.

1902. Before leaving the subject of Populism, apparently stricken to death by the failure of the eighties, and the absence of any response from the Plain Folk to the sacrifices of its champions, we must note its remarkable revival in the Social Revolutionary party. The peasant disturbances in the opening years of the twentieth century gave renewed hope to those who had believed in the revolutionary appeal of the land for the people. Victor Chernov, afterwards one of the successive Ministers of Agriculture in the Provisional Government of 1917, took up the mantle of Mikhailovsky, and set himself to prove the essential identity of the interest of the peasant with those of the town proletarian and the solidarity of the whole working class. The idea was in essence identical with the "two-class party of workers and peasants" which reappears in the Oriental and Colonial policy of the Third Communist International, and is the subject of some of Trotsky's destructive analyses. Chernov's thesis was directed against the contention of a famous Austrian Marxist, that the peasant was a property owner and, as such, an unconditionally hostile element in a socialist revolution. The Bolshevik view was rather that the peasantry fell into two groups, one of which was proletarian while the other was virtually capitalist, "petty bourgeois", as the jargon runs.

Victor Chernov, who published a full statement of the Social Revolutionary position in his *Constructive Socialism*, after the Bolshevik Revolution, stood for a triple alliance of the workers, at the plough, at the factory bench, and at the writing desk. He wanted a *Green* international, and he fixed his hopes for agriculture on small independent working farmers, a union of labour and property, with a collective superstructure, in the form of agricultural co-operation, and on individual farming. Instead of the nationalisation of land, and the centralised machinery of administration which that involves, he wanted its *socialisation*. That is to say, he wanted the land to be inalienable, and the right to it to be based on labour, and to be equal for all. But the forms of management were to be as various as local sentiment might demand and the methods were to be those of democratic self-government in each locality, with the right to appeal to a central authority against the deprivation of equal right of enjoyment.

Such a policy could not but make a wide appeal to the peasantry at all events until it was actually put into force, and the Social Revolutionaries received a majority of the rural votes for the Constituent Assembly of 1918, and actually dictated the main lines of the first Communist Decree on the enjoyment of the land. The subsequent history of the party, known familiarly as the Eseri (S.R.'s) falls outside the scope of this study. It had not the definiteness of principle or the rigour of internal discipline which characterised the Communist Party: and the reasons of its failure are the explanation of Lenin's success.

Chapter 8

Some Religious and Anti-Rationalist Thought

"Le niveau de notre âme est trop bas sur la terre!
Il faut monter encore, il faut monter toujours." [1]

MADAME ACKERMANN.

I SHALL FAIL in my aim of providing a glimpse of the currents of thought in pre-revolutionary Russia, if I do not supplement my sketch of the pre-Marxian rationalists with some account of the religious and anti-rationalist thinkers, other than the Slavophils. Few of these are revolutionary in intention, in the sense of proposing the overturn of the Russian State—though Leo Tolstoi comes near to that in his advocacy of elimination by negation: but all, with perhaps one exception, are preparers of the soil of revolution and symptomatic of the coming harvest. More than one of them strike the note of religious expectation: that Man must surpass himself.

There were shocks in the early life and youth of Fyodor Dostoievsky sufficient to account for morbid lesions. One, of which we do not know the precise nature, affected him in childhood and produced a nervous disease which took the form of lethargic crises. When he was eighteen years old, his

---

[1] "The level of our soul lies so low upon the ground!
It must ascend again; it must ever be ascending."

Madame Ackermann

father was murdered, and the old disease turned to epilepsy. Having joined a circle which occupied itself with the reading of Fourier and other Socialist writers, he fell into the hands of the police, when the repression, following on the European revolutions of 1848–49, was most active. He and other young men were led out for execution. Perhaps there was never any intention of carrying out the death-sentences. Anyhow they were commuted on the execution ground. The revulsion of feeling drove one of the youths mad, and Dostoievsky's mind probably received a lasting shock. Four years were spent by him in penal servitude in Siberia, followed by service in a disciplinary battalion, and it was not till 1859 that he was allowed to return to Russia. The experiences of the ten terrible years bore fruit in his story *The House of the Dead*.

Sigmund Freud has analysed his history and tells us more of the causes of the neurosis which affected him. A diabolical woman figures in more than one of his stories, and he thought ill of love, and ill of women in general, regarding them as a pit for men. He was married twice and had four children, of whom two survived him.

It is obvious that psycho-analysis must find in him a case of absorbing interest, for strange twists of soul manifest themselves in his work. Into one of these a political opponent, Mikhailovsky, "the great Doctor of the Populist Church", fixed his powerful intellectual teeth. In a long article entitled *A Cruel Talent* he showed that Dostoievsky not only loves suffering but takes a pleasure in inflicting it. It was easy to substantiate the charge by quotation. The man from the underworld who torments, quite causelessly torments, the girl Lise, tells her that one may intentionally torture a person out of love, and that love, for him, always meant to tyrannise. In fact he sometimes thinks that love consists in the right, freely given by the loved object, to tyrannise over it. He says he *always began love for hate,* and finished it as a piece of moral enslavement, and afterwards could not even imagine what one could do with the conquered object.

And then follows the startling reflection: what if these monstrous feelings are not monstrous at all, but only deep unknown secrets of the human soul, in which love and tyranny flourish side by side, or perhaps of the educated soul of the nineteenth century?

He discovered—or he rediscovered—the irrational element in man which philosophers—or at all events recent philosophers—had overlooked. It is as the great irrationalist rather than the anti-rationalist, that his title to originality is established. His Shatov, in *The Possessed*, says: "science and reason have from the beginnings of time played a secondary or subordinate part. Nations are built up and moved by another force which sways and dominates them. It is the force of the persistent assertion of one's own existence, and a denial of death. It is the spirit of life, as the Scriptures call it, 'the river of living water', the drying up of which is threatened in the Apocalypse."

He found in mankind a love of the horrible and outrageous. In his story of *The Brothers Karamazov*, a drama of parricide, intended by one, perhaps by two, brothers, and executed by a third, which might have been written to illustrate a central topic of the psycho-analysts, there is a conversation between the youngest Karamazov and a hysterical girl. She says: "Listen, your brother is being tried now for murdering his father: and *everyone loves his having killed your father*. . . . Everybody says it's awful, but secretly they simply love it. I for one love it." (There is something very like this in Synge's *Playboy of the Western World*.) After the young man has left her, the girl "unbolted the door, opened it a little, put her finger in the crack and slammed the door with all her might, pinching her finger", so that the blood oozed from under the nail.

Dostoievsky's interest in suffering seems sometimes a mere Sadist delight in it. Sometimes it seems a passionate desire for regeneration by means of it, a religious conception of expiation for sin. And he believes, and frequently says, that the Russian people (in that limited sense which excludes the gentry and the educated) loves and desires it. Salvation is conceived as something corporate rather than individual, and the sins of all are to be expiated by each. As Khomiakov jested, "even into paradise the peasants enter only by communes". It follows that the cleansing fires are to be sought and endured communally, each for all and all for each.

This means a profound and general conviction of sin, a sense of the Fall, as a theologian might put it. Perhaps the psycho-analysts would tell us that the age-old prevalence in Russia of the patriarchal family, and the savage tyranny over the women and children which this institution meant, had created a universal sense of guilt in all, who had desired the removal of the ever-present tyrant.

It is certain, at any rate, that the passion of self-chastisement was common, and that Dostoievsky looked deep into the soul of his countrymen when he revealed it. What else he saw in that daring analysis, an analysis which takes us far beyond and below the bounds of reason into some lower stratum of unconscious will, he himself could tell only, by fits and starts. There are in him all the contradictions and unevennesses of the prophet, now at the zenith of his power, now at the nadir of depression and banality. But he clearly saw, or believed he saw, something which was new to the knowledge of mankind, or had been forgotten by it, and that was the polarity of the human soul, seeking for opposite things, even yearning for opposites, correspondences the conjunction of which should produce new powers and new values. The story of the peasant who betted that he would shoot at the Eucharist—a believing peasant too—is an illustration of this fluctuation between extremes. Why has man a passion for destruction and for chaos—evidently Dostoievsky feels this in himself as well as in others—though he also has the wish to make a new path through the wilderness? There is a doubling, or a cleavage, of the spirit. Perhaps it is new, something which has appeared as the soul has grown more complex. Perhaps it is a struggle as of the butterfly within the chrysalis. Perhaps it is a prophecy of the changing of man into the God-man, the contention between the human and the divine which are in the end to be mutually complementary. That Dostoievsky himself saw something like this in the antinomy which he revealed, seems certain. This particular thought was not new, for the Greek theologians did not regard the natures of God and Man as fundamentally separate, though they used the word Θεος in a sense which is not adequately translated by our word God.

It has frequently been noticed that Dostoievsky's religion is more concerned with Man than with God. This present life on the material earth is, in fact, the great opportunity in which Man is working out the possibilities of a great destiny. The Elder Zosima, in *The Brothers Karamazov,* speaks of the agony of the man who has missed this opportunity, even after he has risen up to the Lord. "Once, in infinite existence, immeasurable in time and space, a spiritual creature was given, on his coming to earth, the power of saying: I am, and I love. Once, only once, there was given him a moment of active living love. And, that happy creature rejected the priceless gift." So that thereafter he must say to himself: "there is no more life for me and there will be no more time. Even though I would gladly give my life for others, it can never be: for that life is past which can be sacrificed for love, and now there is a gulf fixed between that life and this existence". Perhaps it was of the infinite preciousness of this earthly opportunity that Dostoievsky was thinking when he said that he belonged to a people capable of making a religion out of materialism.

In the Near East there is something holy about a madman, though whether the madness came from god or devil is not clearly settled. There is inspiration in his very folly. Dostoievsky, if he does not repeat this idea, at least raises the question whether disease is the necessary condition of the reception of the transcendent. For him, will must have the primacy over reason, and, it seems, the weakening of reason sets the will free. This is why he detests utilitarianism and the conformity of action to calculated advantage, and all that he describes under the satirical name of the *Crystal Palace;* presumably Chernyshevsky's Fourierist picture of the life of the Phalansteries: and organised Socialism in general: even happiness, or at least the deliberate search for it. If man's will could be completely subjected to his judgment, he would become a machine: whence the dionysiac side of Dostoievsky, the desire to break away from all restraints, the anarchical element which many have noted in him. In the ordinary sense of words he is the very reverse of a revolutionary: but there is in him revolution under the mask of reaction. As one of his successors said, he carried within him the principle of the great overturn, though he desired to fortify the structure. It is in his successors, in the school of thought which proceeded from his influence, that we find the extravagances into which the irrational tends to plunge, when the firm ground of reason is left behind.

Dostoievsky is no systematiser: perhaps he is not even a believer; but he passionately desires to believe. He even passionately loves orthodoxy; and says that no one can love or understand the Russian people who does not love orthodoxy. But his orthodoxy is not the orthodoxy of dogmas, but rather that "congregational" conception of the Slavophils (and of the Old Believers), the conception of mutual love and trust among brethren, in which, as Khomiakov taught, truth resides. For him, the atheist and the unorthodox were not those who disbelieved this or believed the other, but those who had torn themselves away from the native soil which nourished the orthodox Russian folk. "It's all like an ocean, I tell you," says the Elder Zosima, "and mutual love, and mutual acceptance of responsibility of each for all and all for each, will make the unity which is bliss." For him, as for so many—I had almost written for all—Russian thinkers, but under different terms and phrases, Russia was the "God-bearer" having a Messianic mission. To the reactionaries, the Messianism is one of reaction; to the revolutionaries it is one of revolution. In Dostoievsky's imagination the mission ceased to be one to the Slavs, it became one to all the world; but always a mission of Russia herself: of the Orthodox land and the Orthodox folk. The mission was to be attained by the conversion of the State into a Church, by a Theocracy gathering the peoples under Orthodox wings. In *The Idiot*, Prince Myshkin has a vision of the whole of humanity rising again, renewed by the Russian thought (the idea of Theocracy), and of the "astounded world, astounded and dismayed, because it expects of us nothing but the sword . . . because, judging us by ourselves, the other peoples cannot picture us free from barbarism."

In the famous speech in praise of Pushkin, which the Slavophils greeted as a historical event, Dostoievsky spoke of the Russian people as possessing a special gift for embodying in itself the idea of the unity of all humanity, and made the poet's depiction of this all-human quality one of the leading justifications of his panegyric. He even saw in the reforms of Peter the Great the unconscious aim of the attainment of the unity of mankind, and declared that "the task of coming generations in Russia will be, in the end perhaps, to utter the final word of the great universal harmony, of the final brotherly agreement of all peoples in Christ's evangelical word". We must take it as an echo from contemporary politics, that Tsargrad (Constantinople), in Russian hands, was to be the centre of this new all-human federation. The mood was not always the same, and Dostoievsky was quite capable of railing at foreign nations and at Jews, and of declaring the necessity of wars.

He was an intimate friend of Konstantin Pobiedonostsev, of whom we have already heard something in this study. His eyes were not closed to the social evils of Russia. He saw that "money-lenders and devourers of the Commune were rising up: the peasants rotting in drunkenness: and what cruelty to their wives and to their children! I've seen in the factories children of nine years old, frail, rickety, bent and already depraved." He scoffed at the "Liberal" freedom, which was so obviously for the rich man only, having power and means to satisfy his desires. But his remedies for these evils were not, after his early days in the Petrashevsky Circle, which took him to Siberia, the remedies of the Socialists. "Equality is to be found only in the spiritual dignity of man. If we were brothers, there would be fraternity; but without that, men will never agree about the division of wealth. . . . But God will save Russia. Salvation will come from the people, from their faith and their meekness." We note that, as with the Populists, it is the plain folk, the *Narod*, which is the saviour.

There were many phases and there were many moods: but in most of the phases, and in most of the moods, Dostoievsky was agonising, wrestling, like Jacob with the Angel, when he cried, "I will not let thee go unless thou bless me." Sin and expiation were the themes which occupied him most: and sin and expiation raised the elemental problem of liberty and destiny. There is a long conversation between Ivan and Aliosha Karamazov culminating in Ivan's apologue of the Grand Inquisitor, which has exercised the imagination of many Russian thinkers. I shall offer no apology for analysing it here, because its meaning is fundamental to a comprehension of Dostoievsky's thought. The two brothers talk together of the existence of God. Ivan says that he accepts God, simply, and without understanding anything beyond what a three-dimensional mind can grasp, accepts His wisdom and His purpose, believes in the underlying order and meaning of life, and believes that, in the end, something so precious will come to pass that it will comfort all resentments, atone for all crimes, and make it possible to forgive and justify all that has happened to men.

But *"in the final result, I don't accept this world of God's"*.

Ivan gives harrowing examples of cruelty to children and says the tears of the innocent child must be atoned for. What good can Hell do, since the children have already been tortured? And what becomes of the final harmony, if there is Hell? He wants to see justice, and present justice, here on earth, to see with his own eyes the hind lie down with the lion and the victim rise up and embrace his murderer. This justice is not done. Is there anywhere in the universe a being who has the right to forgive these crimes? Too high a price, he says, is asked for the ultimate harmony. "And so I hasten to give back my entrance ticket. . . . It is not God that I don't accept: only, *I must respectfully return Him the ticket.*"

Ivan is outraged that Man, and in particular the child, should be used as a means. Man is an end in himself, not a means, and the ultimate harmony is not a harmony if it is reached in this way.

Aliosha, the novice monk, replies to the question, who has

the right to forgive, by saying that Christ has the right, because He gave His innocent blood for all and for everything: —a somewhat unexpected stress on the Redemption. Ivan ignores this suggestion and proceeds to his apologue of the Grand Inquisitor: in which we are presumably to seek his answer to the question.

The story has a definite historical setting in Seville of the sixteenth century, on the day after an *auto-da-fé* on a hundred heretics. But before he tells the story, he quotes an old Russian poem, taken from the Greek, in which the Virgin Mary, having visited Hell, prays to God for mercy on all sinners. God asks how He can forgive the tormentors of His Son: but concedes a respite from punishment each year from Good Friday to Trinity day. The story is this.

Christ comes to Seville, is recognised by the people and raises a child from the dead. The Grand Inquisitor makes Him a prisoner, visits Him in His cell and tells Him He will be burned on the morrow. Freedom was His gift to man. Man has made all things over to the Pope, and He has no right to encroach by a new revelation on the freedom which He gave. Man has brought his freedom and laid it at the feet of the Church: and for the first time it has become possible to think of the happiness of man, which the fatal gift of freedom exercised by himself, and not through the Church, could never secure to him.

The Church has her secret. *She is on the side of the Tempter of Christ in the wilderness.* She has appropriated to herself the gift of *freedom,* and instead of it will give *happiness* to beings too weak and too base to use the original gift made to man.

"In what, in the Book, is called the Temptation", the Devil, wise and far-seeing, warned Christ that His gift of freedom would be insupportable for man: that man seeks three things, Mystery, Miracle and Authority: and in the three so-called Temptations he offered these three things to Christ: the Mystery of Bread, earthly bread, bread that feeds man and is transmutable in the Sacrament to something transcending earthly bread: the Miracle (that is, the invitation to Christ to cast Himself down), for Miracle is what man, in his most agonising spiritual struggles always prefers to the free verdict of his heart, making sham miracles out of sorcery and witchcraft rather than forgo them: and the Power over all the kingdoms of the earth, by which the universal State and the universal peace could have been secured to man. Christ rejected these things, and His gift of freedom was a boon only to the few, to the elect. All the rest, the vast majority of weak and base humanity, are left unredeemed.

But the Church has accepted the Tempter's gifts.

"*We have corrected thy work,* and founded it upon Mystery, Miracle and Authority. The task is only beginning. But we shall be Caesars, and we plan the universal happiness of man. Thou hast saved only the elect, but we work for all, to give peace to all. Freedom, free thought, and science will lead men into such straits and bring them face to face with such marvels and mysteries, that some will destroy themselves, others will destroy one another, while the rest will crawl to our feet. We shall give them the quiet humble happiness of weak creatures, such as they are by nature. We shall allow them even sin, and they will love us, like children, because we allow them to sin.

"And all will be happy: *except the hundred thousand who rule over them.*

"We are told that Thou wilt come again in victory, Thou wilt come with Thy chosen, the proud and strong, but we will say that they have saved only themselves, but we have saved all. I will stand up and point out to Thee the thousand millions of happy children who have known no sin. *And we who have taken their sins upon us for their happiness* will stand up before Thee and say: Judge us if Thou canst and darest."

If this is perverse, it is sublimely perverse, a self-sacrifice of deception beyond imagination. Aliosha breaks in with: Your inquisitor does not believe in God, that's his secret. (We might question this conclusion, and suggest that the Inquisitor does not believe in Man—in the potentialities of the nature of Man.) But Ivan justifies his Inquisitor, who could not shake off his incurable love of humanity, and had reached the

conviction that nothing except the advice of the Tempter—
so-called—could build up any tolerable life for the feeble,
unruly, incomplete, empirical creatures, created in jest (so
Ivan does not believe in Man either); and he continues his
apologue thus.

Christ made no answer, but continued to look gently in the
Inquisitor's face. The old man longed for Him to say something however bitter and terrible. But He suddenly approached
the old man and kissed him on the lips. The old man shud-
dered. His lips moved. He went to the door of the cell and
opened it and said to Him: "Go and come no more . . . come
not at all . . . never, never." The prisoner went away. The
kiss glowed in the heart of the old man: but he did not change
his conviction.

What did Dostoievsky mean by this apologue: and how
does it answer the question, out of which it arose: who has
the right to forgive?

Aliosha asks how Ivan can endure such a Hell in heart and
head, as this conviction that only a nobly inspired lie can
give an endurable life to man. Ivan says: "There is a strength
to endure everything . . . for everything is lawful" and, when
he is thirty, he will "dash the cup to the ground". He means
that he will plunge into debauchery and end with suicide. Is it
because he does not believe in God, or because he does not
believe in Man?

On this remedy of suicide—so inevitably an often recurring
thought to one for ever agonising over the problems of life
and eternity, of hope and despair—Dostoievsky has dwelt
elsewhere in the picture of Kirilov. There also the question of
free will and of destiny is raised. As Kirilov sees it, the will
of God and the will of Man are mutually exclusive. "If there
is no God, I am God. If God exists, His will is all and by
His will I am helpless. If not, *my* will is all, and I must
declare independence of will. I kill myself to show that I submit to no force outside myself, and to declare my new and
terrible freedom." And this self-destruction, as he sees it, is
not only self-liberation, but the liberation of humanity: a sort
of inverted redemption, a sacrifice for the sake of all. It is

sufficient for one man to kill himself, to assert his own will, to free all men from the subjection to another will, that of God. All are unhappy because they fear to declare their freedom of will. Hitherto man has shivered on the brink like a schoolboy and feared to declare it. Man, alone in the Universe without God, has full freedom because there is no limiting will. But he can only prove this to himself and his fellows by the act of self-destruction, thus acting as their saviour from doubt, and leaving them to their mortal godhead, in which all things are permitted to all. For it is but a mortal godhead after all. All things man can conquer. Only death he cannot conquer.

I repeat, Dostoievsky is not a systematiser. He is a dramatist, who makes his characters speak. They utter separate fragments of his own thought. He sees by fits and starts, and we catch his meaning only by glimpses. He does not always mean the same thing. But if I may venture to interpret, the answer to Ivan's question, as here conveyed, is something like the following.

There are those who would take away freedom to give happiness: but freedom, not happiness, was the gift to man, and freedom carries with it possibilities far transcending happiness. Freedom is the power to do good, or to do evil, and works itself out as much in the torture of innocent children as in the noblest deeds. There is no such thing as forgiveness. Consequence follows cause as night follows day. There is a God, but He is not all-powerful. He has limited His own power by giving freedom to man, and man is free to co-operate with God or to oppose Him.

The freedom of man's will limits the omnipotence of God. Either there is no God, or there is a God whose will is only one among a multitude of warring wills. It follows (unless we shelter ourselves behind the wings of mystery) that either man is God, or that man is needed *to help a weak God—perhaps a God in the making*. The conclusion that God—if there be a God—needs man in order to complete Himself—ennobles man, but lays upon him the burden of the Titan. We are breathing the air of the Prometheus of Aeschylus and Shelley.

Man is a being that must surpass himself. That is the final lesson of Dostoievsky. And despite the value which he attaches to suffering, it is an active, not a passive, mood. The young neophyte Aliosha, by some supposed to be a youthful portrait of Vladimir Soloviev, is bidden by his Elder to leave the monastery, and go out into the world and play his part there.

Nietzsche, who owned Dostoievsky for one of his masters, said: "Man is something that must be surpassed." There is a difference, of course: for Nietzsche meant that man must be superseded: but superseded by his own effort.

In his review of *A Cruel Talent*, Mikhailovsky warned his readers that a great artist and sublime thinker such as Dostoievsky must create a school of imitators who would carry his extravagances into extremes. We shall see that the expectation has been fulfilled. The Western world has passed through experiences and disciplines which have (externally, at all events, whatever the sleeping fires underneath) taken the primitive savagery out of man. In the Russian, who is not an obedient Westerniser, taking his cue from Hegel, or Mill or Comte, or Marx or the Liberal Reformers, there survives something strange and horrifying. We are back with Saturn and his bloody sacrifices, with Attys in the wild rout of the priests of Cybele, with the Bacchantes on Mount Taygetus or the Thracian hills, with the phallus-worshippers (or the phallus-haters, for the two run strangely close), with the forgotten heresies of the early Christian centuries, with a freedom which terrifies and yet allures, because it seems to open into the very abyss. With the writers on whom this barbarous afflatus has descended, Christianity herself drops her decent robes to play the Maenad or the Corybant, and God the Father and God the Son show themselves at variance. It is more than licence, it is a dionysiac ecstasy, exulting on the edge of madness. And it is no decadent eccentricity of absinthe-drinkers and drug-addicts. It has roots deep down in the darkness of popular superstition, where the frenzies of the primitive religious instinct breed monstrous births. Nor is it only among the ignorant that the wild spirit is found. Among us, says

Prince Myshkin, in Dostoievsky's *Idiot,* even highly educated people join the sect of flagellants.

1890. V. Rozanov, one of the successors of Dostoievsky, has been described by a penetrating Russian critic as the greatest writer of his generation (that is, in the purely literary sense). It is with the substance of his writings, not with their form, that we are here concerned. Among his earlier works was an essay on the interpretation of the legend of the Grand Inquisitor. He sees in it the divine in man, his feeling of justice and his consciousness of his own dignity, rising up to challenge God. It breathes love to man, along with contempt for him, boundless scepticism along with ardent faith, doubt of his tottering strength along with strong belief in its sufficiency for any great deed, the purpose to combine the greatest crime in history with an inexpressibly lofty conception of justice and holiness. But the sufferings of the children which set Ivan off upon his tirade against injustice in the order of the world, are only the necessary cleansing from original sin, communicated by the parents to the innocent embryo. Sin, redemption, and eternal judgment, are the three pillars of life, the three mysteries by faith in which man lives. Anyone who lays a finger on any of these three supporting columns is rewarded by hatred and persecution, for they are the source of man's knowledge of himself and the source of his strength.

So sin is necessary, and suffering is desirable: and the suffering by itself is not enough: there must be Redemption and Eternal Judgment too. The Inquisitor denies, not the truth of Christ's message to man, nor the value of the gift of freedom which He brought, but the correspondence between the message, and the gift and the nature of man, and the possibility of building man's life upon His commands. He therefore invents the great falsehood. The legend expresses the thirst of man, not for freedom, but for peace, and this thirst for peace, according to Rozanov, is Dostoievsky's own, since he has grown weary of the old brave determination to live by the gift of Liberty. The new gospel of peace without freedom is an admission that only by crime can the demand of man be satisfied. The Rome which built the lie is the deceiving scarlet woman of the Apocalypse, and her fall is at hand as is there prophesied. "Thus with violence shall that great city Babylon be thrown down and shall be found no more at all." And Rozanov ends on the note of the sins of the West. Only Eastern Orthodoxy, avoiding alike the universalism of the Roman, and the individualism of the Protestant Churches, sits with Mary at the Master's feet.

The apocalyptic tone, so truly echoing Russian popular imagination, is absent from the Slavophil writers, but is characteristic of Dostoievsky and of his successors in religious speculation. Antichrist, and the tremendous imagery of the Book of Revelations, are present realities to them, as they are to the masses of the Russian people whenever the strain of life is intensified by suffering and calamity. One of his editors calls Rozanov "scattered and tormented and ridiculous". But his contradictions are not like those of Dostoievsky, the partial and incomplete utterances of a thought too great to be fully expressed, and assuming different shapes in different moods. There is something more cynical about them than that. "It is surprising how I manage to accommodate myself to falsehood. It has never worried me and for this odd reason: what business is it of yours what precisely I think? I was careless because an inner voice told me that everything I said God wanted me to say." As a journalist on the staff of the conservative *Novoye Vremya*, he defended the excommunication of Tolstoi, and proved that the Jews committed ritual murder: while he was writing, under a different pseudonym, diametrically opposite articles directed against the Church and against dogmatic conceptions of Christianity. Artistic caprice no doubt there is. Sometimes he is a lover of Christianity and of Orthodoxy, always, we may be sure in the sense in which Dostoievsky spoke of it, as the congregation of the faithful, where love is. Sometimes he rails upon the New Testament and says that Christ has emasculated God. In *The Apocalypse of our Time* he attacked Christianity for its impotence to help man, for its abstractions, and for its ignorance of the Cosmos. He says the sun was lighted before

Christianity, and it will not be extinguished, were even Christianity to come to an end. With Christianity alone man cannot live. Speaking of the works of the Spirit as opposed to those of the Flesh, Christ showed that He and the Father were not one. The Father's teaching differs from the Son's, in His ceaseless solicitude for man. It has been suggested that Rozanov really loved Christ but rejected historical Christianity: and this may have been true of him—in some of his moods—as it was of Tolstoi. He combined psychological love for the Jews—in whom alone he says there is a true union with sex —with political anti-semitism, and he believed, or said he believed, that the Jew Beylis, whose trial was a *cause célèbre* of the years preceding the Great War, actually tortured and killed a Christian boy. In one place there is an outburst of admiration for Chernyshevsky, whose energy is compared with that of Peter the Great. But elsewhere there is a fierce attack upon him. Often there is in him the pettish impatience and inconsequence of a child. He dislikes the Westernisers: "but someone must make constitutions and boots and start pawnbrokers' shops and banks. Let *them* do it." Above all things he is the artist, sensitive to beauty. "I would restore the old Princes of Tver and Novgorod, with short purple mantles and little coronets: and down, below, the tramps and riff-raff of Maxim Gorky." Whether these are good or bad for the people, he is indifferent. He has no patience with the Russian yearning after "the good". As to morality, "I am not hostile to it. It simply never occurs to me. People with rules of conduct have always been disgusting to me". Here Oscar Wilde is recalled to us.

Yet pity, tenderness, and charity, appeal profoundly to him, and this at least is no mere mood. He is not merely the eccentric individualistic artist having no bond of union with the Russian people, but a phenomenon illustrating the Russian nature: and going far to explain the union of the typical Christian virtues with outbursts of Sadist fury and excess.

In certain of his moods, he is a priest of Cybele, straight out of the pages of Catullus. *The representation of the phallus drove him to ecstasy*. The series of books expounding his own religion show that it was naturalistic, in fact phallic. One of his books was suppressed for pornography. He was surprised: for, he said, he was only talking of Egyptian marriage, when they thought he was describing a brothel. If any one desires to see in what wild extravagances the frenzy of the dancing dervish may end, he is recommended to look at the appendices to *Solitaria* (which has been translated into English).

On the outbreak of the Great War Rozanov wrote a sort of panegyric of War in general, and of this war in particular, exulting in the spiritual return to the ideals of the Slavophils, and the symbolisation of a Panslavonic attitude in the renaming of Petrograd. He justifies the destruction of the German Embassy and the pulling down of the statues in it, even the "murdered man found in the attic". It was all so good-humoured and so thoroughly Russian in spirit: and a good moment for the people is worth a statute. *Russia in all crimes remembers God.* Her Church is Holy, when Roman and Protestant Churches are merely regular. There follow two chapters on the German monopolisation of well-paid jobs. They are merely industrious, where Russians are loyal. Could any intentional travesty of Slavophilism in decay have been more effective?

The War is called "The war with an aim", and there is a flamboyant picture of the Imperial Life Guards galloping straight at the shell-fire and so "giving the tone of the war" (and, if it really happened so, incidentally making the Germans chuckle).

The closing paragraphs recall Bismarck's gibe: "The Russians are a female race." Rozanov has a vision of a splendid army of giant guardsmen tramping along the pavements of the capital. It is the nursemaid gaping at the Guards in the Park. Strength, strength, strength! There is a paean of greeting to strength, to masculine strength. "My head was clear, my heart beat: as it is with women": and he recalls the Song of Songs: "Where is my beloved? I do not find him. I visited all the town and met him not." Surely, some strangely twisted form of eroticism is here.

1831 to 1891. The thinker to whom I propose next to introduce the reader is of a widely different type, *sui generis*, and illustrating the Russian mind by contrast rather than by likeness. This is Konstantin Leontiev, who spent much of his life in the Consulates of the Near East, and was in love with Turkey and Islam. This is probably what accounts for the impregnation of his Christianity with Mohammedan elements, and in particular for his clearer consciousness of God the Father than of God the Son. Up to 1871, when his religious conversion took place, he was a seeker of beauty: from 1871 he was a seeker of personal salvation, and greatly perturbed by the fear of perdition. Neither the search for beauty nor the search for personal salvation is a Russian characteristic. Russian sympathies have been generally democratic and popular, and the idea of aristocracy, as we know it in the West, has been absent from Russia. Leontiev loved and valued the aristocratic spirit. The absence of belief in the Plain Folk makes him almost unique in Russian literature. He detested equality and regarded the progress towards uniformity, in society as in the natural body, as a process of decay: but equality has always been a Russian aspiration. He detested freedom too, and demanded more discipline for the Russian people, if it is to continue to be the God-bearer: but the normal Russian impulse is almost certainly towards anarchy. Though he valued most the Byzantine principle in Church and State, he saw in Catholicism greater strength, as well as more beauty and a more powerful policy, than in Orthodoxy. His conception of the Church was hierarchical, and he rejected the congregational idea which was the central principle of the Slavophil theologians. He could not see the originality of Orthodoxy, and he thought nothing of the "morality and love which your underground prophet Dostoievsky makes so much of" in the Russian folk, which was the essential of Orthodoxy as Dostoievsky saw it. He was at one with Dostoievsky in despising the ideal of human happiness: but what he wanted to substitute for it was an ideal of power and discipline and beauty.

He hated the middling, townsman, type, that bourgeois whom artists have so often desired to *épater:* and his reasons for this hatred are often naïvely aesthetic. "Is it not horrible to think that Moses, the Greeks, the Romans, the Apostles, the Martyrs, the Knights, did all their glorious deeds, only that the French or German or Russian bourgeois, *in his hideously comic costume,* might enjoy his comfort, individually or collectively, on the ruins of all that past greatness?" He could have pardoned them their sandwiches and ginger beer in the ruins of the Coliseum, if they had been dressed in Arab costume. He loved "the Russia of the Tsar, of the Monks and the Priests, the Russia of red shirts and blue *sarafans"* (it did not matter that they covered disease and vermin and often hungry stomachs), "the Russia of the Kremlin and of the village roads, of benevolent despotism". He had the pictorial eye of the artist.

His principal work was *Byzantium and Slavdom,* published on the eve of the war with Turkey for the emancipation of the Balkan Slavs. Katkov, the nationalistic journalist of whom we have more than once had occasion to speak, had refused to publish it, doubtless because it included a vigorous and reasoned attack upon Panslavism. Leontiev objected altogether to the principle of nationality, which he associated with the principles of democracy and constitutionalism: and he devoted much space to showing that the Southern Slavs were infected with these diseases, and therefore not desirable associates for Autocratic Russia, *unless the combination should be one in which one incomparably great member should organically predominate:* a transparent euphemism for annexation. In Leontiev's view an exceptional respect for personality is a peculiarity of Western Christendom. It came into existence with the fall of Charlemagne's empire, and gradually spread down from class to class, by successive imitations, till it reached the lowest. Such is the origin of his bugbears, equality and democracy. The spirit of Byzantium had no place for an elevated conception of human personality, and Russia, which inherited it, has been saved from this weakness. The Mohammedan East has inherited the same spirit and the same immunity.

Disillusionment with earthly things, the rejection of the

hope of general well-doing, and of general well-being, of all that we associate with humanism, came from the same source and they are negations to be cherished. Instead of the things which they deny, there is the discipline of the Byzantine idea of the State resting upon Roman Caesarism and the Christian Church, and strengthened in Russia by the principle of hereditary right in the monarchy. Without the religious Autocracy, the family bond—already weak in Russia, according to Leontiev—would not be strong enough to maintain order in society. No rebellion could so injure Russia as a peaceful law-abiding democratic constitution. The combination of orthodox Christianity with Caesarism after the Byzantine model, besides defending the family, united all Russia in the Time of Troubles in the seventeenth century, and again in 1812; it was the cause of union between Great Russia and Little Russia, which otherwise had nothing in common; and—here is the characteristic touch of the Great-Russian patriot—determined the issue of the struggle with Poland. Its abandonment must mean decay into the corruptions of the Western world.

The combination of the ideals of asceticism and restraint with a high degree of aesthetic perception and appreciation is unexpected, but both appear to have survived together in Leontiev, even after his entry into a monastery, and his submission to the absolute spiritual and temporal guidance of an Elder. His final political doctrine, as we might expect, was one of extreme reaction, of nationalism, anti-atheism, anti-egalitarianism, the advocacy of severity in the State (to be combined with personal kindness in individuals) and of independence in the Church, contempt for mere morality, and the assertion of the aristocratic ideal. But this final political doctrine was found compatible with an interesting mood of defeatism. He thought, in his latter days, that Socialism would inevitably triumph. In a very remarkable passage he calls for the organisation of the relations of Labour and Capital, in one way or another, by the Monarchical power, "unrestrained by anything except its own conscience, sanctified from above by religion . . . otherwise Socialism will sooner or later take the upper hand, not in the healthy and harmless shape of a new and gradual State-organisation, but amid streams of blood and the numberless horrors of anarchy". In 1890, a year before his death, in a letter to a friend, he sets forth a plan of mystical and monarchical, reactionary, Socialism. "Sometimes I think that a Russian Tsar may put himself at the head of the Socialist movement and organise it, *as Constantine organised Christianity.*" In conquered Constantinople (it must be there, of course) there is to be a concentration of Orthodox government in "congregational" (the word of the Slavophils for the organisation of the Church) and patriarchal form *"coinciding with destructive workers' movements both in the west and with us"*.

A strange dream of the World Socialist Revolution, from the lips of an aristocratic reactionary, conceived as under the leadership of the Orthodox Autocrat, enthroned at Constantinople, with the blessing of the Orthodox Church! But it is not so strange that none could plan to carry it out. The "police socialism" of Zubatov and Father Gapon, a decade later, was an essay in this very direction. There is something in these anti-revolutionary writers which smells of vast impending change, reflects a general expectation in society of revolution to come. Leontiev, judged by all his earlier utterances, hated Socialism, but he is fascinated by a sense of its inevitability, and hopes, by putting Tsar and Church at its head, to preserve a little of the "organised multiformity" and aristocratism which he loves. It is not the familiar British spirit, astutely willing to meet particular grievances as they become urgent, while holding on with a crusty pluck to the central citadel whence the grievances proceed. We might take it to be merely the failure of the courage of an individual, afraid of Socialism for society, as he was afraid of eternal perdition for himself. But it does not stand alone among the evidences of readiness to compromise with social peril, which was one of the factors in the success of the Revolutions. They succeeded, because the possessing classes had ceased to believe in themselves.

1853–1900. A revival of religious idealism in the eighties found a double expression in Count Leo Tolstoi and in Vladimir Soloviev. The latter had aspirations to the establishment

of a Universal Church, and, like Peter Chaadaev, he wished
to see the Roman Church at the head of it. The national
Church, if it was not to become a mere department of the
State, must have a support outside the State and of the
Nation, and it was in Rome that this support was to be found.
In an apostrophe to the Apostle Peter, he says:

"Thou knowest that the Church has need of an earthly body
to manifest herself. Twice already thou hast given her a social
form: first in the Greco-Roman world, and then in the Ro-
mano-German world, thou hast set under her the empires of
Constantine and Charlemagne. She awaits her third and last
incarnation."

There must be a Universal Monarchy as well as a Universal
Church: for the Church, without a secular power distinct
from, but united with her, cannot establish upon earth Christian justice and peace. For the creation of the political power
which is to save and regenerate Europe, Russia is historically
destined.

Such were the basic theses of Soloviev's theory of Church
and State, as expressed in his *Russia and the Church*, which
was published in 1888, not in Russia, and not in the Russian
language, for the Ecclesiastical Censors could not have tolerated the ecclesiastical supremacy assigned to Rome, but at
Paris and in French. We are back among the conceptions of
Universal Dominion, spiritual and temporal, which laid the
foundations of the Holy Roman Empire. There is a mediaeval
flavour too in Soloviev's typification of the twofold government of Church and State by the two-fold nature of Christ
human and divine. One heretic, Nestorius, he says, separated
the human from the divine nature. Even so, the false liberalism separates State from Church and sets the twain asunder.
Another heresy, that of the Monophysites, made the human
nature of Christ disappear in the divine. Even so, some to-day
abandon the earthly world, the states and the empires, and
would absorb the human soul in contemplation of Divinity.
The true Orthodox must avoid both of these errors and maintain the bond which links the human state to the Church of
God, as the humanity of Christ was linked to the divine Word

in Him. The Church must neither dominate nor submit to domination by the secular power, and there can be no question of supremacy as between the two. The line of reasoning may be mediaeval, but the conclusion is clear.

The characteristically Russian conception of *sobornost*, "congregationalism", figures prominently in the thought of Soloviev, and it is a "congregationalism" of the State as well as of the Church. Christians are where Christian society, State as well as Church, is. Christianity is social. There must be a Church and an Empire to enshrine the politically and socially organised world. There is no Kingdom of Heaven for the individual. His salvation must be a corporate one along with his fellows. Christianity has failed, hitherto, for lack of the Church and the Empire, in which the aim is now to enshrine it. The pseudo-Christian, or semi-Christian, doctrine that the Kingdom of Christ, and the teaching of Christ, are for the individual has produced the false ideas of individualism which, in Soloviev's view, are responsible for all the anomalies of history, and, in particular, for the aberrations of the Revolutionists. Within this framework of Christian State and Church, Man is depicted as the Messiah, who is to save the world from chaos by uniting it to God, by incarnating in created forms the eternal Wisdom—that Σοϐία which has become the object of a special cult within the order of the Orthodox Church. The Greeks identified this Wisdom with the Word, the λόγος, which the Gospel according to St. John says was in the beginning. But the Russians, says Soloviev, in dedicating their most ancient temples at Kiev and elsewhere to the Holy Wisdom, have distinguished her clearly both from the Mother of God and from Jesus Christ. She is the Guardian Angel of the earth, future and definitive appearance of the Divinity, the Soul of the World, as he elsewhere calls her: the feminine principle, to which, in the post-redemption cosmic process, human reason mystically supplies the place of an active and creative principle. The East, while avoiding the temptation of materialism, pride, and aspiration to universal ecclesiastical dominion—typified by the Temptations on the Mount—into which the West has fallen, has been deficient in this active and creative principle. In the union of all humanity, the West will supply what the East has lacked.

This is a rarefied air which only the adept can breathe with freedom and security. It is dangerous to change the language of a theologian. But it seems plain that, in the thought of Soloviev, Man supplies something which is lacking to God. It is he, not God, who is the Messiah now: it is he, and not God, who completes the cosmic process in the realisation of the God-man, man made divine by the identification—lost at the Fall—of his will with that of the Divinity. The God-man has already once been realised in Christ—but not by way of an Atonement, which, for Soloviev, is "a casuistical solution of an impossible law-suit", and a purely juridical idea sprung from the legal notions of Rome. He is now to be realised in mankind. But the process is not completed in the individual: it takes place in society, made perfect by the fully Christian State and the fully Christian Church. The end is the creation of the Kingdom of God upon earth, in a new cosmos, in which (this is quoted from N. A. Berdyaev, who is the modern continuator of the thought of Khomiakov, Dostoievsky and Soloviev) "food shall be the Eucharist, union shall be marriage and the awful watery element shall be Baptism", all things shall be transformed into the sacraments of which they are the prototypes. It is to be a universal Salvation, a transfiguration of the Cosmos. *Man must surpass himself.*

We wonder no longer that each and all must do expiation for all and each: a notion widely present in all Russian thought, both learned and popular.

It is not necessary to share these visions in order to see how ennobling is the part which they assign to Man; with how much of Russian thought they are akin in their contemplation of a social, a corporate, salvation; how closely the issue of them corresponds with that belief in the Kingdom of Heaven upon earth, which was the object of so many Russian hopes; how they include all peoples in one transcendent unity. In a society with these infinite potentialities of ennoblement, as Soloviev sees them, nothing mean or base was to be tolerated. For the Orthodox Church, as hitherto conceived, serfdom and barbarous punishment were not contrary to the spirit of Christianity: for physical suffering does not interfere with the salvation of the soul. But a Christian society, conceived as a union of man with God, could not be indifferent to the sin of the oppressor. There is no room in it for distinctions of class, for true social good is union. Baptism is the sacrament of liberty. There must be no serfdom, and no slavery in any form, to contradict in the social sphere the liberty which Baptism has given in the religious. Confirmation gives to each Christian the sacred unction of the King. Communion crowns the other two, making all brothers and sons of God. There is a triple union to accomplish, that of the individual by his union with his complement woman, this is the sacrament of Marriage; symbolic, it seems, of the mystical union of human reason with the feminine hypostasis, the Divine Wisdom: that of social man by reuniting the individual with human society; the type of this reintegration is given in the ecclesiastical hierarchy by Ordination: and of universal man by restoring his union with the organic body of humanity in the sacrament of Extreme Unction.

The last words of *Russia and the Universal Church* are these: "The cycle of the sacraments, as well as the cycle of universal life, is closed by the resurrection of the flesh, by the integration of all humanity, by the definitive incarnation of Divine Wisdom"—that same Σοφία, which is the very stuff and substance of Divinity.

This is no mere Christian Nirvana. We shall see presently that Vladimir Soloviev, however high his head may be set, has his feet firmly on the solid earth. Though it is a transfigured earth. That he does contemplate the immortality of transfigured individual man in a transfigured universe is made plain by another work of his, *The Justification of the Good*. Discussing the spiritualisation of marriage, he says that the children in the present imperfect state are needed to do what the parents have failed to accomplish. But to accept as a permanent condition of the life of man, this succession of mortal generations is to accept the kingdom of death. It is evident that, in the cosmos changed as he expects it to be changed, among men who have raised themselves to participation in the Godhead, marriage as a means of carnal reproduction will cease to exist, because the immortality of individual man will have made the succession of mortal generations unnecessary. This (presumably) represents what Adam and Eve might have been but for the Fall. The Fall brought Death, and it brought Reproduction, inevitable companions unless life is to cease.

Neither in this, nor in anything else, must we look in Russia for the general conformity of realities to ideals. The ascetic attitude to marriage is nevertheless a part of the Russian outlook on the world, and we see its extreme results in the sect of Skoptsi, who take literally the Scriptural injunction to cut off the part which offends. It is interesting to compare Soloviev's solution of the problem with that of Leo Tolstoi. In the *Kreutzer Sonata,* as is well known, the extreme view is taken. The virgin state is the ideal. If it ends human life, as it must, that only means that God's purpose has triumphed and the object for which man was set on earth has been fulfilled. These statements are not limited by any reference to the needs of the imperfect state; but they can only be harmonised with the rest of Tolstoi's teaching by supposing this limitation to be understood. If this be a permissible assumption, Tolstoi may appear to hold a view identical with that of Soloviev. In reality there is a great gulf between the two. Soloviev believes in the personal immortality of the God-man in the transfigured universe. Tolstoi does not believe in personal immortality, and, for him, therefore, the death of marriage as a means of carnal reproduction is the death of man. He merges the individual in humanity—a humanity doomed to death—thus creating a sort of Russian Nirvana: whereas Soloviev foresees an eternity for men who have become gods, merged by organised State and Church into one great congregation of unity and love.

1828 to 1910. For the mystic, it would seem, the missing link in the chain of argument is supplied by the sense that God, or the interpretation of God, explains and satisfies his thought, that things cannot be otherwise, unless thought is to go hungry and vision be stultified. The premises being granted,

Soloviev's system is coherent and consistent with itself, and we must not quarrel with the opinion which sets him high in the ranks of Russian philosophers and theologians. It is otherwise with Count Leo Tolstoi. He was one of the great artists of all time, his vision penetrated to the deepest recesses of the human heart: and he was also a man of the world, a landlord who for many years cultivated a large part of his own estate as a home-farm, and *made it pay;* he was an enlightened schoolmaster on principles learned from Froebel himself: he served as an Arbitrator of the Peace in the distribution of land at the Emancipation of the serfs: and his account of his distribution of famine-relief in 1891–92 shows that he had all the instincts of a first-class administrator. If to all these things he had added the qualities of an original and coherent theologian and philosopher, the combination would have been without parallel in history. Without any desire to depreciate the quality of his thought, we must be prepared to look at it undazzled by the splendour of his literary reputation. If we do so we shall find, among other things, that, like his own Karataev in *War and Peace,* "he often contradicted what he had said before", though, it may be that "both statements were just".

Though he himself talks of having lived a vegetable life for fifteen years, he was never one of the peaceful souls who are untroubled by questionings. Rather he belonged to the type which Russians recognise under the name of "wanderer", and was for ever agitated by moral problems, for ever spiritually on the move: like his Pierre Bezukhov, who wandered from the life of the man about town to Freemasonry, and thence passed under the influence of a peasant ideal. His final departure from his home, in search of something that in his eighty-second year of life he still had not found, is typical of him.

Like all the clever young men of the forties who were not Slavophils or in training for the Episcopate, Tolstoi abandoned Christianity at an early stage: and he was not reconverted till he began to be obsessed, towards the end of his fifth decade, by the realisation of death. In the interval the great novels were written, and they show two influences which persist throughout his life. One, as we have seen elsewhere, was present in the air of Russia. It was the worship of the Plain Folk, and in particular of the Peasant. The other was a strain of Buddhistic or Hinduistic thought, which he derived through Schopenhauer, and which was only modified, not eliminated, by a third influence, that of the ethical teaching of Jesus Christ. The first two of these, not yet the third, merge together in a strange inter-marriage in the conception of the peasant Karataev in *War and Peace*. It is the *ego* and its affections which make sorrow: therefore, be thou merged in the common life of the people, and obey the promptings of the universal life. The little man, with a strong smell of sweat about him (for that, so to speak, is the authentic passport of the peasant in his sheepskin), tells how he was caught stealing wood and sent for a soldier: but all was for the best because brother Michael would have been taken if he had escaped. He is over fifty years old, with not a grey hair, and perfect teeth: he has only to lie down to go to sleep like a stone, and has only to shake himself to be ready at once for any work. He prays before sleeping, and includes in his prayer his horse's saint. He never thought of what he was saying, or of what he was going to say. He knew how to do everything: not particularly well but not badly either. He sang as the birds sing, out of necessity. He was full of peasant saws which seemed to have little meaning, but have a significance of profound wisdom when uttered appropriately. Attachments, friendships, love, he had none (here surely speaks the Buddha or the Gita) but he was on affectionate terms with any creature with whom he was thrown. Pierre felt, in spite of Karataev's affectionate tenderness to him, that he would not suffer a moment's grief in parting with him. He did not know, on beginning a sentence, how he was going to end it. When asked to repeat, he could not recall what he had said. Every word and every action of his was an expression of a force uncomprehended by him, which was his life. But his life, as he looked at it, *had no meaning as a separate life. It had meaning only as a part of a whole of which he was at all times conscious.* In short, Platon Karataev was a part of nature, not a separate personality, or at least not consciously a separate personality: and it is this negative quality of animal unconsciousness which appeals to Pierre Bezukhov, and to his creator.

It is anticipatory Nirvana of undistinguished mass life. But Karataev remained always to Pierre Bezukhov, and doubtless to the Tolstoi of that date, a personification of the spirit of simplicity and truth, and a lesson, it seems, of what life should be.

In *Anna Karenina,* the other great novel written before Tolstoi's conversion, we see all the educated characters drifting aimlessly, unable to find their place or their function, sometimes clashing one with another to their own destruction. Lévin himself, a reflection of Tolstoi, is happiest when he is cutting the hay alongside of the peasants, but sees that they do not understand or approve his departure from the gentry's proper functions. He makes a happy marriage, but is not fully at peace in it, and ends, on a note of qualified satisfaction, in a simple faith in God. "I shall continue to pray without being able to explain to myself why I pray: but my inner life has won liberty: it will no longer be at the mercy of events, and every minute of my existence will have an incontestable and profound significance, which it will be within my power to impress on every one of my actions. *Thus much of good"*: not the language of a seeker who is happy in having found his final goal. Only the plain folk, the peasants, possess, without being concerned to recognise, their place in life. There is a characteristic sentence in the story of Ivan the Fool, which shows the persistence in Tolstoi of the idolisation of manual labour. "There is only one settled custom in the kingdom of Ivan the Fool. Those who have horny hands sit at table, and those who do not must eat the scraps." And of course it is the Fool who is wise enough to establish the custom: for it is precisely in the Fool that wisdom lies. He is a worker without thinking about it: *without attachment,* as the *Gita* would say: and the natural path leads straight to the Bolshevik practice of giving the best dining-room and the best dinner to the shock-worker.

The Orthodox phase of Tolstoi's life was a brief one. He

quickly passed to the so-called ethical Christianity, which is not Christianity in the ordinary sense, because it identifies God with Reason (or with the Universe, for both expressions are used), denies the active intervention in human affairs of this Deity, rejects the divinity of Christ and the idea of Redemption or Atonement, and ranks itself with early Judaism in finding no place for personal immortality. As in Buddhism and in Hinduism, conduct brings its own result, good or evil, inexorably, and by a natural law. There is no original sin, and man's nature is essentially good. Christianity, as professed and practised, is regarded as a heresy far removed from the teaching of Jesus Christ. That teaching, taken from the teacher's recorded words, and sometimes with the interpreter's own corrections of text and translation, is the religion of Tolstoi, and the aim of it is the establishment of the Kingdom of God upon earth.

It is in no way surprising that the authorities of the Orthodox Church excommunicated him in 1901. The surprising thing is that they waited more than twenty years to do it, and that they allowed the publication of so many subversive books: of the *Confession* which rejected the authority of the State and Church, and denied personal immortality: of *What I Believe* and *The Kreutzer Sonata* and *The Kingdom of Heaven is within You* and *The Christian Doctrine* and *Resurrection*. All through these years Tolstoi had been preaching the doctrine of anarchy: of the destruction of both State and Church by a system which his Indian follower, Mahatma Gandhi, would describe as non-co-operation, but, to be directed, not only against a bad State and a bad Church, but against every kind of State and every kind of Church, as in their essence bad. His is the complete individualism which leaves everything to the conscience of each. His anarchism is unqualified by those beliefs in "orthodoxy" and "congregationalism" which modify the anarchism of Dostoievsky, or by the acceptance of the immemorial substratum of Hindu doctrine which modifies that of Mahatma Gandhi. Its quietism and non-violence may have seemed to take the danger out of it: and this may be why he was left for twenty years in nominal communion with the Church, and suffered to publish the most subversive of political doctrines.

And yet when the Revolution of November came, it was much closer in type to the negative conception of a Tolstoi than to the insurrectionist dreams of a Bakunin. True, it was an insurrection in Petrograd which carried the Bolsheviks to power. But the Revolution was something greater and widely different in kind from that insurrection. Society is like a building which stands by the compulsion of its own weight: so long as the natural thrusts continue to be met by the resistance which the architect has prepared against them. Something perishes or is withdrawn; and the eventual collapse becomes inevitable. States exist because men believe and obey: because the social machine divides up the social responsibility so that no one feels to what extent the acts and abstentions required of him are contrary to what his individual desire or conscience would prescribe. If and when each comes to say, as Tolstoi bids him say, "For me, I have no need of the State", and takes his own path accordingly: the belief and the obedience are gone, and the State is at an end. In its essence, the Revolution in Russia was precisely this. *The keystone came out of the arch.* The armies became a crowd of individuals on their way home; the peasants were dividing up the land of the lords.

When such things happen—and they have happened often, and we call them the fall of empires—there is a painful and sometimes infinitely prolonged process of rebuilding, during which a portion of the world reverts to barbarism, and mingles regression with restoration. I take it that this is what we are witnessing in the modern Union of Soviet Socialist Republics: so there is no ground for surprise that friends and enemies both find, in their contemplation of the rebuilding operations, ample material to justify their own sympathies and convictions.

I do not say that Leo Tolstoi made the collapse. Rather he bore witness, with all the power of the artist, to the existence, in the Russian State and in the Russian people, of those fissures which made the collapse imminent. Strongly anti-revolutionary, he was nevertheless a prophet of revolution.

The doctrine of non-resistance was held by him before, as well as after, his so-called conversion. Dostoievsky satirised it in 1877, in an imaginary conversation with Lévin, Tolstoi's representation of himself in *Anna Karenina*. He puts to Lévin the case of a child on the point of being killed by a Turk (these were the days of the Bulgarian atrocities and of the Bashi-Bazuks). Lévin is made to say: "How can I kill the Turk? It is better that he should gouge out the eyes of the child. But I'll be off to Kitty." (That is, to Kitty Sherbatskaya, Lévin's wife.)

A revolutionary view of Leo Tolstoi has been given by Boris Pilnyak, who has never shown servility to the men of the moment and was recently in trouble for his independent views. He has himself declared that he is a non-Bolshevik, but he likes to associate with Bolsheviks "because they have buoyancy and cheerfulness". He speaks of the "holy and idiotic philsophy of Tolstoi's Karataev" as something diametrically opposed to the aims of the Bolsheviks. They desire to regulate life by conscious rational purpose, while Karataev represents an elemental senseless automatism. Indeed, if we attempt to picture a nation of Karataevs, we find ourselves returning to Gleb Uspensky's simile of the shoal of fish rushing together into the net.

There are, however, no signs that the present Government of Russia desires to limit the circulation of *War and Peace*. On the contrary it tolerated a Tolstoyan school at Yasnaya Polyana, gave some measure of support to Tolstoi's daughter against the hostile zeal of local Communists, erected a monument to Tolstoi himself, and still pays a small pension to one of his relatives. Only the books which preach anarchy are banned; for, in spite of the Marxian doctrine of the withering away of the State, the Bolshevik State is a powerfully organised one: and greatly does it need its power and its organisation, if the task of rebuilding is to be performed.

Marxian doctrines were widely current in Russia throughout the greater part of Tolstoi's work on social and religious questions. Their influence upon him, particularly in the story of *Resurrection*, is evident. Nekhludov, the hero, after living the life of a man about town, repents, and follows to Siberia the woman whom he has seduced. In his visits to the prison he sees plainly that peasants are being punished for offences to which they have been forced by economic oppression and for hindering the officials and the rich generally from enjoying the property which they have taken from the people. He discusses the question of punishment with a lawyer: and, when the lawyer says it is just, he interjects: "As if justice were the aim of the law!" "What else?" asks the lawyer, and Nekhludov replies: "The upholding of class interests. The law in my opinion is only an instrument for upholding the existing order of things to the advantage of our class." It is the conception of the class-war, and of Government as the instrument of the dominant class. In 1905 he is appealing to the Emperor to make an end of private property in land.

Such a figure as that of Tolstoi could not but exercise an immense influence on such imitative minds as those of the Russian educated class. Anton Chekhov, whose work for half a dozen years had in it a note of Tolstoyan contempt of culture, and of the Tolstoyan aim of self-perfection, afterwards expressed his protest in a series of stories. He repudiates the Tolstoyan separation of freedom into internal and external, which injured human personality by making light of the external freedom: and laughs at the Tolstoyans who "nibbled at cucumbers and black bread (the peasant food) and thought they thereby became more perfect". "Fidgetiness," he says, "within and without, contempt for life and death, for intelligence, for true happiness, all this is a philosophy most suitable to the Russian lie-a-bed." There seems to have been some chaff current about the "fifth gospel, according to Leo Tolstoi", which prohibited butchers' meat and military service only. Lenin pours scorn on the "worn-out, hysterical, pitiable rags of Russian intellectuals, followers of Tolstoi, who beat their breasts and cry, 'I am a miserable sinner, but I am devoting myself to my moral perfection. I no longer eat meat, and feed on rice cutlets'. " The Maximalist, Ivanov Razumnik, is equally contemptuous of the gradualness and the ideal of little deeds which he associates with the disciples of Tolstoi.

It is seldom that a great man is responsible for all the aberrations of his imitators. Tolstoi was not a Tolstoyan: but for the doctrine of non-resistance to evil he was responsible. It spread far and wide, and, in Lenin's opinion, was one of the causes of the failure of the revolution of 1905: a view which, without committing ourselves to Marxian principles of economic determinism, we may take leave to doubt.

Among Tolstoi's literary descendants two may be regarded as something of a satire on the master. Leonid Andréev, denying the value of culture and intensely conscious of sex and death, was convinced of the holiness of the terrorist revolutionaries. Artsybashev, seeking to get closer to nature, advocated self-abandonment to the passions: so that his work was banned for obscenity by the Communist Government. But the true descendants of the great Realist are to be found in that group of post-revolution novelists who are carrying on in Russia his tradition of psychological realism; the influence of the artist outlives that of the philosopher.

Vladimir Soloviev, who had faced the terrors and splendours of a transfigured cosmos, had enough versatility to write a manual of practical social ethics: in which, without naming either Karl Marx or Leo Tolstoi, he discussed and criticised some of the doctrines of both, which were exercising the brains of the nineties. He takes, for instance, the subject of crime, which Tolstoi declined to punish, accepts the rejection of retribution and deterrence, but asserts the need of measures for prevention and for the amendment of criminals. Forcibly to prevent crime, he argues, is no worse than a surgical operation or the locking up of a lunatic. On the question of economic justice, he admits that Marx is partly right, that the struggle of classes is a cause both of national hostility and crime; but objects to Socialism, for its supposed stress upon material good as an end in itself: adding, with perfect fairness, that plutocracy is the other side of the same error. The solution, of course, is the organisation of the Christian Society. We are conscious that Soloviev has in mind the surplus-value theory of Karl Marx, when he argues that labour does not produce a thing but only a quality in that thing, and that capital does not produce the quality in the thing though it supplies the raw material, and that therefore neither is entitled to own the finished article, so that we are thrown back upon ideal grounds to explain property. His conclusion is favourable to the institution of property, including property in land: and (here he is at Tolstoi again) the idea of right in the economic field involves institutions which are the denial of anarchy. As to the relations of State and Church, the Church must have no power of compulsion, and the power of compulsion exercised by the State must not touch the domain of Religion, and must interfere as little as possible with the inner life of man.

All these precepts are for the imperfect state of humanity, as yet untransfigured by the mystery of universal salvation: but the mystic and the ascetic play their parts in the scheme of practical social ethics. The earth has her rights. She must not be treated as a lifeless instrument for exploitation. We are reminded of the Elder Zosima in *The Brothers Karamazov*. "Love to throw yourself on the earth and kiss it. Kiss the earth and love it with an increasing, consuming love." The exploitation of the earth cannot cease so long as there is exploitation of woman. And so we are brought by a strange and unexpected path to the need of ascetic restraint and the reasonable limitation of the population. It is as though some mediaeval saint had been reading the works of the Rev. Mr. Malthus.

Soloviev stood for that social Christianity which is the natural outcome of the doctrine of *sobornost*. The spirit is not a gift to the individual, but to the congregation. It is something undivided and indivisible. Man—not the individual man, but Man organised in the fully Christian Church and the fully Christian State—is the necessary complement and helper of a God who needs that complement and that help. N. Fyodorov, author of *The Philosophy of Common Work*, carried the same reasoning to a conclusion more immediately affecting the State. The gift of the spirit has been torn into fragments, and must be reunited in the common and active task of the reconstruction, economic and social, of society. This conception of religious duty brought the author so near to the Bolsheviks, that his work retained some of its popularity after the Revolution.

A movement which can be clearly traced to Dostoievsky and Soloviev is the religious-philosophical movement of the early part of the twentieth century. Kartashev, afterwards Minister of Cults in the Provisional Government, advocated the liberation of the Church from the tutelage of the State. He found an associate in D. S. Merezhkovsky who, after an early period of Hellenism, in which he sought for a synthesis of flesh and spirit, turned to a more definitely Christian inspiration. The two together founded the *Society of Religious Philosophy*, which brought together such laymen as Rozanov and Shestov (of whom there is something more to be said below) with cultivated churchmen. The aim in ecclesiastical policy was freedom for the Church, but some of the members at least were adepts of the mystical teachings of Soloviev, and looked for an imminent revelation of the feminine hypostasis, the Divine Wisdom, and the transfiguration of the cosmos. Projects for the revival of the Patriarchate, abolished by Peter the Great, were in the air, and the reactionary newspapers talked spitefully of a plot to create two Tsars and destroy the Orthodox Autocracy. Merezhkovsky and his wife Zinaida Hippius, a gifted poetess, dabbled in Revolution in 1905, and the Tsarist Government doubtless had reasons for looking with some suspicion on the *Religious Philosophical Society*. Indeed the idea of the more complete freedom of the spirit, unless allied with a distinction such as Leo Tolstoi drew, between the inner and the external freedom, was not a comfortable bedfellow for Autocracy. In it we see yet another of those influences which seemed to be making for revolution among non-revolutionaries.

1907. The Christian Revival (for it is not too strong an expression to use) extended into another and a very unexpected sphere. Hitherto not only Socialism, but even Liberalism, had been associated with the negation of the Christian metaphysics. Now religion passed into the ranks of the political reformers. A group of religious Liberals, including such distinguished names of former Marxists as Peter Struve and N. A. Berdyaev, published a volume formulating the new political philosophy; but it will be convenient to postpone an account of their views to the chapter in which we shall consider the coming of Marxism.

In the years immediately preceding the Great War, there were further indications of the activity of religious thought in the establishment of the Imaslaviye movement, for the worship of the Name of God, which, Berdyaev says, is characteristic of Orthodox Mysticism. The Holy Name, he tells us contains the divine energy which penetrates and changes the heart of man: and he assigns the cult to the influence of Platonism, which was preserved by the Eastern Patristic tradition, when St. Thomas Aquinas and the Scholastic philosophers turned to Aristotle, and affirmed that man and the world belonged exclusively to the natural order. In Platonism, as the Eastern Fathers conceived it, the earth is only the symbol of the heavenly and spiritual. The Holy Name, in the same way, is the symbol of something not otherwise to be grasped or formulated, the vehicle of the incommunicable. In the worship of the Name I cannot but recognise a kinship with the religious conceptions and practices of Asia, and catch a glimpse of something which Western thought has lost—or escaped: for I prefer to leave open the question whether it be loss or gain.

1844 to 1889. The gigantic figure of Nietzsche, who owned Dostoievsky for one of his masters, had for long loomed large upon the Russian imagination, but it was not the most characteristic ideas of the master which had the greatest influence. The idea of the Superman was not new. Madame Ackermann had already made Nature apostrophise her creature Man with the warning:

Tu n'es pas mon but, il faut que tu périsses.[2]

But it was the notion of surpassing man by something greater, which contributed to Soloviev's conception of the evolving God-man in a transfigured cosmos, and inspired a group of Russian poets and writers with a contempt of small deeds and gradualism, and a demand such as that of Ibsen's Brand, for

---

[2] "You are not my goal, you must die."

the heroic and the impossible. This group, calling itself the Scyths, combined the influences of Dostoievsky and Nietzsche. In Leo Shestov we see God depicted as transcending human standards of morality and reason, as "demanding always and only the impossible"; only to be achieved by a dionysiac escape from common sense, such as the monks of the Thebaid sought by asceticism, and by the second sight of unreason, such as comes just before death and came to Dostoievsky in the underworld of prison. The Master's order is more imperious than that of Reason, says Shestov. For, having destroyed Reason, you will only be a fool: but, having disobeyed the Master, you will lose your soul. It is precisely reason and common sense which block the vision, because that which is to be perceived is beyond reason and common sense. The natural vision must be confuted by the supernatural vision which is the gift of the Angel of Death.

This maximalism of the Scythian group, demanding always and only the impossible, was championed and expounded by Ivanov Razumnik, the despiser of smugness and respectable philistinism, and it passed into Russian poetry, where it grew into a revolutionary messianism, as entirely foreign to Nietzsche's outlook on the world as was the racial and the nationalistic maximalism of which he was the unintentional parent in Germany. What was new in Nietzsche, or what was newest in him, was that he was a revaluer of values, neither immoral nor amoral, but the sceptic of an old morality and the seeker of a new. Previous philosophy had left Christian ethics alone, while striking deadly blows at Christian metaphysics. But Nietzsche placed himself beyond good and evil, in order to ask whether that which has long been held to be good and evil is really good and evil. He saw the old morality as something fit for *slaves*, and insisted on the creation of a new one fit for *masters*. By an irony of circumstance, which is perhaps less rare than we suppose, these Russian Nietzscheans, transformed into revolutionary Messianists, found themselves championing the older morality which their master despised and rejected. For, if we tear from our minds the veil with which anticlericalism and the jargon of irreligious profession have obscured them, we shall see the Bolshevik revolutionaries in the true line of succession of the Christian moralists: seeking, in the language of the Canticle, to cast down the mighty from their seat and to exalt the humble and meek. The revolutionary ethics were those of which Nietzsche had sought to make an end: and when the poet Blok set the stamp of eternity upon his vision of "the twelve" with the figure of Christ marching at their head, he was denying him whom the Scyth Maximalists took to be their master.

We have Ivanov Razumnik's own account of the central idea of these Scythian revolutionaries. The introduction of Christianity to the world, nineteen hundred years ago, was a revolution, but a revolution which the old world captured and brought to naught. Christianity made a new man, and the new man was spiritually free. But his spiritual freedom was left uncompleted by physical, economic and social freedom, because the victory of the old world marred the work. A new revolution has now come to complete the old. The gospel of the new is the gospel of the old, that is of the liberation of man. But, this time, there is to be a complete liberation, physical, economic and social, as well as spiritual. It is the mission of the Scyths, of the newer nobler Russia which they represent, and indeed of all the Scyths in spirit, of whatever country they be, to break up the smug,[3] respectable, philistinism of Europe, and effect this apocalyptic transformation. As we might expect, these ideals found a natural home among the poets.

If we are to attempt to summarise the attitude of the Russian people to Religion, at the time of the Revolution, we must begin with the definite affirmation that the Church, as an organised institution, had lost all religious influence. She col-

---

[3] The word which I have tried to convey by smug, respectable and philistine is *Myeshchantsvo*, which might literally be translated by townsmanship or bourgeoisie. It seems to mean the opposite of the heroic spirit of Ibsen's Brand, a pursuit of comfort as an end in itself, lack of courage, smallness, meanness: the sort of thing which some artists have had in mind when they expressed a wish to *épater le bourgeois*. Gradualness and small deeds are part of the idea. Courage and activity are its negatives.

lapsed, as the State collapsed. She was to be rebuilt, on new foundations, before she could become again the God-bearer. Dostoievsky and Vladimir Soloviev were, perhaps, the beginners of the new construction. Because the Church, as such, made no appeal to man, the religious cry in the Civil War never roused the masses. There was nothing similar to the Pilgrimage of Grace in sixteenth-century England, or to the use made of the Clergy in the revolt of the Right in twentieth-century Spain. On the one side there was the desire to recover property and domination: on the other side the determination to cling to what had been won; and not even the pretence of a spiritual import illuminated the struggle on the side of the reactionaries.

But when we have said this, we are left with the deeper question of Religion apart from the Church. Merezhkovsky, describing a meeting of clerics and laymen in 1902, says: "The holy words of the Scripture in which we heard the voice of the seven thunders sounded to them like catechism-texts learned by heart." Little though we may be convinced by those who discover a profound religiousness in every peasant, the Russian people were more religious than their Church. Of the brotherhood of all the "orthodox" they had a profound sense, and the ethics of the Sermon on the Mount, however frequently ignored and flouted, were their ethics. It is questionable whether they gave any thought to personal immortality. In this respect, as in many others, Count Leo Tolstoi is a mirror of the Russian people. For the rest, the rites of the Church were a piece of necessary and salutary magic, which it was imprudent to omit.

Berdyaev's epigram was: The people has given up Christianity and the Intelligenstsia is coming back to it. There were certainly some grounds for the second half of this dictum. In the nineteenth century, outside of the Slavophils and the aspirants to ecclesiastical careers, Religion had no following among the youth of the Universities or in Russian Society. In the twentieth century, the tide was setting the other way, and the poets and the philosophers, even the politicians, had turned with it.

Chapter 9

The Coming of Marx

"However strange it may appear at first sight,
yet it is actually Marxism—at first critical rather
than orthodox Marxism—which has supplied us
with an idealist, and, later on, a religious, current of thought."

BERDYAEV, *Origins of Russian Communism.*

"There are parts of what it most concerns
you to know that I cannot describe to you: you
must come with me and see for yourselves. The
vision is *for him who will see it.*"

Plotinus: as quoted by DEAN INGE.

"Marx introduced into revolutionary theory
and practice the order, method, and authority,
which had hitherto been the prerogative of
Governments, and thereby laid the foundations
of the disciplined revolutionary state."

PROFESSOR E. H. CARR, *Michael Bakunin.*

"The living core of Marx's doctrine was that
he transformed a demand for economic justice
into a demand for a just organisation of society:
for a society so constituted that, in it, justice
would, in virtue of its very structure, be done.

PROFESSOR HERFORD, *Contemporary Review,*
May 1927.

283

THE HEBREW PROPHETS proclaimed a vision of history and of its inevitable continuation into the future. There was in Karl Marx something of the passion for justice which inspired their utterances. But he was more than a Prophet, because he initiated the world into his method. He claimed to be scientific where the Hebrew Prophets claimed to have a revelation, and to show how Man could carry the work of Prophecy further and play a part in its realisation.

He had a close friend and collaborator in Freidrich Engels, who made large contributions to the joint work. It is possible to separate the contributions of the two, but for my purposes I shall not attempt the separation, but shall continue to call the joint work by the name of Marx. Earlier Socialists had for the most part depicted the desirable, and had assumed that the idea of the desirable would win its way to acceptance and reform the world according to its own image. They had not asked for the help of history to tell them what conditions were in process of development and therefore actually capable of realisation. Marx called his own Socialism scientific, and the earlier Socialism utopian, because he made a new departure in this respect. *He plotted the curve of history,* as mathematicians say, and his prophecy was the continuation of the curve as plotted by him. Whether the curve was correctly or incorrectly plotted can only be decided by the event.

It is this plotting of the curve of history that is the essence of the Marxian method. And the method is more important than any of the results so far attained by it. For, without the method, prophecy degenerates into dogma, and, if right, is only right by accident or by inspiration. With the method, if it be sound, there is a vista of further results, ascertaining, perhaps controlling, the evolution of human society. They may even contradict Marx himself, as the Hegelian dialectic, in the hands of the young Hegelians, ultimately contradicted Hegel.

But there can be no plotting of the curve of history without the assumption that history follows laws of its own. At the back of the Marxian method lies this assumption. It adopts from the biological sciences the conception of evolution, and applies it to the life of human societies. History, in the sense of the activity of social man, enters the domain of law and becomes the subject of scientific investigation. Accidents, in the sense of events which have historic consequences but no historic cause (earthquakes, for instance) may deflect its course. Great personalities are accidents, but the field in which they operate has been prepared by history, and is not accidental. Just as we have to assume, for working purposes, that the order of nature continues unchanged, so it is assumed that the "accidents" will not suffice to disturb more than temporarily the working of the laws of history, and that the curve of human affairs can be plotted. But, as an Einstein arose to correct the work of a Newton, so some later thinker may teach us that the curve is to be plotted otherwise than Marx plotted it. Neither Marx nor Engels fancied that they had completed their own theory: any more than the theory of the origin of species had been completed by Darwin.

In plotting his curve, Marx went back to a very ancient theory of the universe. He accepted the doctrine that all things are permanently in flux, always in a state of becoming, that every form contains in itself the germ of its own destruction, but that the destruction is only the birth of a new form, which in turn must be destroyed and give place to a newer. This doctrine that all things are in flux he extended to the forms of social life. It is evident that we ought to change our metaphor and, instead of the plotting of a curve, speak rather of observing a stream of historical tendency, and of tracking it where the natural configuration of the country suggests that it must flow; but the nature of the soil offers possibilities of erosion and avulsion which may modify its course, and sudden alterations of level may quicken it into a destructive torrent.

Behind all this there was a philosophy, going down to the very roots of being and of thought: but Marx and Engels never formulated such a philosophy in separate form. Their followers and commentators have done it for them (as they have done much else): but there is no doubt of its general character. One group of philosophers puts the idea before the thing. The philosophies of the great Religions, at all events of all the Religions which postulate a Divine Creator of the Universe, inevitably put the idea before the thing. Another group puts the thing before the idea, existence before consciousness. Hegel, of whom Marx in his early days was a worshipper, and whom he never ceased to admire even when he had, in his own language, turned him upside down, conceived that there was a logical idea at the basis of life, and that this logical idea developed itself progressively and was the cause of all change, as a theologian might speak of a power within us, not ourselves, that makes for righteousness. The mature Marx rejected this pre-existent or co-existent idea, and substituted, as the cause of growth and change, social facts of an entirely different order, arising out of social life and social relations, and having no mystical character.

We are now prepared to consider what we mean by Dialectical Materialism. It owes a sad grudge to its godparents for a name wholly unintelligible to most of us, and of doubtful intelligibility to all. How doubtful is its intelligibility, is shown by a recent suggestion that *materialistic*, in its application to the interpretation of History, means objective, realist, positive, and not materialistic at all in the philosophical sense of the word. At any rate it does not mean that History is mechanistic, but rather that it is to be treated as a branch of Biology. The present writer takes the materialism of Marx to consist primarily in the fact that he belonged to the group of philosophers who put the thing before the thought, who do not believe in the mystical pre-existence of the idea, who believe that thought grew out of a particular form of motion in matter, that there was no Divine Creator who "thought" of the Universe before it came into existence. It is materialism, secondarily, because it explains social life in terms of economic relations. In the Marxian view, history is, in the final resort, always to be explained by the social relations arising out of material production: though the connection of these relations with the facts is frequently obscured by a layer of intermediate causation.

This is why Dialectical Materialism is materialistic. Why is it Dialetical? We must expel from our minds all association of the word with local variations of language: and get back to its original significance of the art of discussion: of conversation and dispute, of the interchange of arguments, where A. takes one view, B. takes another, and finally, if they are reasonable people not too wedded to their preconceived opinions, they agree on something which is not precisely what either of them said at the beginning of the discussion. The Dialectic may thus be conceived as consisting of a statement, and a contradictory statement, and of a third statement which reconciles or embodies the other two. Let us now remember that in the view of Marx, to which he succeeded as the heir of a long line going back to the Greek Heraclitus, nothing is static, all things are in flux, in process of becoming. In such conditions a simple Yes, or No, is not the answer to any question. Yes, is still true, while No is becoming true, and No is already passing into something that is neither Yes nor No. The Dialectic is the syllogism of a growing and a changing world, where truth also is a rushing river. He who argues dialectically must travel with that river, not stand on its bank and observe it as a stationary phenomenon.

Mr. H. G. Wells, little as he likes the Marxian doctrine, gives us precisely the appropriate metaphor in his autobiography, when he speaks of "running as hard as I can by the side of the marching facts, and pointing to them." We see him, in the light of this metaphor, as an enthusiastic collegian running by the side of his college boat, along the towpath of time, and pointing out from moment to moment how B. gains upon A., till C. comes from behind and successfully bumps B. At each moment his bulletin of information is correct, and at each moment it is contradicted and made untrue by the next phase of the eternal spectacle, fulfilling perhaps what the intelligent amateur has foreseen of the temporary issue. This is just what happens to the user of the dialectical method. There is indeed a singular correspondence between the method of Karl Marx and the method of Mr. H. G. Wells. The latter is trying to "disentangle the possible drift of life in general, and of human life in particular, from the confused stream of events," precisely the first part of the Marxian undertaking. He is also trying to do what our imaginary collegian can hardly be trying to do: that is to find "the means of controlling that drift," like Marx, and probably with an equal amount of *parti pris*. When he speaks of the "change from life regarded as a system of consequences to life regarded as a system of constructive effort," he comes even nearer to Marx. Both are prophets, both base their prophecies on an observed curve in human affairs, or an observed stream of tendency, they have the same suspicious outlook on the national state, the same aspiration to internationalism, they have the same determination to help the fulfilment of the prophecy by the addition of human effort to the factors which contribute to it. The method of Mr. Wells is the method of Marx—without the jargon, or shall we say, with the substitution of the jargon of natural science for that of German philosophy, with new inductions from new facts, and without the conception of class-struggle, which is no part of the method, but a particular induction from history, coloured and flavoured by the juices of an eupeptic in lieu of a dyspeptic nature.

As the conversation, which gave its name to the dialectic, proceeded by statement, counter-statement and agreement upon a third statement, which reconciled or included the other two, so the dialectic is conceived as proceeding, in this eternally changing universe, by thesis, antithesis and synthesis: each synthesis serving in turn for a new phase in a further similar process. Each successive phase in the process contains in itself a contradiction which must ultimately destroy it and cause it to give place to the new phase. It is the disruptive force of the eternally repeated contradiction which moves the world and makes its history. If I may be pardoned for adding yet another metaphor to those which I have already ventured to employ, the contradiction is the force which produces the explosion, and the series of explosions is the motive power which impels the machine. Thus if we consider, for the moment from the Marxian standpoint, that particular balance of economic forces known as the Capitalist system, we see that, as the result of an earlier dialectical process, it superseded the Feudal system, because it provided an immensely greater range of economic satisfactions to man. No sooner has it done so, than internal contradiction begins to make itself apparent. The Capitalist system, as Marx sees it, is increasingly unable to find markets for its own products at prices profitable to itself, is compelled to restrict production, and becomes a fetter upon the growth of wealth. It therefore perishes and gives place to a new synthesis, that of Socialism, which does not need to demand a separate profit in each portion of the field of production, so long as outgoings are balanced by incomings over the field taken as a whole.

Truth itself is not something absolute or static. It is a perpetually shifting goal, to be approached only by successive approximations, each of which requires to be verified by practice.

In the particular example taken, the new synthesis, of Socialism, is not an automatic product of self-determining forces, independent of the will and action of man. There must be a concurrent activity of thought, feeling, and will, and Man must, so to speak, fling himself into the balance, in order to determine the result. The Capitalists and their supporters may prefer a smaller output of wealth for society as a whole, in consideration of retaining a larger share of it, and a dominating position for themselves. They may make a fight for it, with the help of the tremendous machinery of modern warfare, and defy the less well-organised majority. In short they may make the synthesis something other than Socialism, and may be successful in the making of the alternative, *if the conditions are ripe for their success.* This is where the power of man to make his own history comes into the dialectical process. He has that power, but it is not an absolute power, because he can only win that for which the course of history has prepared the conditions. The Capitalist victory will be only a temporary setback, if a system other than the capitalistic one is the one which fits the conditions of the time and gives the greater scope for the development of the productive forces.

If we assume, for the moment, that Socialism is the synthesis, and that, as a further development of the dialectical process, the classless society, which is the Marxian aim, is attained, we are not to infer that this is the end of the process. It was not the affair of Karl Marx or of Friedrich Engels to follow the future of man beyond the termination of his economic antagonisms. Their purview extends to the attainment of a social constitution which gives scope to the forces of production, and their task ends there. But the dialectical process continues to infinity in the development of human personality. Set at liberty from economic preoccupations, man has before him a limitless future, which it is for other eyes to explore. As Lenin put it, the immanent contradictions will remain, and their continuance is the necessary presupposition of further development. The whole of history is nothing but the progressive transformation of human nature, first unconscious, and afterwards conscious. A perspective of endless possibilities opens before us, with ample room for all the apocalyptic imaginations which for so long have occupied the Russian soul.

But this is not the point which concerns us at the moment. I have tried to convey my notion of what is meant by Dialectical Materialism. The operator—for he is more than an investigator—proceeding with the assistance of the dialectical method, seeks to foretell the historical process by using economic relations as his clue through the darkness of the labyrinth, and by observing the internal contradictions whose function it is to produce the new phase by the destruction of the old; and to complete the process according to his own aim. Human will (it is human will conditioned by economic relations and environment) is one of the factors in the production of change, but only one of them.

Such is the method, which might be described as a method of induction assisted by certain special clues, and accompanied by an effort. As a method of inquiry it is one which might be used by any investigator, with or without the revolutionary bias, and has doubtless been employed, consciously or unconsciously, by most of those whose attention has been directed by the influences of Marx to the bearing of economics upon history. But the Marxian doctrine covers a much wider field than the Marxian method. In the first place, there are certain of Marx's inductions from his study of history and economics which have virtually passed into dogma. They spring out of his method, and they are presumably liable to be contradicted by the same: but their origin and their possible fate have been forgotten in reverence for the master. The most significant of these inductions is the class-struggle. We shall see presently that followers of Marx have not always and everywhere attached equal weight to this induction. It is obvious at all events, that the class-struggle is not a permanent factor: for it comes to an end with the establishment of the classless society. A second induction, following closely upon the theory of the class-struggle, is the dictatorship of the proletariat in the period after the defeat of the bourgeoisie and before the attainment of the classless society. It seems that Marx was indebted for this conception to a Russian source—Michael Bakunin. It has played an enormous part in Russia, where it has merged with the older conception of a messianic mission of the Russian people, and has, under the Constitution of 1936, lost its original significance of the domination of a class. Another induction of importance is the theory of Surplus Value, which shows us the capitalist employer taking from his workers an increasingly excessive share of the value of the product of their work. It was valuable to revolutionaries for the theoretical justification which it provided for the expropriation of the expropriator: regarded as the statement of the fact that the worker produces more than he consumes, it is almost a truism: and it has furnished to Russian Marxians one of their firmest principles: that one man must not be allowed to make a profit out of the work of another.

Apart from particular inductions which have found their way in a greater or less degree into dogma, Marx, the revolutionary, embodied in his works a mass of quite avowedly biased advice and instruction. Just as John Tanner, in G. B. Shaw's *Man and Superman*, wrote a Handbook for Revolutionaries, expanding Mrs. Poyser's thesis that "we must be born again and born different," so Marx provided, and intended to provide, the materials for a Revolutionaries' Manual, not a manual of tactics, but a manual of strategy, not the arithmetic of Revolution but its algebra. He passionately desired the reconstruction of society on such a principle as would ensure economic justice: he did not believe that this reconstruction could be carried out unless it fell within the curve of history as plotted: but he believed that it did fall within that curve, and he wished to convince men that this was a true forecast. How far he thought that it could be brought by the conscious will of man within the curve, is one of the controversies. The elements of human will and activity being once introduced into the chain of causation, it seems impossible to resist the conclusion that the same method, in different hands, may lead to different results. At any rate there was no pretence of the enquirer's impartiality, on this side of his work. He wrote his Revolutionaries' Manual with the intention of teaching Man how to think, and whither to direct his energies, *if he desired the Socialist Revolution.* A natural consequence of this combination of intentions, of the provision of a method of enquiry, along with a manual of revolutionary strategy, not clearly differentiated, is that the critics have questioned the value of the method. To announce, as some of the successors and commentators have announced, that the Marxian method is a means to a particular result, is to discredit it entirely as an instrument of scientific enquiry. That this is precisely the line taken by the representatives of the mystical philosophies, who demand the activity of the enquirer's will, as well as of his thought, in the search for ultimate reality, would not appear to invalidate the criticism. I suggest that method and handbook are separable, and ought to be separated: but to abandon the method, while retaining some of its results, is to invite dogma to run riot; and, man's brain being what it is, he is already only too willing to spare himself pains, by making a dogma and clinging to it. We must therefore retain the method, while leaving open the question of its results.

We are dealing with Russia: and the point which interests us is not so much what Marx himself meant as what his Russian followers and expositors understood him to mean. Michael Bakunin had been in close touch with Marx for some years before the publication of the *Communist Manifesto,* and he published a translation of it into Russian in Herzen's *Bell* in the early sixties. *Das Kapital* was first translated into Russian in 1872, and from this time there was a slow, very slow, infiltration of Marxist ideas among the Russian revolutionaries. The followers of Lavrov were popularly described as Marxists, presumably because he stood for propaganda, against the Bakuninist doctrine of conspiratorial insurrection, which was anathema to Marx. An illustration of the difference of the ways in which the works of a master may be interpreted is given by the notion, current in Russia in the early eighties, that the Marxists were the friends and supporters of Capitalism. A story was published in one of the magazines in which a disciple of Karl Marx was represented as glorying in the provision of agricultural machinery on an estate of which he is manager, and in the capitalistic developments there. The picture was not drawn without a reason. To the Marxian, or to the Marxian of one type, the capitalist system was one of the links in the chain of history, a desirable successor to feudalism, and an inevitable predecessor to Socialism. He really desired the fuller growth of capitalism: so much so that, at the time of the disastrous famine of 1891–92, some of the orthodox Marxists of the day protested against assistance to the peasants, on the ground that the growth of capitalism must not be impeded. Engels had said something similar much earlier, but, in informing the capitalist of the services which were expected of him, he had added the significant reminder: "But the executioner is at the door."

From 1893. There was even a tendency to identify Marxism with the Manchester School of economics, which perhaps accounts for the Tsarist Government's long toleration of what was known as "legal Marxism," that is, Marxism expressed in the columns of the press legally published within Russia. This legal Marxism became the philosophy of the new class of managers and engineers brought into existence by the developments of economic policy by Count Witte. The nonterroristic character of the Marxian doctrine was doubtless a recommendation, but the Tsarist Censors were never remarkable for perceiving the ultimate tendencies of any teaching: and were evaded with an ease which strikingly illustrates the comparative efficiency of the present Government of Russia.

We have seen that Marx supplies a method of social enquiry, and also—quite separate from the method—a manual of strategy for the revolutionary in making the revolution. He also supplies some scattered hints which help the revolutionary in deciding what to do when the revolution has been effected. But he is quite misunderstood if he is supposed to supply a scheme of policy for the Dictatorship of the Proletariat when the Proletariat has come into power. The general aim is plain enough; the attainment of a classless society. But that is scarcely more definite than the Kingdom of Heaven upon earth, to which it has some remarkable resemblances. The Dictatorship of the Proletariat, in conducting its affairs towards the dimly envisaged goal, has a thousand things to do each day, and it is not part of Karl Marx's function to give instructions how they are to be done. Certain lines, mostly negative, are made plain. An end is to be made of exploitation of class by class, of man by man, and of woman by man. An end is to be made of private profit, whether it be made out of direct labour or out of the exchange of commodities. Socialism depends primarily upon the system of production: only secondarily upon the system of distribution. Production is to be recognised as a social function. Whether it is to be in the hands of some central organisation, or of local organisations, or of voluntary co-operative societies, or even of individuals socially controlled and prevented from exploiting others, there is no attempt at definition. Engels did indeed suggest co-operative farming as the best method of dealing with peasant agriculture, but that hint stands alone. Distribution is left undefined: except that it is quite clear that it is *not to be egalitarian*. The worker's share will depend upon the work he does. Later on, when the classless society is attained, and the increase of production has removed the difficulties in the way of gratifying all desires, it will depend upon his needs. The factory is to be the centre of social and political, as well as of economic life. Woman is to be in every respect the equal of man, and the family is to take the new form, which her emancipation and her work side by side with man will dictate.

These are important principles supplying the foundation for

a commonwealth aiming at the attainment of Socialism; but they leave the whole architectural superstructure to the wisdom and taste of the builders. For dogma, in the conduct of day-by-day business, the teaching of Marx offers no justification: and its crystallisation into dogma, if that were to take place, would be fraught with results, only comparable with those of the petrification of religious teaching, and more immediately ruinous.

Marx does not present his followers with an ethical system. He provides a method of ascertaining what will happen, not what ought to happen. But an ethical system based upon social justice must inevitably flow from the Marxian doctrine; and it will not be a Nietzschean system, built upon the exaltation of the superior few, but rather one in which all humans count equally as social units.

1883. The first systematic explanation of Marxist doctrines in the Russian language was given by George Plekhanov, whom we last saw as the exponent of the *People's Will,* in its new determination to use the political weapon, and work for a political constitution. His alternative hopes of a "Black partition," that is of the allotment of additional land to the peasantry, were disappointed, and he went abroad and plunged into Marxist studies, the fruits of which were seen in a series of publications and in the formation of the *Liberation of Labour Group,* the first Russian Marxist association. In his *Socialism and the Political Struggle,* he took as his point of departure the decision of the Revolutionaries to aim at a political constitution for Russia, and showed that the logical consequences of the departure had not yet been appreciated by its authors. If the State is to be used to effect economic change, it must be a State inspired and worked by those who understand and sympathise with the spirit of the change. In other words, the political weapon must be used. Though each country has its own economic peculiarities, one and the same scientific Socialism supplies for all the strategic principles by which the change is to be effected. This doctrine is the head of the movement: and the propertyless workers of the cities are its heart. Their merit as a class lies precisely in the fact that they have none of the prejudices created by the possession of property. They, therefore, are the instruments of the change, and they must be fitted for their task by participation in political life. It is a slow and gradual process: but economic justice is not to be produced by the mere transfer of land and the instruments of production to new hands: it is only to be achieved by the socialistic organisation of production. Even if momentarily achieved by more summary means, it will be rapidly undone, unless those who constitute the State understand and are in sympathy with the aim. Still less will any sudden seizure of power, before the necessary education has been effected, produce the results which are sought. Those who obtain power by such means before their natural supporters are ripe for it, will find themselves inevitably using the power in the interests of those who *are ripe* for it, that is of another class.

The book opens with a quotation from Marx on the class-struggle: "Every class struggle is a political struggle," and Plekhanov tells us that history shows a political struggle between classes, *wherever classes exist, having their economic interests as their ultimate aim.* But his emphasis is on the need of the political struggle rather than on the existence of a class-war. He does not deny the need of the ultimate capture of power on behalf of the revolution, but he denies its immediate possibility or desirability. He regards the peasant as an ally, because the peasant desires the land: but reliance is placed upon the propertyless worker of the town, because his interests are not warped by the possession of property.

1884. In the following year Plekhanov published a second exposition of Marxism, entitled *Our Disagreements.* It is interesting to observe in it the modest pretensions of the Russian Marxians at this stage of their preaching. Marxism, says Plekhanov, is the true algebra of revolution, and "though it includes defects and impracticabilities, it is a first attempt to apply scientific theory to the analysis of complicated and involved social relations." He only points to the solution, and hopes that *People's Will,* the organisation of the revolutionary Populists who aimed at a political constitution for Russia, will itself become Marxist. *In hoc signo vinces.* Marxism will show

how to utilise the progressive aspects of the Liberal revolution, while remaining true to the worker class.

Plekhanov is writing with the object of converting Populists to Marxism, and he deals tenderly with the peasant-worship which was a central feature of their social thought: but he points out that the Mir is in process of decay. He damns with faint praise the practice of terrorism, which "does not widen the sphere of the revolutionary movement, but on the contrary narrows it down to the heroic acts of small partisan groups."

1884. The same ideas are embodied in the programme of the group of *Liberation of Toil*, which was established in 1884, but the latter is more definite in regard to the political institutions which are to be set up. The workers are to conquer political power, and to make a democratic constitution with a popular legislative assembly and organs of local self-government. They are to be organised for struggle, both with the existing Government and with the future bourgeois parties which may be expected to arise under a democratic system. This clause provides for the "permanent Revolution"—we should rather call it continuous than permanent—of which Karl Marx foresaw the necessity. The classes are to be eliminated: economic emancipation is to be attained by means of collective ownership of the instruments of production, for which the present development of technique is already preparing: the coercive State is to wither away and to be replaced by purely economic organisations: the coming economic organisation is to be international: all Marxian anticipations. The standing army is to be replaced by the general arming of the people: the land is to be divided among the peasant communes: and reforms of taxation and factory inspection and State aid to producers' associations are specified as desirable. The value of the revolutionary movement in the villages is recognised, but "Populist traditions are to be maintained only in so far as they do not contradict scientific Socialism." The new group recognises the need of the terroristic struggle against absolute Government, but differs from *People's Will* in respect to the seizure of power, and in respect to the direct activity of the Socialists of the working class (by which is meant insurrectional adventure). Except the reference to the elimination of classes, the document contains nothing about class-war: it puts forward the Intelligentsia rather than the proletariat as the leader in revolutionary activities: the process is evidently to be a gradual one: and it is contemplated that the revolution will in the first place be one which will place the bourgeois in power, but the workers are to be active in preparing for their own succession to the first place.

The general result of these discussions of 1883–84 is to show us a Marxism somewhat different from the one with which we are most familiar: especially in the small prominence assigned to the class-war: and noticeably gradualist in temper. Neither of these two points appears to the present writer to be absolutely vital to the Marxian system. One vital question is the attitude to human freedom. If the historical process works itself out according to inevitable laws, and man's interventions are entirely predetermined by similar laws, the philosophy is one of apathy at the best, despair at the worst. But if man can make his own history, subject only to the limitations imposed by the historical process on the range of possibilities, and by social environment, on the direction of his own will; if he can make it, in the same sense in which he can boil a kettle, by moving the sticks which make the fire, and by placing the water where the fire will make it hot: then the philosophy is one of hope. George Plekhanov does not appear to me to emphasise the freedom of man, so much as he emphasises the inevitability of history. In this his interpretation was at one with the general interpretation given in Germany, where it was probably the cause of the final defeat of the Marxist party. It passed into the Menshevik doctrine, where it threw a pallor over the native hue of resolution. The Bolsheviks on the other hand transferred the emphasis to the freedom of man. They interpreted Marx as meaning, not that Communism is fated to be realised: but that, if society is to survive, Communism is the only way of escape from Capitalism's inability to provide a good life for its wage-earners. Marxism in this form, or thus coloured, is a call to man to make his own history, and the enthusiasm which it ultimately evoked in Russia becomes more easily intelligible.

A second vital question is that of the ultimate economic aim: whether it is a redistribution of good things on a principle of justice: or the establishment of a society so constituted as to provide a guarantee of justice: whether the keynote is distribution or production. Plekhanov seems to stand for the latter interpretation, which is indeed the inevitable one for the close student of Marxian teaching. Mere redistribution does not take the world beyond the stage of a generalised poverty. Production, freed from the fetters imposed by the condition of a separate private profit to be achieved in each section of the field, and from the quarrel between employer and employed, is capable of giving the material security and the leisure which man requires. As I have already noted, but venture for the sake of emphasis to repeat, it is production, not distribution, which the form of Marxism adopted by the Bolsheviks emphasises. The assumption is made that when the artificial limits, imposed by the individual entrepreneur's need to make a profit in his own section of the field of production, are removed, and when full and free use is made of the possibilities of science, by a society in which no motive for restriction persists, production will advance in an infinite degree, and it will actually become possible to give to everyone in accordance with his needs. Until this stage is reached, Communism is not attained: and since some, or even all, must continue to go hungry of material satisfactions, all the old conflicts must continue. That is to say many will grab, and some will steal, and all the old apparatus of the State with its coercive authority and its policemen (however they be named) must persist. Only when all can find satisfaction, can the State wither away, as Marxians anticipated that it would.

I diverge here for a moment to point out the possible consequence to these anticipations of a shortage of certain raw materials such as the rarer metals. In so far as these should prove to be irreplaceable, a perfect organisation of production might still leave the world with causes of friction and dispute. But this difficulty was not present to the mind of Plekhanov.

By 1887 Marx's *Capital,* in a Russian translation, was the most widely read book among Russian students. The Populists continued their terroristic attempts, for this was the year in which Ulianov (the brother of Lenin) made his attempt on the life of Alexander III and suffered the death penalty. Tolstoyan influences were strong, and somewhat depressing. The Maximalist Ivanov Razumnik calls the eighties a period of contentment with little deeds and smug philistinism. A disastrous famine in 1891–92, and the evident failure of the administration to cope with its destructive effects, ushered in a decade of great intellectual and economic activities, which was contemporaneous with Count Witte's financial administration. Labour began to use new means of defence and to make larger claims. About 1893 the name of *Social Democrats,* already in use in Germany, began to be applied to the Russian Marxists, to distinguish them from the Anarchists, and to emphasise their acceptance of democratic methods. They stood for the combination of Socialism with the political struggle, but used the day-to-day economic needs of the workers to press the political lesson upon them. In 1895 a Petersburg Fighting Union was formed with Lenin as one of its leaders. It was the germ of the Russian Social Democratic Party. The textile workers' strike of 1896 confirmed in Lenin and Plekhanov the Marxian conviction that the proletariat would be the instrument of revolution. A year later the Jewish Social Democrats, always well in the van, formed the Union known as the Jewish Bund, and in 1898 the first general Social Democratic Congress was held at Minsk, and formally inaugurated the Party which Plekhanov had advocated.

This was the decade in which Maxim Gorky rose to literary fame. Though he was far from being a Marxist in these early years the spirit of his writings, buoyant and combative, and the source of his inspirations in street and field, were sympathetic to the Marxian outlook. His faith in life attracted youth, to which Tolstoyan principle made no appeal. His robust and cheerful engine-driver Nil, in *Townsmen,* may be drawn with something less than the highest of dramatic gifts, and may have in him a good deal of that satisfaction with small deeds against which the Maximalists protested, but he is the New Man, the portent of a new era, and the forerunner of the Bolshevik worker, convinced that "he who works is master of the house," and with some of the narrowness of his class. He has his bitter fling at the "swine, fools, and thieves, who command honest men," but says "they will pass like boils from a healthy body." He comes in with a lot of young people who have been rehearsing a play to be shown to soldiers, and someone says: "It is pleasant to be with them. There is something healthy, such as you feel out in the forest." Speaking to a young lady, with a very different turn of mind, the turn of mind of the intelligentsia which Chekhov satirised, he says: "I love to live. I love noise, work, jolly simple people. But do you live? You are perpetually groaning for an unknown reason, and complaining. Against whom, why and for what? I don't understand." He goes on to describe his own particular hobby: "I'm awfully fond of forging metal. In front of you is the red formless mass, malicious, fiery. To beat the hammer on it is a joy. It spits at you with fizzing, blazing, sparks, seeks to burn out your eyes, blind you. . . . It is living, malleable . . . and with mighty blows from the shoulder you make of it what you need." All this is an unmistakable anticipation of the Bolshevik attitude to life.

Again, in an argument with the educated and restless youth, who tells him that "we shall see what answer life will give," he says: "I will compel it to give the answer which I want. Don't try to frighten *me*. . . . I know that life is a serious thing, and all my capacities and powers are needed to order it. And I know that I am no hero, but only an honest healthy man and yet I say: Never mind! We shall win. And with all the powers of my soul I satisfy my desire to plunge into the very depth of life, *to knead it this way and that, to prevent this and help the other. This is the joy of life."*

To which the educated youth replies: "Devil knows what he means: it is as though he were drunk."

It is the New Man, unintelligible to the old Intelligentsia, and, let us add, failing in turn to understand it: and the New Man is, at bottom, on the side of the Marxists, at all events of those Marxists who believe that man can make his own history. With an incomparably greater gift, Anton Chekhov depicts the old, and leaves us in little doubt of its weakness. It tends to futility, boredom, and despair of life.

1891. The epoch of Count Witte's financial reforms was also that of a new interest throughout the world in the problems of industrial labour, of the adoption of the Erfurt programme by the German Social Democrats, of the Encyclical of Pope Leo XIII dealing with the condition of workers. In Russia, Tolstoi's gospel of non-violence and non-co-operation with the State was still a living force. Religious thinkers were straining the eye of faith to follow the eagle flight of Soloviev into the empyrean of mystery where the realisation of the God-man was awaited. Poetry was awakening from a long contempt. The triumphs of the Moscow Art Theatre were being prepared by its greatest dramatist Chekhov and its greatest producers Stanislavsky and Nemirovich-Danchenko. New wealth seemed to promise the growth of new branches on the tree of civilisation, and more insistent political claims by the enriched middle class seemed imminent. Socialist thought was divided between the opposite camps of Mikhailovsky and the Populists on the one hand and of the Marxians on the other. The former stood for democracy and the federal form of the State, the rights of personality and of the individual, for an ethical basis of legislation, for the claims of Labour in general and for land for the peasant. The Russian Marxians laid no emphasis for the present on the rights of personality, but much on the struggle of classes, denied the validity of any distinction between evolving reality and right, and aimed at the hegemony of the urban working classes. The more fatalistic among them were willing to co-operate in the expropriation of small proprietors in order to hasten the advent of capitalism. Those of them who emphasised human will, while recognising the inevitability of the capitalistic phase, were intent upon active revolutionary intervention in human affairs. To all appearance the Marxian doctrine was marching triumphantly upon the broken forces of Populism, and about to secure the undivided allegiance of the progressive Intelligentsia. A turn of opinion reversed this anticipation. By the time that

Kerensky, for a few months of 1917 to hold supreme power in the Russian State, was a University student, the first ardour of enthusiasm for Marxism was at an end, and the Social Revolutionary Party, which had revived Mikhailovskyian Populism, was gaining ground against it.

1899. Peter Struve was the author of the first Marxian work legally printed in Russia and of the manifesto of the first Social Democratic Conference. But his "legal" Marxism proved to be a stepping-stone to the revision of Marxian theory, and ultimately to a religious Liberalism. The revisionist movement originated in Germany, with Eduard Bernstein, who, while still an Orthodox Marxist, held that the economic revolution works itself out automatically. This theory contained in it the germ of quietism and conservatism. It explained away the most characteristic features of the Marxian doctrine: its materialism, the primacy which it assigned to economics as a motive force in history, its lack of emphasis on the claims of the individual. In Peter Struve's hands, revision took the form of criticism of the dialectic as a method of enquiry: he declared that social evolution proceeds by gradual steps, not by leaps, thus eliminating the expectation of a violent revolution: that the theory of surplus-value is subject to revision and to ultimate negation: and that a State rising superior to the influence of class is possible, so that a conflict of classes is not inevitable, and the withering away or destruction of the State is not necessary. In 1899 he was demonstrating that the standpoint of Marxism is not unconditionally anti-individualistic: on the contrary that it tends to the elevation of real personality: social and economic organisation being only the means, while the all-round development of personality is the end. This was another way of putting the truth, too seldom understood, that the removal of economic anxieties is the way to set man free for the pursuit of true individuality. Struve had previously, in his *Critical Observations,* minimised, in the orthodox Marxian fashion, the part to be played by the Intelligentsia, the mere men of ideas, who have no part in production and do not constitute "a class." He still holds that they are powerless from the social and economic standpoint, but recognises their politi-

cal value, and, by implication, the power of ideas. The orthodox
Marxist does not deny the power of ideas: but he minimises
it by his insistence upon the fact that ideas are conditioned by
the state of economic relations. To emphasise the power of
ideas is to return to Populist conceptions, and to adopt an
idealistic rather than a materialistic standpoint. Orthodox
Marxians recognised no absolute ethical standard, and no such
thing as natural right or natural law. In 1901 Peter Struve was
claiming that natural right, rooted in the ethical idea of personality, is the criterion of all positive law. "No objective law,"
he wrote, "denying the freedom of the expression of thought
and will, can be recognised as in accordance with right, even
though it be reduced to the form of law, with every formality,
and receive the sanction of universal suffrage." N. A. Berdyaev,
a brilliant member of the Struve group, who has for many
years continued to illuminate the dark places of religion and
philosophy, was arguing, like Mikhailovsky (and like Kant),
for man as an aim in himself, and claiming that every new form
of social organisation must justify itself as a means of realising
the ideal aim—the natural law of personality, freedom and
equality.

1898. Revisionist Marxism became the doctrine of a large
part of the Intelligentsia and of the majority of the University
students: who accepted the historical justification of Capitalism given by Marx, while dropping his expectation of revolution. About the same time, the new Social Democratic Party
was divided by the emergence of a section which called itself
Economist, returning to the earlier doctrine of the Populists,
disclaiming the use of the political weapon, and the aim of a
political constitution, and limiting the activities of the working
class to the economic sphere. It found its theoretical support in
"legal" Marxism purged of the revolutionary spirit.

The stars in their courses were fighting for the stability of
the Tsarist State by robbing its most dangerous enemies of
their ideological basis. Policy carried the advantage further: by
the establishment of the peculiar system of Police Socialism
known by the name of Zubatov: which offered the prospect
(precarious, perhaps, but temporarily real) of robbing political

agitation of its grievance. The quarrel between Bolsheviks and Mensheviks, of which I shall have occasion to speak presently, was quite unintelligible to working men, and played into the hands of the authorities. But the Emperor, and the camarilla which surrounded him, unconscious of what the future had in store, threw these strategic advantages away, by the Far Eastern policy which led to the Japanese war.

1904. Lenin sought to make good the weak places in the Social Democratic armour by pressing upon his colleagues the fateful policy which is responsible for the existence of the Communist Party—a disciplined order of devoted adherents more nearly resembling the Society of Jesus than any of the lax aggregations of political sympathisers to which we are accustomed to apply the name of political party. There was nothing characteristically Marxian in this idea. We can trace the germs of it to Bakunin, Nechayev and Tkachev. But, almost certainly, it is to this idea, realised by Lenin in fact, that the Bolsheviks owed their emergence at the top of the revolutionary wave in November 1917. As described by Lenin in *What is to be done?* the plan is one for a "small compact core, consisting of reliable and hardened workers, with responsible agents in the principal districts, and connected by all the rules of strict secrecy with the organisations of revolutionists. Let the roots go as deep and wide as they can, but the struggle against the political police can only be conducted by professional revolutionists who can keep secrets, and whose organisation demands far greater training than that of Trade Unionists. A strong and disciplined revolutionary organisation can alone prevent the danger of premature outbreaks, before the ferment and anger of the working class are ripe for them. It is because of the need of restraint and of secrecy that democratic management is inapplicable to a revolutionary organisation."

Lenin was aware of certain weaknesses of his countrymen: the perpetual discussion, and the fissiparous tendency, the loose talking and the premature action, which (as Khalturin said) brought down the police upon them and ruined organisation. The disciplined "party" was the remedy for these things.

The "Economist" group stood for subservience to the spontaneous action of the mass as well as for the elimination of political aims. Lenin's pamphlet insists that without leadership from above, the movement must degenerate into the use of such weapons as lie ready to hand, in particular of terrorism, which is a mere waste of forces: and that the aim must be the political aim, of the seizure of power. Economic grievances must be used to illustrate the necessity of the political aim: for only a Workers' State will redress them. Unity of object must be secured by the establishment of an all-Russian newspaper: a plan not fully realised till the publication of *Pravda* in 1912. The Jewish Social Democratic organisation, the Bund, was at this time claiming autonomy: and Lenin, true to his instinct for discipline and organisation—qualities not often to be found among his fellow-countrymen—insisted upon unity.

1903. At the Second Party Congress, begun at Brussels and finished in London, the battle was joined between the "softs" and the "hards" on the subject of party discipline. The youthful Trotsky was on the side of the "softs". He tells us that he "did not at that time fully realise what an intense and imperious centralism the revolutionary party would need, to lead millions of men in a war against the old order". The looser formula, requiring mere co-operation or sympathy from candidates for membership, was temporarily victorious: and the "softs" shortly obtained control of the *Spark (Iskra)* which was the journal of the party. George Plekhanov almost immediately joined the "softs", with whom the general trend of his writings had already shown him to be in sympathy. The formal separation of the sections took place on the issue of co-operation with the Liberals, which Lenin condemned. The "softs", hereafter known as *Mensheviks* (Minority Party), were defeated by the "hards", *Bolsheviks* (Majority Party), on this issue: and the former abstained from attending the Third Party Congress in 1905.

As might be expected from the favour which they showed on this occasion to the policies of co-operation with the Liberals and of elasticity in the organisation of the party, the Mensheviks represented reformism and gradualism rather than revolution. With the typical Marxist, it was an axiom that the first theatre of the Socialist Revolution would be one of the advanced capitalist countries. The Mensheviks were gradualist and opposed to the seizure of power, and, in the Revolution of 1905 they desired the summoning of a Constituent Assembly and deplored the armed rising at Moscow. They distrusted the peasantry as allies in the struggle for revolution, thought that Russia was ripe only for democratic, that is for parliamentary institutions, and stood for co-operation with Liberal non-socialists. Trotsky, young and fiery, can never have found his spirit's home in so much moderation, and he tells us himself that he left the Mensheviks in 1904, after vain attempts to dissuade them from their alliance with the Liberals; though he did not join the Bolsheviks till August 1917. Lenin and the Bolsheviks, already clear in their conception of the class-struggle and its logical consequences, hoped for nothing from Liberals or from middle-class politicians. To them, as to the newly-formed party of the Social Revolutionaries, peasant disturbances had brought home the value of the peasantry as a revolutionary ally. But they saw that the industrial proletariat must lead, because the peasantry is attached to rights similar to those of property, from which the town-worker—perhaps only until he acquires vested interests in social insurance—is completely dissociated. Inspired by that particular brand of Marxism which calls on man to make his own history, and, as we shall presently see, also by something which was Bakuninist rather than Marxian, they looked forward to armed insurrection, ultimately for the conquest of power, and immediately for the creation of a historical example: having before them the memory of a heroic failure, that of the Paris Commune. Where such differences of temper and outlook existed, the division between the Bolshevik and the Menshevik groups of the Social Democratic Party explains itself. It may be that the Mensheviks were the truer Marxists: but controversy over such a question is barren.

It will help us to obtain a correct perspective if we realise how small was the *apparent* importance of the Bolshevik section, and indeed of the Socialists in general, at the time of the Revolution of 1905. Even eleven years later, M. Maurice Paléologue, the French Ambassador in St. Petersburg, admirably informed though he was on most aspects of Russian life, believed that the leader of the Bolsheviks was Alexander Kerensky, who was actually a member of the Labour group of the Social Revolutionary Party. The Bolsheviks were the stronger in the industrial north, in the centre and in the Urals: the Mensheviks in the south and in Georgia. In November 1904 the Bolshevik Party numbered only three hundred, and in September 1905 only eight thousand. The Mensheviks had a stronger hold upon the upper ranks of the workers, as we shall see by their predominance in the St. Petersburg Soviet of 1905: and, if we may judge by the fact that the Teachers' Conference in 1906 excluded the Bolsheviks altogether, also upon the rank and file of the Intelligentsia. The Social Revolutionaries made a wider appeal in rural areas than did either section of the Social Democratic Party. As all Socialists alike boycotted the elections for the first Duma, we can draw no inference from the voting for that body. But, for the second Duma, when the policy of boycott had been dropped, and the franchise was still a wide one, thirty-five Social Revolutionaries and fifty-four Social Democrats of both sections were elected. On the other hand, the Kadet Party (representing the educated middle class in general) won a hundred and fifty seats, and Aladin's Labour Group won ninety, in the first Duma. In the second Duma, from which a large number of Kadet and Labour deputies had been excluded for their participation in the Viborg manifesto, the Kadets won a hundred and twenty-three, and the Labour Group two hundred and one seats. We gather that all the Socialists taken together were not able to win one-third of the number of seats captured by the parties which stood less far to the Left.

The St. Petersburg Soviet of 1905, which became the original example of an afterwards famous institution, was not a Marxian, nor even a Socialist, invention, but rather a spontaneous device brought by the factory hands from the villages, something quite as genuinely Russian and popular as the Mir, or the workers' co-operative association, though not so early discovered by the sociological student. The Soviets, in this their earliest form, consisted of representatives of the workers in the factories. At a later date they included also representatives of peasants and of soldiers. Lenin being absent in Finland, a section of the Bolsheviks misapplied his canon of a limited and disciplined party organisation, and threatened to secede from the Soviet unless their terms were accepted. This incident provided a new descriptive nomenclature for the tendency to dictate to the non-party masses, which Lenin envisaged as having a far wider degree of freedom than the disciplined party. Those who showed this tendency were described as Ultimatists—pronouncers of the Ultimatum—or Otzovists—from the Russian word which means to *recall*: and it was vigorously resisted by Lenin as destroying the basis of non-party co-operation with party. In so far as the Party, at a later date, has taken up a dictatorial attitude, beyond its guiding and inspiring functions, it is likely to be charged by the Bolsheviks of the older school with an Ultimatist, or Otzovist, deviation from the principles of Lenin.

Even if Lenin had been in Russia when the St. Petersburg Soviet was set up, there are reasons for doubting whether he would have given it a particularly warm welcome. But, as usual, he learned from the facts: and, having seen how the Soviets of St. Petersburg, and of the score of other towns which followed suit, served in practice to embody the will of the workers, he recognised them as "organisations of power, despite all the embryonic, unorganised, scattered elements, in their make-up and functioning". In October 1915 he is still speaking with some reserve about the value of the institution. The Soviets must be looked upon as "organs of insurrection and of revolutionary power. But, only in connection with a mass strike of a political nature and with an insurrection, can such institutions be of lasting value."

The leading facts about the institution of the Soviet are: that it represents not a geographical constituency, but is a microcosm of a particular class: that is of a body of workers engaged together on common work, who have intimate knowledge of their fellows: that there is a power of recall as well as of election: and that the function of the elected is administrative as well as legislative, resembling rather that of a county council than that of a parliament. But perhaps the most significant fact about the Soviets, is that they involve the creation of a series, or successive tiers, of administrative authorities: the lowest of which is directly chosen by the workers, while each higher body is chosen by the body below. It thus brings the workers, or their representatives, into immediate executive touch with every kind of public business from the humblest of everyday concerns up to the supreme tasks of the head of the State. These characteristics fit it better than a parliament for a rapidly changing situation, but the Soviets of 1905, as of 1917, were far from keeping pace with the impatience of revolutionaries, and represented the moderate man rather than the extremist. The first chairman, Khrustalev Nosar, was an orator rather than a leader. Trotsky, who succeeded him, was criticised for attention to economic objects when he should have aimed at securing the power of the State. But the temper of the members was not such as to support extreme measures. The Mensheviks never lost the advantage which they gained from the aloofness of the Bolsheviks at the establishment of the Soviet. Its measures were moderate because its temper was moderate: perhaps because it was really representative of a working class which at that time did not contemplate the overthrow of the Tsarist Government, and contained large elements of the purely "economist" way of thinking. It went nearest to attacking the régime when, doubtless under the inspiration of Trotsky, it repudiated Romanov debts, and called on the people to withdraw their deposits from the Savings Banks. It was convinced that Count Witte aimed at provoking disorders, in order to crush them effectively: and it desired to disappoint him in this aim.

Dec. 1905. The opportunity of joint action with the really dangerous agrarian movement was missed. When that was over, and the Soviet had been broken up, and its leaders imprisoned —in other words when the advantage was already on the side of law and order—the Moscow insurrection occurred, against the wishes of the Menshevik section. The tactics of this rising were deplorable. Mr. Maurice Baring says it was conducted by boys and girls. But a more important question here is that of its policy: which was evidently deliberate. It was an imitation of the Paris Commune, deliberately "insurrectionist" in design, in the sense in which Bakunin and Tkachev might have used the expression. It was intended to give to Russia and to the world an example of what the proletariat could do, in the hope of establishing a provisional government of the city of Moscow, *for a time;* but without the expectation of overthrowing the Tsarist Government. This interpretation is supported by former utterances of Lenin himself. In May 1901 he proposed preparation for armed insurrection in connection with the massacre at the Obukhov works. In November 1904 he wrote that the working class must extend and strengthen its organisation and prepare for insurrection. In May 1905, having said that the people could not defeat the army, he continued: "that the people may rise, together with a small handful of the army, against despotic rulers, is a reality of to-morrow." And, after the mutiny on the battleship *Potëmkin* in June 1905, he pointed out that the call for insurrection was timely, and urged Social Democrats to study military questions. After the Revolution of 1905 had been defeated he told the Mensheviks that "it was really a great revolution, and not a chaos . . . not because the Tsar was compelled to proclaim a constitution, and not because the bourgeoisie began to show signs of life, but chiefly because, abortive though it proved, there was an armed rising of the workers in Moscow, and because the world proletariat has for one month had a glimpse of the Soviet of Workers' deputies at St. Petersburg. . . ." He called the rising the greatest historical movement of 1905 and "the signpost to future victory". In other words he was, at all events at this time, an advocate of what we may call *exemplary* insurrection: which is certainly not Marxian.

When Engels gave his advice about insurrection in his *Germany in 1848* he said it must seize the moment when the activity of the vanguard of the people is at its height and the vacillation of their opponents at its extreme. Neither of these conditions was satisfied in December 1905: nor can anyone have supposed them to be satisfied. The timing and preparation of the rising of November 1917 were very different.

1906. All the Socialist parties boycotted the first Duma, probably because the Witte franchise had not then been brought fully into effect. Their participation in the elections for the second and later Dumas was in harmony with the Marxian principle of taking part in politics, and with Lenin's translation of it into the use of legal as well as illegal methods. His line was to co-operate in the election, but to refuse to carry out the Menshevik plan of forming an alliance in the Duma with the Liberal Kadet party. An attempt, classified as Ultimatist, or Otzovist, in tendency, to recall the Social Democratic deputies from the third Duma, because of its reactionary tendencies, was resisted successfully by Lenin.

The counter-revolution was a period of extreme depression, and there was a moment when even he was pessimistic. In the reaction the Mensheviks stood for a legal Workers' party, and for legal Trade Unions, with reformist demands. The party had lost faith, and there were many deserters, intellectuals as well as working men. The practical differences between the different groups of Social Democrats centred at one time in the question of the "expropriations", violent seizures of money and property for party funds. In a single half year of 1907 there were over a hundred of these "Exes" in Lodz alone, and Stalin distinguished himself at Tiflis by the cool audacity of his seizure of bank funds. The attitude of the groups towards "Exes" was characteristic. The Mensheviks disapproved: the Bolsheviks approved, subject to the maintenance of strict party discipline and control. The London Social Democratic Congress of 1907 forbade the practice: and it is said that Lenin organised a secret Bolshevik centre to maintain relations with the perpetrators of the seizures, because of their value as a source of funds.

The fissiparous tendency of Russian thought was in the meanwhile receiving a new manifestation. At the beginning of the last quarter of the nineteenth century, German philosophy took a turn away from Hegel and back to Kant, and produced what seems to have been in its origin a critique of pure experience. The argument was that only sensations exist, and the name of empirio-criticism (which presumably means that experience is the only source of knowledge) was invented for it. Whatever the originators, Avenarius and Mach, may have intended to convey by the doctrine, it was seized upon by Russian thinkers nearly thirty years later, by some to defend the materialistic interpretation, and by others, including Victor Chernov and the Social Revolutionaries, as a useful weapon for the idealists. A Marxist philosopher, P. A. Bogdanov, partly alone, and partly in collaboration with other Machians, expounded the principles of the Machian doctrine as understood by Russians: and A. V. Lunacharsky, afterwards Minister of Culture and Education in the revolutionary Government, took to what was slightingly described as "god-building" on the basis of it. He spoke, for instance, of "deification of the highest human potentialities", of "religious atheists", of "scientific socialism in its religious significance", and said that "for a long time a new religon has been maturing within me". The Immanentist group in Germany who were close associates of Mach and Avenarius, were preachers of Theism, and the tendency in this direction was no mere accident. The Christian revival in Russian thought, under influences which descended from Dostoievsky to Vladimir Soloviev, had created a soil which was favourable to such developments, and the old days when intelligence was regarded as synonymous with disbelief seemed to have passed away. The writings of N. Fyodorov (who died in 1903) combine the Orthodox conception of *sobornost* with that of an active socialism as a Christian duty. There was a moment when Bolshevism might have become Theist, if not Christian.

Under the ministry of Peter Stolypin the Government policy was a combination of vigorous repression of disorder, with the creation of a (presumably) conservative class of peasant landholders independent of the Mir, and the maintenance of a constitution made safe by a restrictive electoral law. There are signs that this policy might have been successful in averting revolution. One of the results of a constitution—even a restricted constitution—was the growth of a capable and influential Liberal group. If it was not precisely a party, in the sense of an organisation having roots in the people, it was at any rate a body of enlightened and high-minded politicians, who showed themselves capable of useful public work. It received a powerful reinforcement in the realm of ideas from a body of former Marxists, for by this time (*1907*) the Russian revisionist group had passed over to a religious liberalism, the principles of which were embodied in a collection of essays published under the title of *Landmarks*. In this volume Peter Struve takes the Revolution of 1905 as the text of his sermon, and blames the principles of the Intelligentsia for the mischief which it caused. The Intelligentsia, or the Socialists, for to him they are one and the same, deny the personal responsibility of man, and attribute all suffering and all crime to economic and social conditions. They preach the idea of service to the people, with no corresponding obligations. Progress can only be the fruit of the inner perfection of man and of the growth of his sense of responsibility. Only religion can supply what is missing. For lack of it, the Revolution of 1905 ended in a harsh reaction as soon as agitation ceased.

N. A. Berdyaev, another of the contributors, is scornful of the Intelligentsia for the weakness of their philosophy, and compares them to Dostoievsky's Grand Inquisitor, who aimed at giving happiness to man, at the cost of truth. They have never understood Hegel, nor Kant, nor Mach, nor even Marx. They have only asked how they can use these philosophies to help their idol, the people. They have admired Positivism, because it deifies humanity. Their love of man is not respect for man as the child of God. It has turned to Man-Idolatry. Chaadaev, Dostoievsky and Soloviev are neglected because they offer no support to Socialism. He complains of the philosophers of the Right, including Merezhkovsky and Rozanov, for an anarchical denial of philosophical reason, and sees a tendency for mysticism itself to become an instrument of social aims (probably a reference to the mystical anarchism of Vyacheslav Ivanov, and the Christian revolutionism of Merezhkovsky). He calls for a synthesis of knowledge and faith, for the recognition of the independent value of truth, and for "congregationalism", *sobornost* (the Old Believers' and Khomiakov's word for the most characteristic feature of the Eastern Church), of the consciousness, which can only be realised in the soil of the national tradition. In this last we hear an echo of Slavophil teaching.

A third contributor, Frank, in an essay on the Ethics of Nihilism, condemns it for its denial of aesthetic and cultural values. Culture is a value in itself, necessary to the completion of human nature. Moralism is nothing without a faith: for it only begets a wish to make the people prosperous. When Marxism first appeared in Russia it brought with it certain good things: a respect for culture: an aim at increased production both material and spiritual: a realisation that what was needed was the completion of human nature, and that the moral problem is in a certain sense subordinate to that purpose: and a sense that an ascetic renunciation of the highest form of life is an evil, not a good. All these good things were soon swallowed up in the returning flood of Russian Populism. To-day the god of the Intelligentsia is the plain folk: and its morality is their service. But the living love for man, which inspired the "going to the people" for altruistic service, has been lost in a religion of the realisation of popular happiness. The pursuit of prosperity for the people is, for this critic, not compatible with the attainment of the higher values. He calls the Intelligentsia "a militant monk of the Nihilistic religion of earthly prosperity" and summons it to "pass from unproductive uncultured Nihilistic moralism to the creative, constructive culture of religious humanism". In the meanwhile he pours scorn on the Marxian "god-builders", and the Machians, saying that the Social Democrats begin to talk of God, to occupy themselves with aesthetics, to make brethren of the mystical Anarchists, to lose faith in materialism, and to reconcile Marx with Mach and Nietzsche.

One criticism which is repeated both by Berdyaev and by

Frank is that the Socialists aim at a purely distributory system. This statement was true of most of the earlier Russian Socialists except Chernyshevsky. But Marxism, as has already been pointed out, laid stress upon production rather than upon distribution. In his *Critique of the Gotha Programme*, Karl Marx was very definite in his repudiation of egalitarian distribution: and his Russian followers have been generally steadfast in their emphasis on production, as the key to scientific Socialism.

Bulgakov, another contributor to *Landmarks*, and now a leading publicist of the Orthodox revival, analyses the qualities of the Intelligentsia, and notices the large contribution of Religion to these. Their aversion from the world, their rigoristic morals, their penitence for supposed sins against the plain folk, their eschatological dream of the kingdom of heaven upon earth, their desire to save man from suffering, if not from sin, are all traced to religious training: and the writer exclaims: "How often, in the debates of the second Duma, did we hear from atheist lips echoes of orthodox thought!" These are very just observations. Many of the advanced thinkers had been trained in the religious seminaries (as was Stalin): and among their thoughts are the reflections of religious teaching. Though the Bolsheviks completely repudiate Christian cosmogony and dogma, their ethics are fundamentally Christian, by contrast with the Nietzschean doctrine of a "master's" morality: and their habits of thought continue to be profoundly influenced by Orthodox conceptions.

1909. There was a time when the doctrines of Mach and Avenarius seemed likely to establish themselves as the standard philosophy of Bolshevism. The Party might have become confirmed in an idealistic, even in a fideistic, tendency which would have altered its history. Lenin, after a period of thought and study, published his one philosophical work, *Materialism and Empirio-criticism*, which was an effective intervention on the side of materialism. The work is more important as a historical fact, than as a body of philosophical argument. The choice of a philosophy was vital to the Party, just as the choice of a theology was vital to the early Christian Church: and deviations, or heresies, were fraught with unforeseeable consequences. In the long run, Lenin's intervention determined the abandonment by Russian Marxists of theories which might have led back to idealism and to religion. But the Communist school at Capri, which was founded by Maxim Gorky and Lunacharsky, and conducted largely under the auspices of Lunacharsky and Bogdanov, continued to pursue the tendencies which Lenin repudiated, and Gorky declined to supply funds for the rival school which Lenin established at Paris. The great leader's attitude to the teaching of Capri is illustrated by the story of his remark to the new-comers from Capri to Paris: "You won't find intellectual liberty, and right of private judgment, here." On the question of discipline on the party-line, there was no compromise for Lenin.

As a statement of Marxian philosophy and fundamental theory, George Plekhanov's *Fundamental Problems of Marxism*, the date of which suggests the intention of a reply to the Machians, is more important than Lenin's philosophical work. Thought is conditioned by being: as the influence of cattle upon Kaffirs, or of camels upon Arabs, clearly shows. The Deed came first, says Goethe. This is the essential of Materialistic philosophy. Dialectic is a theory of social evolution, with recognition of the occurrence of sudden changes. It explains the end of a social order, as well as its existence. Whatever is, is right: but it is coming to an end for all that: and what next is, is also right. History is made by human beings and therefore by great men among the rest. This is not merely *Chanticler*, helping the sun to rise, or the beating of tomtoms to end an eclipse. In sociology, causal necessity is made up of many items, one of which is the conscious action of men making their own history. A dualist, who separates thought and being, can only imagine one kind of necessity, which compels us to act against our wishes, and only one kind of freedom, which enables us to act in accordance with them. But a Marxist, who identifies being and thought, recognises the freedom, which is limited by the necessities of natural law, in the social as in the physical world. One decides to boil a kettle: and it is done by putting the vessel full of water where the fire is. The means of ending the ills of society must be sought in the material relations of production, not invented as a desirable Utopia. History, in its entirety, is nothing but a continuous modification of human nature. Such, in brief summary, is Plekhanov's outline of the fundamental problems of Marxism. The struggle of classes is not forgotten, but it is not emphasised as fundamental. As we should expect, Plekhanov soon figures in the opposite camp to Lenin, as a patriot, a "defensist", concerned primarily with the defence of his country in war: which is precisely the reverse of the mental attitude of those to whom the essential problem was the struggle of class.

I do not attempt to give an exhaustive account of the successive divisions in the Social Democratic Party. But one of them, which took place in the period of counter-revolution, is important because of its effect on the policies pursued during the Great War. This was the movement known as *Liquidationism*, which gave up illegal work, and was supported by the legal magazine *Our Dawn*. The Georgian Chkeidze, who afterwards distinguished himself by his courage in opposing the vote of the Duma for war credits, was at one time its leader, and it included many intellectuals. During the war the *Liquidators*, who had been expelled from the Party, became Defensists, stood, that is to say, for the prosecution of the war to a successful issue, without annexations or indemnities, against the *Defeatism* which aimed at converting the war into an international one of classes.

1912. In spite of the gulf between the Bolshevik and the Menshevik Social Democrats, no separate and independent Bolshevik Party existed before 1912. A Conference at Prague in that year formed a Bolshevik Central Committee, and thus completed the split in the Social Democratic organisation. This conference also decided upon Bolshevik participation in the elections for the fourth Imperial Duma, and upon the foundation of a legal daily newspaper in St. Petersburg. Such was the origin of *Truth (Pravda)*, which, often suppressed but reestablished, survives to-day as the organ of the Party now called Communist. Stalin was associated with Malinovsky (afterwards discovered to be an agent of the Tsarist Police) in the editorial management. The economic depression which had been heavy over Russia up to 1910 had now lifted, strikes recommenced in the period of comparative prosperity, and the Revolutionaries began again to hope.

Chapter 10

The March Revolution

> "The old Government is in prison, and the
> new is under house-arrest."
>
> A Petrograd humorist,
> quoted by TROTSKY.

> "The power slipped into the street."
>
> VICTOR CHERNOV.

> " 'To whom, dear Nicolas, should belong
> The land, the fields, and the villages?'
> 'To you my brothers and sons, to you alone.' "
>
> BORISOV. The peasants' talk with
> St. Nicolas the Miracle-Worker.

WHO, OR WHAT, made the Revolution of March 1917? And
what did the makers of it intend it to be, if there were any
makers of it, and if they had any intentions? Kerensky says
the Tsardom committed suicide: and perhaps it did so, when
the Grand Duke Michael refused to accept power, unless it
should be offered to him by a Constituent Assembly elected by
the Russian people. But there was an earlier stage of the
Revolution than this; and at this earlier stage it looked no
more than one of those Palace Revolutions, or displacements
of one Tsar to make room for another, which have been
occasional occurrences in Russian history. Nicolas II was to

abdicate, and he and Alexandra Feodorovna were to pass away from the stage of their errors and failures, and their son Alexis was to succeed them under the regency of the Grand Duke Michael, or the Grand Duke Michael was to become Tsar. After these plans had been shelved, it was months before a political intention had so crystallised in the minds of those who exercised power as to justify the proclamation of a republic. In the meanwhile, there was so little trace of any resolved intention anywhere, that power, in the language of Victor Chernov, "slipped into the street". The Grand Duke Michael had refused it. The Provisional Government showed an obvious unwillingness to summon the Constituent Assembly which was to determine the future form of Government. The Petrograd Soviet, while meddling continually in affairs of State, refused to accept the responsibilities of power. There was continual search for coalitions to help in bearing the burden, a constant summoning of a variety of popular assemblies. Only one party, or perhaps only one small group in one party, was willing to rush in where others feared to tread; and the other parties laughed uproariously when Lenin expressed readiness to accept power, because the Bolsheviks seemed at that moment so obviously incapable of doing what others with a wider popular support were afraid to do.

Who then made this revolution in which all or almost all shrank back from the consequences of the overthrow of the old régime? Beyond all question, it was not the Bolsheviks. They were taken by surprise when it came. Lenin was in Switzerland, Trotsky, not yet a Bolshevik, was in America. For months the notion that this section of the Socialists might dominate the country seemed an absurdity. Social Revolutionaries and Mensheviks, representing in all except agrarian questions the parties of moderate and gradual reform, had the great bulk of the Socialist vote: and they too had no claim to be makers of the Revolution. It could not have happened without the Army: and yet the Army, as a whole, rather acquiesced in it than made it. As for the Liberal politicians, scrupulous, legally-minded gentlemen, conscious of inexperience in statecraft and administration, the hitherto firm earth had opened into a gulf beneath their feet. They neither planned nor desired the earthquake. In so far as any man can be said, in those March days, to have used his will to direct events, it was the eloquent lawyer Alexander Kerensky. There was a moment when he seemed to be the strong man of the situation. But he did not plan or make the Revolution of March. Perhaps the police officer who reported that it was "spontaneous in the generally propagandised condition of the masses", came nearest to the truth. The peasants, and the rural anarchy which the peasants made in seizing the land, finally shook down the fabric of the State. But the peasants, if in a sense they made the Revolution, did not plan it. No man planned it. But it *grew*, upon the hands of those who seemed to be its actors, *grew*, till it ceased to be the liberal palace-revolution which at first it had seemed to be, and, from the destruction of the dynasty and the creation of a republic, passed, under the impact of a ruinous war and the collapse of the national economy, into the advent of a new Demogorgon, shaking the thrones, and more than the thrones, of the civilised world.

A more pertinent question than that which asks who or what made a revolution, is: what was it that held the State together before the Revolution shook it asunder? It is the building that is the marvel, not the collapse of it. Every political or social organisation is hard upon someone: and most are hard upon the majority of those who are subject to them. A complex of hopes and fears, spiritual and temporal, of inhibitions and habits, traditions and affections, holds men to their obedience, often against what seems their interest. Not in every State are the skill of the architect, and the virtues of the material, of equal power to achieve permanence in the structure. Natural decay may bring it down, even though earthquakes are spared to it, and history has witnessed nearly as many falls as rises. The Tsarist State in Russia was not so much an object of fear, or so much an object of love, had not so much support from those who benefited by its existence, did not so much benefit those on whose good will its existence depended, did not so much bemuse its people with the prestige of greatness, that the illusion of its power should survive the shocks and strains of an ill-conducted and disastrous war. As the present writer sees the Revolution, it was a negation, a slipping of the key-stone out of the arch upon which rested the Imperial Russian State. Count Tolstoi had preached precisely this collapse. Every man was to say: For me there is no more State. The moment came when every man, or nearly every man, said it: and the whole fabric, military and civil, fell into dust.

The immediate cause of collapse was the defection of the army or rather of a small part of it. In the indiscipline of the withdrawal through Siberia in 1905, there had been an omen of future catastrophe. But the war was over, the immediate objects of the malcontents were attained or seemed to be attained, and the danger passed. Between 1914 and 1917, the army had learned to distrust, if not its military leaders, at least the Government behind them; and, in the months preceding the Revolution, discipline was seriously shaken, of which wholesale desertions, bad treatment of horses, of equipment, even of weapons, were symptoms. A peasant poetess, who served in a military hospital, is quoted as repeating the words of the wounded: who cursed the war, and God, and the Tsar; and spoke of "the Tsar's war, which enveloped us all like a terrible black cloud": of course after the first exaltation of sentiment and hope of victory had passed. The efforts made by patriotic organisations, often hampered by the Government, had greatly improved supplies of all kinds: but disease was rife, there was frequent shortage of food, and there was no confidence in the success of the war whether among officers or men. The enormous numbers mobilised in the rear, and, in particular, the huge inactive garrison of Petrograd, were a focus of discontent which communicated itself to and from the civil population. The people of the capital were made desperate by a reduction of the bread-ration: there was a lock-out in the great metal-works, which sent 20,000 men on to the streets: and by March 10th a strike of workers was general. Orders for drastic action against disorder were received from the Emperor at General Headquarters, and the General commanding the Petrograd military district announced that crowds refusing to disperse would be fired upon. The Duma, in what proved to be its last constitutional session, passed a Bill transferring the administration of food supplies to the Town Councils. Its President warned the Emperor that the capital was in a state of anarchy, and asked him to appoint a minister "possessing the confidence of the country". In reply he received, on the night of March 11th to 12th, an order dissolving the Duma. On the same night, a part of the Emperor's own Guard, stationed in Petrograd, including the Engineer Battalion (Volynsky), which was recruited from the pick of the skilled workers, mutinied. It was this mutiny of the Guards, soon extending to other battalions of the same corps, which, together with the unwillingness of the Cossacks to play their old part in maintaining order, allowed the Revolution to occur: in the capital directly: and, in the country, by example.

On March 12th mutinous troops, without their officers, went to the Viborg district in the north-east of Petrograd, where the metal-works are situated, and where revolutionary leaders often took refuge, and joined with the workers in attacking police and breaking into arsenals. The arrival of these mutineers accompanied by a civilian crowd at the Tavrida palace, where the Duma had been in session, resulted in that body's determination to sit again in unofficial session—a tribute to the constitutional proprieties, for the Imperial order of dissolution was thus not technically disobeyed. The Duma also took what seems to have been the first actually revolutionary step, by appointing a temporary Committee, of all parties except the extreme Right, with unlimited powers, and called upon the military officers in Petrograd to report to its military commission and carry out its orders. The ministers of the old régime were arrested or surrendered. The Police, who had been defending themselves against the attacks of soldiers and workmen, surrendered or disappeared. The Tsar sent troops under General Ivanov to "restore order" and they fraternised with the revolutionary soldiers.

Such was the course of events in the capital. At the front neither the Commander-in-Chief nor any portion of the army opposed the abdication of the Emperor. Kerensky says that

they actually insisted upon it. In Moscow the troops passed
over at once to the Revolution. The spread of the Revolution
in the country generally was facilitated by two circumstances.
One of these, which might under different circumstances have
helped repression (if, for instance, the military leaders of a
counter-revolutionary movement had immediately made their
appearance), was the collection in Cantonments of a very
large proportion of the adult male population. Owing to the
general acceptance by the army-commanders of the Revolution in its first stages, the country was literally garrisoned by
armed and organised millions who were at one with their
officers in favouring the Revolution: or what, at that stage,
the Revolution appeared to be. The other circumstance which
assisted the spread of the Revolution throughout Russia was
the underground existence of Soviets, which had survived
from 1905 or even from earlier years. Something like a crude
form of alternative local government was available in all important centres, and came immediately into active operation.
This alternative Government, or perhaps we should say, these
alternative Governments, while excluding counter-revolution,
maintained a doubtful solidarity with the Provisional Government at the centre. In May the local Soviets at Kronstadt and
certain other centres declared themselves the sole powers in
their respective cities. They did not, of course, include representatives of the middle classes, and the middle classes made
no attempt to create corresponding organisations of their own
—a fact full of significance for those who seek to understand
the Revolution.

There is a story, which there is no reason to doubt, that a
police officer was found taking down the names of those
present at a demonstration on March 12th, and was spared by
the crowd. It harmonises with the fact that only seventy-three
policemen lost their lives in Petrograd in the heat of the struggle. Only in the naval centres, where the feeling between
officers and men was particularly bad, was the change attended
by serious excesses. At Kronstadt the Commander-in-Chief
was torn to pieces. The total number of deaths due to the
March Revolution has been calculated at one thousand three

hundred and thirty. It is likely that no equally great cataclysm
in the political world was ever accomplished with less bloodshed. There would have been more, no doubt, if there had
been a tougher fibre in the resistance; but, at this stage, at all
events, there was no class-war: and no common intention
except a negative one: to end the State as it had hitherto
existed.

The inactivity or pusillanimity of classes, and of individuals,
who might have been expected either for reasons of personal
loyalty or for the more sordid motive of interest, to strike a
blow for themselves or manifest devotion to the fallen Imperial family, is a noticeable feature of the March Revolution
in Russia. The mind travels to the French Revolution of 1789,
to the emotion of the courtiers singing "O Richard, o mon
Roi, l'Univers t'abandonne", to the slaughter of the Swiss
Guard, to the gallant Count Fersen planning the escape of
fugitive royalty, and escorting the unwieldy berlin on its risky
journey towards Varennes; and notes the lack in Russia of
anything analogous to these things. Kerensky tells us briefly
that the Imperial staff did not show loyalty or devotion, though
we know that a few humble friends were faithful, and even
perished with their masters at a later date. It is no mere accident that Nicolas and Alexandra found no help in their downfall; but rather a testimony to the flaws in the fabric of the
Russian State. Those who enjoyed the good things of the old
régime lacked the sense of obligation, and the devotion to
the "Little Father" was either a legend or an echo from a
dead past. The Grand Dukes made their submission, and the
Grand Duke Michael, in refusing the Imperial Crown till it
should be offered to him by a Constituent Assembly elected
by universal suffrage, called upon all to submit in the meanwhile to the Provisional Government. The Church blessed the
Revolution; the middle classes hailed it with satisfaction. A
Government was formed with "ten capitalist ministers and
Kerensky as hostage of the democracy" (as Lenin put it),
and a member both of the Duma and of the Petrograd Soviet.
The Premier was Prince Lvov, a consistent advocate of constitutional government, with a record of distinguished service

with the Provincial and District Rural Councils, which he organised for military supply during the war: and the ministry, excepting Kerensky who was a member of the Labour section of the Social Revolutionary Party, consisted of Octobrists—moderate Conservatives, taking their name from the Imperial Manifesto of October 1905—Constitutional Democrats or "Kadets"—whom we might describe as Liberals—and non-party men.

If there had been a plan, and a will, behind the Revolution we might have expected that the Duma, or its temporary Committee, or the Ministry which had taken office, would, expressly and definitively, have assumed the authority of the State, or, since the terms of the Grand Duke Michael's answer demanded an electoral ratification for a new constitution, and liberal opinion since 1905 had been demanding a Constituent Assembly, would have summoned one without delay. In fact, though some problems were attacked with promptitude, the Commission which was to draft the electoral law for the creation of the Constituent Assembly did not meet till May 8th, and the meeting of the Assembly itself, more than once delayed, did not take place till the November Revolution was completed. During the whole period of its existence, therefore, the Provisional Government stood half-way between the position of an authority which has seized power and looks to its deeds for justification, and of an interim holder dependent upon an early response to a popular referendum. Standing, as it did, upon a scrupulous legality, it was yet open to the charge of evading an expression of popular opinion, and was driven to devise a succession of unsatisfactory substitutes—two Congresses of Soviets, a State Conference at Moscow, a Democratic Conference in September, and its offspring a pre-parliament in October—to fill the gap. One of the practical mischiefs which resulted from this procrastination was the postponement of the imperatively urgent agrarian question, till the greater part of the land had passed by violent seizure into the hands of the peasantry. If the delay had been due, as sometimes stated, to the difficulty of consulting the suffrages of the troops in the field, it should have continued till the termination of the war and the demobilisation of the armies. The British Ambassador, Buchanan, who had doubtless discussed the question with Kadet Ministers, tells us that they did not desire a meeting of the Constituent Assembly, until the local elections for the newly-established town and rural councils had provided machinery for organising and controlling the general elections. This explanation involves the inference that the urgency of an early and definitive regularisation of the Government, and of a settlement of the land question, was not understood.

If there had been a definitive assumption of power by the Duma or its temporary committee, another cause of weakness might have been eliminated. A parallel authority, which disclaimed responsibility, and yet participated in State affairs, established itself almost contemporaneously with the first revolutionary action of the Duma. This was the Petrograd Soviet of Workers' and Soldiers' Deputies, which was provided with a room alongside of the Duma in the Tavrida Palace from the afternoon of March 12th. The temporary Committee of the Duma gave it recognition by negotiating with it to obtain its support. This was no local body for the affairs of the capital city. Theoretically its function may have been to deal with the Petrograd garrison and proletariat. Actually, it assumed from the outset functions which clashed with those of the Provisional Government: and it was led by some of the ablest thinkers and economists of Russia, many of whom were among the recently amnestied political prisoners. Among its early interventions were its insistence upon the arrest of Nicolas II and his family on March 21st, and upon their detention in Russia: and the introduction of an eight-hour labour day, without waiting for the Provisional Government's decree. Alexander Guchkov the new Minister of War, told the Commander-in-Chief on March 22nd that the Provisional Government was at the mercy of the Soviet, which controlled troops, railways, and postal and telegraph services. It was not an extremist body, like the "sections" in revolutionary Paris, but largely composed of moderate Socialists, and, until the Kornilov fiasco of September had effected a complete reshuffle of parties, markedly anti-Bolshevik in temper. The mischief which it did was the creation of what Trotsky calls a "dvoyev-lastiye" or dyarchy, in the Revolutionary Government, which divided authority up to the very day of its fall.

The present study is not concerned with the history of events after the revolution of March, except as a means of showing what the nature of that revolution was. I repeat that it was in essence a collapse, a reversion to a condition in which the State ceased to exist, or at all events to function, though its forms survived, and the humbler institutions at the basis of society continued to be effectively operative. It is hardly an exaggeration to say that Russia became, for a time, a mere confederation of communes without organic link between them. It is not true that every man did what was right in his own eyes: but it is almost true that every commune did so. The Tsarist police force disappeared at once: and no body of men has since then borne the hated title in Russia. They were replaced by a militia with heads chosen by popular election, and we learn that foreign residents were employed with this force as special constables. There is abundant evidence that this militia, hastily formed and ill-trained, and uncertain of its ground with the people, was not efficient. Some squadrons of Cossacks were employed for the maintenance of order in the capital. In rural areas it was necessary, later on, to strengthen the militia by detailing selected soldiers on special pay. But the cry for troops for the maintenance of order in rural areas was constant throughout the period of the Provisional Government: and crime was rife in the cities. No detective police existed: but Alexander Kerensky was occupied with a plan for the re-establishment of a department similar to the Tsarist Okhrana, when he was driven from power by the November Revolution. The lack of an adequate Police must be placed high among the causes of the overthrow of the Provisional Government: for rural anarchy involved a virtual severance of the economic tie between town and village, and cut off supplies of food and fuel from the capital and from the army at the front.

After a short interval in which an attempt was made to make use of the Chairmen of Rural Councils as local Gover-

nors, Provincial and District Commissars were appointed by
the Provisional Government: and the demands of these func-
tionaries for military help in the maintenance of order, and the
exhortations of the central authorities to them to put down
anarchy, fill a large place in the official correspondence. It is
evident that they lacked the regular machinery for the work
of administration: and that the locally elected bodies, the
Soviets in the towns, the Canton Committees in the rural areas,
and the Village Mirs (which exhibited all the vitality of their
indigenous origin) took their own course, without much regard to orders from above. The course of the agrarian movement gives ample evidence of this dis-co-ordination of central
and local machinery. The Tsarist Land-Captains were not
abolished till July, but it is evident that their authority was
completely paralysed from the early days of the Revolution.

Canton Committees, of the nature of Soviets, were formed
with the acquiescence of the Provisional Government in
March, and played a prominent part in the agrarian movement, till the new bodies provided by the legislation of May
1917 came into existence in September. We see them, in the
Tver province, collecting grain and money for war-require-
ments, organising a Canton library, and ultimately arranging
for the elections to the new legally authorised body. But a
good deal of their activity was more strenuous and less innocent than this. Both the Canton Committees and the Village
Mirs clashed, often violently, with the Committees set up by
the Central Government for dealing with food-supply and
with land. The Food Committees were organised in connection
with the grain monopoly which the Provisional Government
found it necessary to establish. The Bolsheviks, whose policy
towards the Provisional Government was largely a wrecking
one, raised the slogan of: Down with the Food Committees:
and there were at least some cases of the destruction of the
local food offices, due to dissatisfaction with the fixed price or
with the method of requisition. The Land Committees were
established to settle disputes between peasant and landlord, or
peasant and peasant, with respect to land, rent, and wages:
and to help to secure seed, implements, animal and machine

power, for the cultivators. Where they took their colour from local influences, the Land Committees joined vigorously in the movement for the seizure of land from the landlords. Where they stood aloof, as representatives of the central authority, they often found themselves virtually set aside by the purposeful determination of the locally elected bodies. The picture is, in general, one of centrifugal tendencies too strong for the Central Government.

The relegation of final legislation on the subject of the land to the Constituent Assembly, itself indefinitely postponed, gave time for abortive attempts by the landlords to defeat the claims of the peasants by the sale of their land, and there was a long struggle over a Bill to prohibit such anticipatory disposals. There was a crescendo of agrarian crime reaching its maximum after the harvest had been garnered. Beginning with the seizure of estates and agricultural property, it went on to the destruction of libraries, works of art, bloodstock, conservatories and experimental stations, the hamstringing of animals, the burning of houses, even the murder of their owners. Landlords were destroying their own crops to keep them from the peasants. Apart from the grosser outrages, there was, paradoxically, a certain system, even a certain order, in the proceedings. Peasants did not seize the land which had not been cultivated by them or their forebears, and one commune did not invade the domain of another. The Mir was a living and active institution, though the State was in a state of suspended animation. State and landlord were ignored; but the primitive commune was rehabilitated in what tradition persisted in regarding as its natural rights. Those peasants who had left the Mir, under the operation of the Stolypin legislation for the creation of separate peasant property in land, were, in the Central Agricultural and Middle Volga zones (which were strongholds of the Mir, as well as storm centres of agrarian disturbance), often forced to return and pool their land again: another evidence of the vitality of the indigenous commune.

The collapse of State authority was almost as evident in the Army as in rural Russia, though the habit of discipline survived longer in the former. Much has been made of the disintegrating consequences of orders which were aimed at securing certain rudimentary rights to the rank and file, or at removing the men's suspicion of counter-revolutionary tendencies in their officers. More serious was the temporary abolition of the death-penalty for offences at the front. But indiscipline was worst among the troops at the rear. Five thousand uniformed men are said to have taken part in one attack upon State liquor-stores. Desertion, stimulated by the first consequences of the Revolution, afterwards diminished for a time: but ultimately became catastrophic in its dimensions.

Of the fighting qualities of the men there is some definite evidence in the history of the renewal of the offensive in Galicia in July, 1917. It is natural to compare it with the achievements of the French revolutionary armies, in the eighteenth century, which triumphantly turned back advancing Europe. The French had in their favour the burning enthusiasm of an awakened people: and simpler conditions of training and equipment made a hasty reorganisation an effective one. Alexander Kerensky, the persuader-in-chief of an already war-weary army and people, lacked those inspiring slogans which made Frenchmen forget the limitations of their mortality. He did not attempt a reorganisation which was perhaps impossible in the face of an efficient and enterprising enemy: and the resumed offensive ended in a failure, made disgraceful by outrages perpetrated upon the peaceful population of Galicia in the retreat. Nothing less than a complete collapse of *morale* will explain the shocking facts, of which the former Minister of War, Alexander Guchkov, gives convincing testimony.

The Provisional Government showed a liberal spirit in its legislation, much of which was based upon the best Western models, and in its forbearing treatment of political opponents: it removed all the worst grievances of the non-Great-Russian Nationalities, recognised the "constitutions" of Finland and the independence of Poland; it restored the Patriarchate to the Orthodox Church: it incurred a ruinous internal risk, in a generous attempt to fulfil Russia's military obligations to the Western Powers.

There was one moment, after the defeat of the *émeute* in July 1917, when it appeared to have reached a position of real authority: but the opportunity which this seemed to offer was either not what it looked, or was, at all events, not grasped. When the end came in November, the triumph of the one Party which, however small, possessed the strength given by organisation and masterful guidance, and promised to meet the popular demands for peace, land, and the freedom of the nationalities, was almost incredibly easy. On the early morning of the 7th, all the centres of public business and communication in Petrograd were occupied without a blow being struck. On the following night, the Winter Palace, the Headquarters of the Provisional Government, along with all the Ministers except Alexander Kerensky, was captured. The event took place amid scenes of comedy rather than of tragedy. The warships on the Neva fired blank. Sir George Buchanan, the British Ambassador, examined the Palace and found only three marks where shrapnel had struck. On the side of the town were many marks of bullets from machine guns: but not one shot from the field gun on the other side had struck the building. Not one of the defenders was killed. Five sailors and one soldier were killed on the attacking side and a number slightly wounded. Only in Moscow was there a fierce struggle for the possession of the Kremlin. Lenin and his Party had picked up the power, which had fallen into the street.

A detached critic, a Baltic Baron of Russian nationality, has pointed out how respectful of free speech the Provisional Government was, and has said that it was beaten because it treated the Russian people, not like slaves, but in terms of European democracy; thus showing an excessive belief in the miracle of Government by consent. We cannot, indeed, but feel, in the later stages of the Provisional Government's agony, that the old-fashioned statesmanship would have effected a prompter and more drastic extirpation of dangerous enemies, and that suitable opportunities for such action could have been found or made. But the March Revolution was a breaking up of the foundations of the State, an anarchy in which the instruments of compulsion themselves were shattered, a storm in which the winds took their will. No Government could have survived which had endeavoured to compel these elemental forces. The error of the Provisional Government was, not that it tried to govern by consent, for that was inevitable, but that, while maintaining all the forms, and suffering from all the weaknesses, of Government by consent, its leaders did not discover and fulfil the will of the people. They did not make peace and they boggled over the land.

When it was the turn of the Bolsheviks to ride the whirlwind, they did not immediately attempt to direct the storm. *Temporarily* they gave the people all that they wanted: they gave them peace, though at an appalling sacrifice: they confirmed the claim of the peasants to the land, on terms which their own judgment did not approve: and they eliminated the private employers, and gave the workers control of many factories, with consequences temporarily disastrous to industry. But, behind the cover of these concessions to the inevitable, they began to plan the restoration of a new discipline. Even so, the victory was precarious, and bought only by three years of civil war and famine, to be followed by a long retreat.

Index

337